# Between Market and Myth

**Campos Ibéricos**

**Bucknell Studies in Iberian Literatures and Cultures**

**Series Editors:**

Isabel Cuñado, Bucknell University
Jason McCloskey, Bucknell University

*Campos Ibéricos* is a series of monographs and edited volumes focusing on the literary and cultural traditions of Spain in all its rich historical, social, and linguistic diversity. The series provides a space for interdisciplinary and theoretical scholarship exploring the intersections of literature, culture, the arts, and media from medieval to contemporary Iberia. Studies of all authors, texts, and cultural phenomena are welcome and works on understudied writers and genres are specially sought.

**Titles in the Series**

Andrés Lema-Hincapié and Conxita Domènech, eds., *Indiscreet Fantasies: Iberian Queer Cinema*

Katie J. Vater, *Between Market and Myth: The Spanish Artist Novel in the Post-Transition, 1992–2014*

# Between Market and Myth

## *The Spanish Artist Novel in the Post-Transition, 1992–2014*

KATIE J. VATER

Bucknell University | University Press

LEWISBURG, PENNSYLVANIA

Library of Congress Cataloging-in-Publication Data
Names: Vater, Katie J., author.
Title: Between market and myth : the Spanish artist novel in the post-transition, 1992–2014 / Katie J. Vater.
Description: Lewisburg, Pennsylvania : Bucknell University Press, 2020. | Series: Campos ibericos | Includes bibliographical references and index. | Summary: "In its early transition to democracy following Franco's death in 1975, Spain rapidly embraced neoliberal practices and policies, some of which directly impacted cultural production. In a few short years, the country commercialized its art and literary markets, investing in "cultural tourism" as a tool for economic growth and urban renewal. The artist novel began to proliferate for the first time in a century, but these novels-about artists and art historians-have received little critical attention beyond the descriptive. In Between Market and Myth, Vater studies select authors-Julio Llamazares, Ángeles Caso, Clara Usón, Almudena Grandes, Nieves Herrero, Paloma Díaz-Mas, Lourdes Ortiz, and Enrique Vila-Matas-whose largely realist novels portray a clash between the myth of artistic freedom and artists' willing recruitment or cooptation by market forces or political influence. Today, in an era of rising globalization, the artist novel proves ideal for examining authors' ambivalent notions of creative practice when political patronage and private sector investment complicate belief in artistic autonomy"—Provided by publisher.
Identifiers: LCCN 2019042568 | ISBN 9781684482214 (paperback) | ISBN 9781684482221 (hardcover) | ISBN 9781684482238 (epub) | ISBN 9781684482245 (mobi) | ISBN 9781684482252 (pdf)
Subjects: LCSH: Spanish fiction—21st century—History and criticism. | Spanish fiction—20th century—History and criticism. | Künstlerromane, Spanish—History and criticism. | Artists in literature. | Art in literature.
Classification: LCC PQ6147.K85 V38 2020 | DDC 863/.6409—dc23
LC record available at https://lccn.loc.gov/2019042568

A British Cataloging-in-Publication record for this book is available from the British Library.



∞ The paper used in this publication meets the requirements of the American National Standard for Information Sciences—Permanence of Paper for Printed Library Materials, ANSI Z39.48-1992.

www.bucknelluniversitypress.org

Distributed worldwide by Rutgers University Press

Manufactured in the United States of America

# Contents

# Between Market and Myth

# Introduction

In 2012, author Rafael Reig published a brief piece in the Spanish online newspaper *El Diario* titled "Desde dentro de la burbuja" (From within the bubble). The title referred not to the housing or the dot-com bubbles, or any of the others of the post-2008 era with which we have all become familiar, but rather to the notion of a Spanish "literary bubble" whose bursting led to a "crisis" in the novel. In this piece, Reig posits that, just as the housing bubble had grown as a result of increased demand and overzealous, avaricious speculation, the public's call for culture in the years following Francisco Franco's death created a bubble, as well. The "speculators"—editors, publishing houses, critics, et al.—attempted to meet the public demand and profit handsomely by investing in artistic products, even when they were of dubious quality. Like potential home buyers, cultural producers were extended loans of "good faith" in the form of prizes, even when it was unlikely they could repay their debt with products of consistently high quality; Reig uses the metaphor of a risky subprime mortgage to describe "premios literarios a locutores de la tele" (literary prizes given to TV presenters).[1] He imputes blame for the growth and subsequent deflation of this bubble not only to the nebulous "system" or the impersonal market but also to the desires of artists and authors themselves. It becomes personal as he sums up his own writerly desire with a plea to the God of Literature: "Hazme un escritor insobornable, pero no te des demasiada prisa por favor, déjame disfrutar un poco de las burbujas." (Make me an incorruptible writer, but don't do it too soon, please. Let me enjoy the bubble a little.)[2] Reig knows from experience that contemporary authors want it both ways, but can they remain "pure," free from external constraints on their work, and profit at the same time?

To illustrate this tension, and to present it as a timelessly human trait as old as literature itself, Reig cites the Roman poet Persius's *Satire I*, in which the ancient stoic harshly chastises *other* poets for coveting fame and giving in to trends to achieve it. In this critique of the unnamed "others," Reig contends, Persius actually gives voice to his own contradictory desires: "[Persio] se desdobla para expresar sus dudas y temores. Se pide a los dos y así nos da un magnífico retrato psicológico de una burbuja vista desde dentro." ([Persius] splits himself in two to express his own doubts and fears. Drawing on both, he offers us a magnificent psychological portrait of a bubble seen from the inside.)[3] Very little has changed since Persius's time, Reig suggests. On the one hand, contemporary authors and artists want at least the appearance of the purity that has defined the autonomous, and therefore "authentic," artist for centuries. On the other hand, the changing conditions for producing cultural work have presented more tempting opportunities for material success than ever before. Reig summarizes this inconsistent position with another rhetorical question that illustrates the conflict between autonomy and opportunity: "¿Quién no quiere ser un escritor ajeno a las modas, independiente, al que no le importe el aplauso de los lectores ni el de la crítica? ¡Nadie, por favor, pero si todos queremos eso, precisamente eso!" (Who doesn't want to be an independent writer, unaffected by trends, and who doesn't care about applause from readers or critics? Nobody, but come on, that's exactly what we all want!)[4]

Reig's question is one that the protagonists of the eight artist novels studied in this book are all searching to answer. In their depictions of the labor of artists, art historians, and even a writer asked to moonlight as a performance artist, each of the novels discussed in *Between Market and*

*Myth* offers its author's perspectives on the aesthetic and political dimensions of creativity. These novels also reflect and respond to changes in the field of cultural production that occurred as a result of Spain's rapid embrace of neoliberal practices and economic policies in the early transition to democracy after the death of Francisco Franco in 1975. In just a few short years, the country experienced swift commercialization of its art and literary markets at the same time that both the national Spanish government and the regional governments of autonomous communities began investing in "cultural tourism" infrastructure that positioned culture as a tool for economic growth, urban renewal, and job creation. The authors explored here—Julio Llamazares, Angeles Caso, Clara Usón, Almudena Grandes, Nieves Herrero, Paloma Díaz-Mas, Lourdes Ortiz, and Enrique Vila-Matas—have crafted texts about artists and art historians whose central conflicts revolve around questions of autonomy and artistic identity formation that stem from the shifting relationship between art and commerce. In their largely realist narratives about the life and work of "creatives" living in the late twentieth and early twenty-first centuries, these Spanish authors reveal the changed conditions of production and accelerated distribution for art and literature alike, but the function of the novels is more than documentary. Often, the novels represent a clash between the myth of total artistic freedom that has long been a hallmark of the artist novel and artists' willing recruitment or co-optation by market forces or political interests. As these authors critique a system in which they themselves are deeply embedded, their responses to this clash are unsurprisingly ambivalent. Often, they vacillate between heralding autonomy as the artist's defining aspiration and suggesting the fundamental impossibility of achieving it in the current conditions. For centuries, the depiction of creative practice in the artist novel has been bound up with the notion of autonomy, reflected in the belief that the artist, when free from external constraints, is able to create work that is unique and therefore valuable. For that reason, the artist novel proves ideal, even today, for examining Spanish authors' notions of their own creative practice in an era when political patronage and private-sector investment complicate belief in that autonomy.

The artist novel saw a veritable revival in the 1980s and 1990s, when it began to proliferate for the first time in Spain since the turn of the twentieth century.[5] Every major Spanish press has published art-world novels in the past several decades—not only about artists but also about art dealers, gallery owners, museum curators, and art historians. Yet, as a category, these novels have received very little critical attention that goes beyond the enumerative and descriptive.[6] The transformation of the artist novel shows how authors interrogate the ambivalence of cultural producers' identities today, but I argue that the study of contemporary artist novels is useful to understanding broader questions about the way we conceptualize work, especially "cultural work," that, as Mark Banks describes it, is often banally perceived as "more self-expressive, creative, and fulfilling than conventional work."[7] I read these novels, at times explicitly and other times against the grain, to contextualize and historicize the myth of the individual creative genius long represented as the "radically" autonomous bohemian artist who works differently and with singular motivations that set him apart from the average worker. Examining this myth as a discursive construct facilitates understanding of the way cultural industries and artists themselves have been able to mobilize this construct for their own varied ends. These novels are set in the age of cultural industries, the age in which, simultaneously, neoliberalism has become an inescapable norm. Therefore, their study also allows us to form questions about the impact of neoliberalism's market-oriented logic on subjects' identity formation as professionals (and especially as artists), as well as its effects on the formation of their class, gender, and national identities.

The notion of artistic autonomy has informed understandings of creative work since the Romantic era. Banks defines autonomy in cultural production as the "freedom from the particular demands and constraints of the commercial world."[8] Of course, most cultural work is not radically autonomous. One of the few places where that radical autonomy could exist is in the fictional world of the artist novel, which also has its literary roots in Romanticism. Outside of its pages, cultural work has always been characterized by a "socially embedded, compromised, or 'negotiated' autonomy."[9] At least some level of creative autonomy underpins all practices—painting, writing, et cetera—that we understand as cultural work today. Works of art are differentiable from standardized, mass-produced commodities and are appreciated as unique because they bear the imprint of an individual and original creator. However, as Banks asserts, the same autonomy that allows for the creation of unique works of art has become a "structural precondition for effective capitalist cultural production."[10] In other words, a shared belief in autonomy and its value both allows artists to express their individual creativity and lets creative industries successfully commodify their work. Therefore, when an artist signals distance from the market, his or her work may actually become more valuable within that same market.

Cultural industries—defined by Banks as "commercial activities that involve the production of aesthetic or symbolic goods and services"—first became a topic of both academic and policy-making debate in the 1970s.[11] As a result, many thinkers began to question the existence of artistic autonomy "as a foundational normative principle of cultural work," with Michel Foucault, Pierre Bourdieu, Theodor Adorno, and Max Horkheimer leading the charge in different ways.[12] A thorough review of these critical approaches is outside the purview of this book, and it is something that both Justin O'Connor and Banks have cogently undertaken.[13] However, one of these critiques of autonomy has informed my own understanding of the art world as it is depicted by the Spanish authors I study: Bourdieu's reflexive sociology of art that claims that "cultural workers' own status-seeking behaviors" undermine the possibility of radical autonomy.[14] Bourdieu's work can be understood as a vigorous argument against the concept of autonomy, also defined as "disinterestedness" in his parlance. In this book, I do not take the stance that some mediated autonomy is utterly impossible, but Bourdieu is still a useful starting point for understanding how the concept of "artist" has been socially constituted and how the concept of the "Great Artist" came to be.

Bourdieu's work in *The Rules of Art* (1992) and *The Field of Cultural Production* (1993) examines the social processes of differentiation, commodification, and classification of culture in late capitalist societies that result in the emergence of cultural economies.[15] It can be situated within a branch of sociological critique that sees the cultural industry as "a collective project" that requires a contextualization of individual artistic practice.[16] Bourdieu explains that the very terms *art* and *artist* have meaning because of a collective *belief* in the notion of autonomy.[17] Throughout this book, I use the term *charismatic myth of the artist*, derived from Bourdieu's lexicon, to refer to that discursive construction of the individual creative genius. Using Bourdieusian parlance, Sigrid Røyseng, Per Mangset, and Jorunn Spord Borgen define the charismatic myth as the belief that artists "are people with extraordinary talents possessing the ability to create unique and sublime works of art . . . [, which] should be carried out in a disinterested manner with a pure aesthetic vision as the only guiding light."[18] In other words, the charismatic myth sees "artist" as an inherent category, a subject position inhabited from birth and "irreducible to any condition or conditioning."[19] Bourdieu posits, however, that artists are recognized as artists because they are embedded in and legitimized by a larger social framework. He calls the structure of the field in which artists' work is produced and legitimated, especially the elite or "restricted" field of cultural production, an "economic world reversed." It is dominated by a "winner-loses logic," which means that the artist who enacts the most autonomous behaviors is the most successful, and so those who enter it, even those who appear most disinterested, actually "have an interest in disinterestedness."[20] In Bourdieu's words, performing the most "anti-economic and visibly 'disinterested' behaviours" in no way excludes "their authors from even the 'economic' profits awaiting those who conform to the law of this universe," and, in fact, it often encourages it.[21] Performing freedom and disinterestedness can ultimately lead to pecuniary gain, and the "disinterestedness" that characterizes the charismatic myth can be adopted as a long-term commercial strategy.[22]

My approach to the eight artist novels chosen for this study is informed by this notion that performing autonomy can be marketable. This is represented diegetically in many of the novels as artist protagonists mobilize "disinterested" strategies that lead to symbolic consecration and financial reward. In some of the authors' public statements about their work, the same kind of performative disavowal of honors and financial reward can be seen. It is undeniable that cultural production has responded increasingly to market demands in recent decades, but my own position aligns more with Banks's assertion (and less with Bourdieu's) that it is "never reducible to those demands."[23] Even if artistic autonomy is employable as a commercial strategy, cultural industries will never completely standardize artistic output if they wish to remain economically viable, because the culture-consuming public continues to demand original products made by a unique creator. Those who work in the cultural industry, like authors, editors, and publishers, understand that the consumers of art and literature find a "use value" in cultural products that are defined as authentic and unique. Profit is generated from marketing novels to a contemporary readership that Sarah Brouillette describes as "inclined to disavow instrumental goals as secondary to, or as inhibitors of, immaterial goods like self-knowledge, authenticity, originality, and happiness."[24] However, in contemporary society, where materialistic motivations increasingly "exist in tandem rather than in tension with the desire for self-expression," the search for artistic authenticity does not have to lie only in radical autonomy from the market.[25] Rather, authenticity is often expressed in these literary texts as a mediated search for some kind of autonomy within capitalist confines.

I argue in this book that the post-Franco rise to prominence of the artist novel is related to a desire to market "authenticity," but this can only be understood by taking into consideration the "ideologies of authorship," often informed by the charismatic myth of the artist, that make artistic expression a topic interesting to readers. As Brouillette has shown, whether one is a proponent or critic of the market's impingement on artistic practice, the "idea of the artist's special position vis-à-vis capitalist value has been structured into the field and by now thoroughly permeates all its parts."[26] This can be seen reflected in two different points of view she describes: either the artist is so special that capitalist processes will annihilate his or her creativity or those same capitalist markets will offer the artist the opportunity for a creative career and liberate him or her from financial constraints that might prevent independent creation. The recognition that the discursive construct of autonomy is fundamental to generating profit from culture is key to understanding the way artists—both the authors of the novels studied and the artist protagonists they create—participate in the new cultural economy.

---

The revival of the artist novel after 1992, with its narratives about individual creativity and artistic autonomy, cannot be separated from the definitive implantation of neoliberalism in Spain. All of the artist novels studied in this book were published in what Mitchum Huehls and Rachel Greenwald Smith call neoliberalism's "ontological phase," during which neoliberalism became no longer a set of ideological beliefs but rather "what we are, a mode of existence defined by individual self-responsibility, entrepreneurial action, and the maximization of human capital."[27] To understand neoliberalism this way is to see beyond actual economic policies and understand "market-based" thinking as having infiltrated every aspect of human life, including the art world and the university. As Wendy Brown explains it, neoliberalism in the contemporary age is a pervasive and agentic "governing rationality" that has the power to organize states and shape subjects.[28] Taking this context into account, one of the central questions of this book is how authors represent or negotiate the concept of artistic autonomy when there is no longer an "outside the market."

Spain implemented a neoliberal economic program nearly immediately after Franco's death as part of the same modernizing and integrating impulse that motivated its embrace of "culture" as a political tool. Helen Graham and Antonio Sánchez explain that, after decades of ostracism, the Spanish government's desire for symbolic European integration meant incorporation into a "specific political and economic entity which has at its center (both ideologically and economically) the market."[29] Though some progressives had hoped that the dictator's demise would usher in a sort of anticapitalist program of the Republican era, when the Partido Socialista Obrero Español (Spanish Socialist Workers' Party; PSOE) took over the first democratically elected government, it surprised and disappointed its hard-liners by embracing neoliberal economic policies. David Harvey defines neoliberal practices as those that propose that "human well-being can best be advanced by liberating individual entrepreneurial freedoms and skills within an institutional framework characterized by strong private property rights, free markets, and free trade."[30] From a set of economic policies in the 1970s and 1980s, neoliberalism was transformed into a political ideology, and later, as Huehls and Smith suggest, it suffused "the sociocultural landscape until it [became] a post-ideological mode of existence."[31] One of the hallmarks of the Transition was the endurance of certain Francoist institutions, values, and leaders, whose presence in the government continued for years after the dictator's death. Despite this continuity, there was little support for Franco's state corporatist economic model.[32] As Paul McVeigh notes, neoliberalism was embraced by leaders and the public alike in this context because it enjoyed a "symbiotic relationship with European integration" and with the related and highly prioritized goals of "democratization, modernization, and an end to Spain's isolation."[33]

So important was the realization of those goals that the anti-Francoist progressives, represented largely by the Partido Comunista Español (Spanish Communist Party; PCE) and the democratic socialist PSOE, abandoned in the name of pragmatism the idealism that had fueled their resistance through the Franco years. A version of the liberal democracy they envisioned, in which modernization and normalization would be achieved, needed to be palatable to the still deeply entrenched Francoist establishment, and this reality led to a fundamental deradicalization of both parties' platforms.[34] When the PSOE came to power in 1982 as the first democratically elected government of the post-Franco era, its business-friendly economic policies earned it the unexpected backing of Spanish capital, policies that the right-wing Partido Popular (Popular Party; PP) would sustain and strengthen after its electoral victory in 1996.[35] The Spanish electorate, including a large part of the progressive base, accepted these neoliberal policies with vigor as they saw in them the promise of that much-desired integration within Europe, concretized in an economic sense with the signing of the Treaty of Maastricht in 1992.

In this context, a vibrant Spanish creative economy emerged in which "culture" in all its forms was approached as a resource to be mined and exploited for sociopolitical and economic ends. In fact, investment in culture came to be intimately associated with the success of the PSOE's neoliberal and democratizing project. As Jorge Luis Marzo and Tere Badia explain it, culture was lifted up as "el símbolo más aplaudido a la hora de promocionar el nuevo sistema político" (the most lauded symbol used to promote the new political system).[36] Spain was not the only country in Europe with a left-leaning government that would invest in culture this way. But, while culture was also being wielded in places like the United Kingdom as a "branded tourist product" and a "gentrifying force," similar projects in Spain were meant to demonstrate the country's right to inclusion in the international art world and to herald its membership in the larger European economic community.[37]

The construction of the Museum of Contemporary Art in Barcelona (MACBA), which opened in 1995, offers just one such example of a project designed to signal Spain's modernization and its overcoming of the dictatorial past. "Culture" was considered both economically productive and key to the consolidation of democracy that made investments like this one a win-win situation for the PSOE government. MACBA was designed by the high-profile U.S. architect Richard Meier and was to be constructed in the impoverished Raval neighborhood, where, it was hoped, it would promote urban renewal.[38] The museum was slated to open in 1992, a year that for many marked the definitive end to the Transition and the consolidation of Spanish democracy. It was also a watershed year for culture; Barcelona was to host the Olympic Games, Seville would be home to the World's Fair, and Madrid had been named that year's European Capital of Culture. However, the case of MACBA exemplifies the Spanish cultural policy that Marzo and Badia define as "política promocional en detrimento de una política productiva" (a promotional policy at the expense of a productive policy).[39] In Vila-Matas's novel *Kassel no invita la lógica* (discussed in chapter 4), the narrator, in one of his critiques of the Spanish art scene that pepper the book, recalls MACBA's opening this way: "Los barceloneses se paseaban por el museo admirando las blancas paredes y solidez de la construcción y otros detalles arquitectónicos, orgullosos de haber pagado aquello con sus impuestos y diciéndose que las obras de arte podrían esperar" (The people of Barcelona wandered through the museum admiring the white walls, the solidity of the construction, and other architectural details, proud of having paid for it with their taxes and telling themselves that the works of art could wait).[40] The existence of the building itself was enough to promote local and national pride and court tourists at the same time. In this context, constructions like MACBA—as well as the Bilbao Guggenheim, Valencia's Institute of Modern Art (IVAM), and Madrid's Reina Sofia museum—allowed for the performance of a "new dynamic Spanish identity" at a time when all eyes were on Spain.[41]

The government's promotion of cultural policy had different effects in Spain than in other parts of Europe. O'Connor observes that such promotion in many other places created a split between the sponsored art that embodied the "privileged representation and exemplification of national cultural identity" and a more "autonomous art" whose relationship to the former was often antagonistic.[42] Community arts and urban social movements were commonly privileged sites for this more autonomous cultural expression, but in Spain these types of movements were short-lived in the 1980s and all but disappeared in the following decades. One notable exception is the *movida madrileña* (the Madrid scene), that "explosión cultural y creativa que se vivió en el Madrid de finales de los setenta y primeros ochenta como producto de una condensación diversa y heterogénea de toda la pasión vital y creativa que se forjó en las cloacas de las culturas *underground* del franquismo" (cultural and creative explosion that Madrid experienced at the end of the seventies and early eighties as a result of the diverse condensation of vital and creative passion that was forged in the sewers of underground cultural movements during the Franco era).[43] However, as Hamilton Stapell details in his book *Remaking Madrid*, the movida had been almost entirely co-opted by the local government around 1983, less than ten years after it began.[44] Stapell asserts that the movida did not dovetail neatly with any political party's aims, but rather it "symbolized the belief that there was something more to life than simply production and consumption."[45] After the death of Madrid's mayor and movida champion Enrique Tierno Galván, a shift in the local government policy withdrew funds from many of the artists and groups associated with the movida. At the same time, the rapid solidification of a mass consumer culture in Spain meant that, in both governmental and private sectors, less time and money was being spent on the sort of independent cultural enterprises the movida had represented.[46] The end of the movida also meant the end of large-scale spontaneous cultural movements for the next several decades.[47] The movida had promised a grassroots, autonomous art that would remain distanced from the state and from private-sector involvement. It had suggested that capitalism alone could not satisfy Spaniards' desires for a meaningful life, and this belief seemed to disappear, or at least attenuate, along with the movida itself.

The largely antagonistic relationship that politically progressive Spanish culture had held with respect to the state for centuries dissolved in the early democratic era. The arrival of democracy was accompanied in Spain by what Ignacio Echevarría refers to as "la ofensiva cultural neoliberal desacreditadora de la dialéctica y de la crítica y legitimadora de la fatalidad intrínseca de la realidad y la internalización capitalista del sentido de la historia y de la cultura" (the neoliberal cultural offensive that discredited reasoned debate and criticism and legitimated the current reality as intrinsic inevitability as well as an internalization of a capitalist sense of history and culture).[48] For the first time in many of their lives, young writers, artists, and intellectuals found themselves living in a country in which they saw themselves allied with the government in power, and many had to rethink the kind of political engagement possible or necessary in these new conditions. Journalist and author Guillem Martínez, one of the most vociferous critics of this new and largely tacit arrangement between the state and cultural producers, considers the years of the Transition and the decades that followed it as the era of cultural "deactivation" in the name of political stability and social cohesion. He describes the newly reconfigured relationship this way: "La cultura no se mete en política—salvo para darle razón al Estado—y el Estado no se mete en cultura—salvo para subvencionarla, premiarla, o darle honores" (Culture doesn't get involved in politics—except to agree with the state—and the state doesn't get involved with culture—except to subsidize it and give it awards and honors).[49] This symbiosis would come to define cultural production in Spain for years to come, imposing limits of possibility for novels, films, and art of all kinds that their authors hoped would be successful.

Martínez coined the term *Culture of the Transition*, or CT for short, to refer to these widespread and inescapable limits of possibility, whose political and cultural correctness would develop a censoring function.[50] Literature and art published or produced within this context had to uphold a broad social consensus that Luis Moreno-Caballud describes as "la incuestionabilidad de unas bases políticas y económicas fundamentales: el sistema de partidos y el capitalismo" (the unquestionability of a couple of fundamental political and economic foundations: the party system and capitalism).[51] The result of engagement in this tacit agreement was the production of what Martínez calls "productos aproblemáticos" (unproblematic products) that tended to ultimately re-inforce the status quo by refusing to challenge the accepted political or cultural norms of the Transition.[52] The author Belén Gopegui, whose work of the 1990s often *did* reflect some disillusionment with Transition-era values, described the CT as the only possible context for literary production long after the political Transition had ended. To exist outside it was to inhabit a no-man's land: "No existía una literatura española al margen de la CT. Existía sólo un completamente fuera, un lugar muy frío donde no había CT, pero tampoco C." (There was no Spanish literature on the margins of the CT [Culture of the Transition]. You could only be completely outside it, in a very cold place where there was no CT but also no C.)[53] In other words, it behooved any author who hoped to make a living by writing to obey the CT's unwritten rules or face ostracism from critics, cultural supplements, and the like.

Throughout this book, I refer to the "CT" as the cultural context that ineludibly marks the artist novels in question. It facilitates understanding of the authors' and their protagonists' vacillations between defending autonomy as central to artistic identity and embracing the market as a space of possibility. It also helps us understand how and why contemporary Spanish authors have transformed the artist novel genre. Historically, the protagonists of artist novels have been positioned as oppositional figures, and readers' interest in them lies in their difference from the "common man." Their embodiment of the charismatic myth of the artist, and particularly artists' disinterestedness, has provided a source of fascination to readers anxious to plumb the depths of their unique psyches. However, as I explore in greater depth in chapter 1, contemporary interest in artist characters in the age of the CT is not exactly in their distinctive eccentricity but rather in their search for authentic creative expression that mirrors readers' own desires for authenticity. In other words, artists prove a compelling subject for a novel, not just because they are special, but also because they are relatable. Since its origin in the Romantic era, the artist novel, or *Künstlerroman*, has told the story of the artist's formation and development as an exceptional kind of person.[54] Maurice Beebe, in his influential 1964 study of the Künstlerroman, *Ivory Towers and Sacred Founts*, described the artist-hero's singularity in terms of his "divided self." According to Beebe, the artist protagonist of nineteenth- and early twentieth-century novels can often step outside himself, to see that the "man" and the "artist" are separable and driven by different and often opposing impulses.[55] The impersonal but omnipotent force of "Art" moved the artist in ways that even he did not always understand, and his moral superiority was grounded in this innocence. The higher power of Art chose the artist as a vessel and he was motivated solely by an intrinsic desire to create, so cynical calculation or interested desire could not form part of the equation.[56] The key conflict in many artist novels of the past was the irreconcilability of art and life occasioned by the artist's own divided self, especially that between a bohemian existence germane to the artist and the painfully limiting bourgeois lifestyle, complete with familial and professional obligations. The bourgeois "philistine" was often positioned as the artist's enemy, for were he to impose on the artist his own desires to follow rules, create useful and productive products, and champion the nuclear family, the artist's creativity would be severely limited. In short, the artist's resistance to "normal" life was precisely what positioned him as a hero and what attracted readers to stories about him. The pursuit of autonomy, still fundamental to the social category "artist," continues to draw readers to these texts, but rather than see the artist as someone who stands apart, contemporary authors present him or her as a source of potential identification for readers.

I argue that three related factors help explain the surprising revival and transformation of the artist novel in the post-Transition period. The first concerns changes in the Spanish literary market produced in the context of the growing creative economy. As large publishing houses began to swallow up smaller ones in the 1980s, they became less willing to take risks on work not guaranteed to sell. In this context, the experimental novels by the likes of Juan Goytisolo or Juan Benet that had dominated the elite literary field in the 1960s all but disappeared and were replaced by the mass publication of "easy-reading" literature.[57] As Laura Freixas describes it, the boundaries between the "literary" and the "commercial" became blurred in this context, leading to the production of what she calls the "best-seller culto" (highbrow best seller), works that combine the theoretically antithetical traits of being "literariamente estimables" (literarily worthy) and at the same time "se izan en la lista de los más vendidos" (climb the best-seller list).[58] The turn away from experimental fiction could be perceived as an aesthetic deradicalization that mirrored the political one happening in progressive circles. Antonio Gómez López-Quiñones defines the new aesthetic as one marked by a privileging of plot over form, its "carácter anti-elitista" (anti-elitist nature), and its capacity to "dialogar con la cultura de masas o la cultura popular" (dialogue with mass or popular culture).[59] Most important to understanding the revival of the artist novel, however, is the notion that readers of this new novel read to learn more about themselves. As María del Pilar Lozano Mijares notes, the novels that enjoyed the greatest success both in terms of critical reception and copies sold are those that offer the reader the chance to "sentirse identificado con alguien que se encuentra en la misma situación que él" (identify with someone who finds himself in the same situation).[60] The traditional Künstlerroman with its distant and hermetic artist-hero did not generally offer such opportunities for identification. However, a reconfiguration of artist-protagonists as "creative workers" in light of the aforementioned changes in cultural work outside the fictional realm has altered the ways readers can relate to their struggles and triumphs, limits and losses.

The second influence on the artist novel's contemporary popularity is a social trend that emerged in the second half of the twentieth century and encouraged people "to imagine themselves as constantly pursuing better versions of themselves."[61] Put another way, it became culturally normative for people to seek the truest expression of themselves by engaging in practices of self-development and self-care. In her discussion of literature and the creative economy, Brouillette argues for a consideration of how the "authentic self" came to have market value, and while she does not mention artist narratives specifically, this consideration is key to understanding why an audience would take interest in them.[62] For many people, authenticity is valuable in the sense that being one's "truest self," however that is defined, will lead to greater satisfaction, creativity, and productivity. But for the artist, authenticity is often synonymous with creative autonomy, and stories told about artists tend to highlight a relentless quest for those conditions that would facilitate their creativity. The commitment to finding the conditions and relationships that would allow for the development of this "best self" involves dedication to self-evolution and requires motivation in achieving nonmaterial goals. At the same time, it eschews stasis and demands, at minimum, a tolerance of instability, indeterminacy, and flux. The dedication to goals higher than the self, as in the case of the charismatic myth of the artist, "helps to make the risks and insecurity of artistic life seem more bearable," and in this artists provide a model of other kinds of workers.[63]

The third issue that may help account for the artist novel's newfound popularity, closely related to the second, is that more work, even outside of creative fields, has come to resemble artists' work.[64] In the neoliberal era, employers have capitalized on this adherence to therapeutic notions of betterment and the pursuit of nonmaterial goals to effectively extract more work from their employees by casting the "career as [the] primary site of self-discovery."[65] If workers believe that careers offer them the opportunity to "work on themselves," or to reach those nonmaterial goals they may have, they will undoubtedly dedicate more of themselves to their jobs. David Brooks identified this tendency in 2000 when he published his book *Bobos in Paradise*, describing what he called the United States' new upper class of "bourgeois bohemians." Of the "Bobo" at work, Brooks claims: "Companies learn that Bobos will knock themselves out if they think they are doing it for their spiritual selves."[66] They do this because, as members of this new educated class who are paid to use their minds, they "often regard work as an expression of their entire being, so of course they devote themselves to it with phenomenal energy."[67] This has long been the way that artists' own existential devotion to their work has been described, and since more and more people have begun to conceptualize their own relationship to work this way, stories about artists struggling with this dedication to their craft become newly relatable.

In sum, the Spanish readership in the post-Transition bought novels to connect with artists, who as paragons of authenticity and as models for intellectual labor offered them opportunities for connection. In my readings of these artist novels by Julio Llamazares, Angeles Caso, Clara Usón, Almudena Grandes, Nieves Herrero, Paloma Díaz-Mas, Lourdes Ortiz, and Enrique Vila-Matas, I consider the ways these authors respond to the market demand for such narratives about artists' lives and how those representations and negotiations of autonomy figure into their work. Though readers might see artists as models for work, these narratives show that finding fulfillment is not easy or uncomplicated for any of the creatives they represent. For these novelists, the question seems to be whether or not it is possible, or even desirable, to engage in artistic practice only to satisfy oneself.

---

All of the artist novels I discuss in the following chapters of this book were published in what I call the post-Transition, meaning that they were published in or after 1992, when democracy had been consolidated in Spain. With the exception of Vila-Matas's *Kassel no invita la lógica* (2014), they were also all published before the 2008 financial crisis, and in the conclusion, I discuss the possible repercussions of a "literature of crisis" on the genre. The chapters are organized thematically, beginning with novels about male artists in the first chapter, then turning to women artists and art historians in the second and third, and ending in the fourth chapter with a hybrid novel that resists easy classification but that interrogates the concept of "avant-garde" identity and the Spanish artist's position in the global art world. I also identify the ways that the artist novel lends itself to adaptation and combination with other genres popular in Spain at the time including the novel of memory, the postfeminist *novela de mujeres*, and the campus novel. This book does not advance chronologically, as I am not arguing that there was any marked linear progression of the genre in this period. Rather, my readings of these novels compare themes within the same broad post-Transition era.

In chapter 1, I concentrate on novels about male artists that I consider emblematic of a neoliberal re-imagining of the Künstlerroman in which the relationship to artistic autonomy is extremely ambivalent. Julio Llamazares's *El cielo de Madrid* (2005) and Angeles Caso's *El mundo visto desde el cielo* (1997) are retrospectively narrated, first-person novels of memory in which a famous artist recalls the story of his life and work for his child. Neither of the artist protagonists denies the commercial world, but rather each seeks some degree of autonomy within the capitalist markets that are considered an inevitable reality in post-Transition Spain. They continue to signal that autonomy in their retellings by privileging the parts of their life stories that align with the charismatic myth: their bohemian beginnings and their relationship with the art market that never got *too* cozy. However, in both cases, artistic autonomy is not the source of fulfillment or satisfaction. These two novels suggest in very different ways that autonomy—the full, radical autonomy the charismatic myth of the artist demands—allows the artist little freedom to pursue and prioritize social bonds, especially those between family members. Success is identified—either by its realization in *El cielo de Madrid* or by its absence in *El mundo visto desde el cielo*—as being highly individualized and located within the family unit. While artistic fulfillment may be a part of that success, it is hollow without the familial bonds; the artist's "authenticity" lies not in his distance from the market alone but also in realizing affective connections with others. Taken together, these novels demonstrate the way that the neoliberal age has accommodated the charismatic myth of the artist.

The second chapter of this book is dedicated to artist novels by and about women. These novels have been separated into their own discrete chapter because their fictional women's artistic trajectories are so different from men's and show how possibilities for experiencing autonomy are gendered. Hopelessness and resignation permeate the women's artist narratives in *Todo fue nada* by Nieves Herrero (2005), *Castillos de cartón* by Almudena Grandes (2004), and *Corazón de napalm* by Clara Usón (2009). I study all three of these novels in the context of postfeminism, as conceptualized by Angela McRobbie, Yvonne Tasker and Diane Negra, and Shelley Budgeon, among others, because its representational paradigm of women's labor helps us understand women's struggles to succeed as artists. By reading the novels as postfeminist, it is easier to see why their narrators fail to highlight the structural injustices and disadvantages women still face in the art world today, casting them instead as personal shortcomings. The study of these three novels allows for reflection on the highly contingent and socially produced nature of the charismatic myth of the artist, namely, to reveal that its extreme individualism has always been gendered male. For the women artists, the market is seen as not always jeopardizing to their careers and identities, but fundamental to it, as they have less privileged access to the symbolic category of "Great Artist" (whose image depends on distance from economic imperatives). In the women's estimation, autonomy is often a pose that can be performed in order to gain a foothold in the field. These artist novels by women are not aspirational tools for facilitating readers' imagination of a liberated future. Rather, they depict women's highly ambivalent relationship to the art market, and by extension the authors' own literary market, in which they are simultaneously highly visible and often marginalized.

In chapter 3, I turn to a different sort of narrative about cultural work by examining two representations of art historians, Lourdes Ortiz's *Las manos de Velázquez* (2006) and the final chapter of Paloma Díaz-Mas's *El sueño de Venecia* (1992), which parodies an art historical academic essay. I situate these texts within the genre of the campus novel because it shares a similar conceptualization of "culture" with the artist novel, by identifying intellectual practice as an inherently different kind of labor. Comparable to the way many artist novels represent artistic practice, these academic ones also set up a dialectic between "scholarship as a means to an end [and] an end in itself."[68] Therefore, these novels can be used to show what happens when the model of the artist's "flexible" and self-motivated labor is applied in other nonartistic contexts. I examine *Las manos de Velázquez* and *El sueño de Venecia* as historiographic metafiction because their awareness of their own textuality and fictionality highlights the constructedness of the historical discourse each art historian produces. Seeing how that historical discourse is produced invites the reader's consideration of the enunciative situation of each protagonist, situated within the neoliberal university where tensions between "disinterested" research and a "publish or perish" imperative are high. Each novel represents, in its way, changes to professorial labor in the era of neoliberalism. Ortiz accomplishes this through a more direct and decidedly self-conscious representation of her art historian protagonist's writing process as he completes a monograph about Diego Velázquez and the effects of his workload on his psyche. Díaz-Mas's representation is subtler, as she represents these changes in the academic world not through process but through *product* in the form of a parodied art historical essay by an unnamed professor. In "Memoria" (Memory), *El sueño de Venecia*'s final chapter, she shows the way the pressures to publish lead to a distortion of facts in the name of scholarly originality.

Finally, in chapter 4, I draw the art and literary worlds together through the study of Enrique Vila-Matas's semi-fictional novel *Kassel no invita la lógica* (2014), which focuses specifically on the category of "avant-garde" as an artistic identity. Vila-Matas's novel centers on the author's actual participation in 2012 at the quinquennial art exhibition Documenta(13) in a performance piece called *Chorality, on Retreat: A Writer's Residency.* The fictionalized Vila-Matas wants to know what it means to claim the title "avant-gardist" and wonders if the avant-garde still exists or if the biennial circuit has simply engineered a formula for creating art that *appears* avant-garde. I concentrate largely on the narrator's understanding of his participation in *Chorality*, with its direct links to commerce, as a threat to his charismatic and avant-garde identity that is rooted in the concept of disinterestedness. I consider the novel itself a response to that threat, as Vila-Matas is able to scale his experience at Documenta through a concrete product under his control that contrasts sharply with the performance that depended on visitor interaction to function. Through the novel, I argue, Vila-Matas restores his privileged position as an authentic avant-gardist that he feels has been stripped from him in the *Chorality* performance. At the same time, the eccentricity that he displays, as well as that quest for and questioning of the existence of an authentically autonomous art, once again, is one of the things that makes this novel marketable.

In sum, the novels by Llamazares, Caso, Usón, Herrero, Grandes, Ortiz, Díaz-Mas, and Vila-Matas demonstrate that those who perform cultural labor are complex, and their motivations are myriad. They reveal that there are varying and mediated ways to exercise autonomy, and they often depend on factors like gender, class, or the level of artistic consecration already achieved. They also depict the cultural producers as multifaceted and embedded in other social structures, like families, that influence their choices about their careers. Authors' explorations of the lives and work of other cultural producers give them the opportunity to explore and respond to changing conditions for making art. They show different visions of what it means to be a creative professional in Spain today, as well as the anxieties and contradictions that characterize this work. Artist novels like these have proliferated because so many cultural producers are still negotiating the conflict between the charismatic myth of complete artistic autonomy and their conscription by competing interests, whether private or public ones. These texts offer us, even as we are still living this period of flux regarding artistic work, an important tool for understanding cultural producers' own critical evaluations of that experience.

CHAPTER 1

# The Weight of Fame

## MEMORY IN TWO CONTEMPORARY *KÜNSTLERROMANE* BY ANGELES CASO AND JULIO LLAMAZARES

Although the artist novel had been popular in Spain at the turn of the twentieth century, it all but disappeared as a genre with the onset of the Spanish Civil War in 1936. The preoccupation with "pure" aesthetics that commonly lies at the heart of the artist novel clashed with the social realism that prevailed in the years following the war. But after the death of Franco and the subsequent transition to democracy, the artist novel experienced a revival. As the twentieth century drew to a close, a new breed of artist novel reconfigured for the age of late capitalism appeared in Spain. The novels discussed in this chapter—Angeles Caso's *El mundo visto desde el cielo* (1997) and Julio Llamazares's *El cielo de Madrid* (2005)—exemplify this new tendency. After decades of its virtual disappearance, one way to account for the artist novel's resurgence during the Transition is to situate it within María del Pilar Lozano Mijares's category of the *novela del desencanto* (novel of disenchantment), which she describes as a predominant expression of Spanish postmodernism. Artist novels share many of the characteristics of the novela del desencanto. Authors of the novela del desencanto implicitly rejected the formal and thematic experimentation of many mid-century novels by returning to narrativity. These are novels that privilege story, often blurring the lines between the highbrow and the popular.[1] Another hallmark of the novela del desencanto is a privileged depiction of the individual, marking a turn away from representations of collectives (social, political, or cultural). Lozano Mijares describes this change as the "reprivatization" of Spanish fiction.[2] Many artist novels typify the turn toward a supposedly "traditional" kind of fiction whose primary function is to tell stories and center on the consciousness of a single individual. The novels by Llamazares and Caso exemplify these newly "private" novels, centered on the formation or recuperation of personal identity and that often employ emotion and memory as tools to explore the self or reconstruct it from its state of fragmentation.[3]

*El mundo visto desde el cielo* and *El cielo de Madrid* are "novels of memory." They both evoke the bygone years of the artist characters' early careers through subjective remembering, and, as such, they participate in a kind of identity formation that appeals to the contemporary Spanish reader.[4] In *Narrating the Past*, David K. Herzberger describes novels of memory as ones in which an "individual self seeks definition by commingling the past and present," or by situating one's current self within history.[5] In the postwar novels that Herzberger discusses subjective remembering "saps the roots of myth-producing narrations," namely, those related to the Franco regime's single-voiced historiography.[6] In these artist novels, the myth that is rejected by the characters' subjective recollections is related less to the history of Spain under Franco—especially in Caso's novel, where references to national history are largely eschewed—than it is to the charismatic myth of the artist that informed and structured the typical Künstlerroman. In *El mundo visto desde el cielo* and *El cielo de Madrid*, the protagonists' own private, remembered experiences contrast sharply with the myth of how the artist should be—antibourgeois, nonconformist, socially radical, et cetera—and instead justify a vision of artistic life and work that fits comfortably within the confines of neoliberal capitalism. At the time the novels are narrated, both protagonists have achieved fame and, if not fortune, then relative economic comfort. The artist characters' confessional telling of their life stories are attempts to justify their actions and ideas, which some—especially their former selves, young artists just beginning their careers—might deem selling out. In other words, the act of narrating allows them to explain the breach between their youthful, bohemian aspirations to be "pure" artists and their adult reality of full incorporation into the creative economy and the longing to be part of a bourgeois family unit. Though the stories are ostensibly written for their young children, who are positioned to bear their fathers' stories into the future, the narrative justification of their own material success in the art world is much more about articulating a coherent sense of self than about leaving a legacy for their progeny.

Many novelas del desencanto adopt a tone of nostalgic and melancholic contemplation of the past similar to the one found in Caso's and Llamazares's novels. That nostalgia often serves to highlight the distance between current realities and past ideals, especially political and social ones. The novels of Belén Gopegui, especially her work of the 1990s, like *La conquista del aire* (1998), provide a clear example of this tendency because her protagonists must reconcile "sus ideales de democracia, igualdad y revolución con sus deseos de mejora económica y éxito social" (their ideals of democracy, equality, and revolution with their desires for the improvement of their financial situation and social success).[7] Eva París-Huesca makes an apt comparison between *El cielo de Madrid* and *La conquista del aire*, noting that both question the official discourses of the Transition's success and offer a "nueva interpretación del tiempo y de la historia [que] se basa en una mirada melancólica y en una crisis de identidad" (new interpretation of time and history [that] is rooted in a melancholic gaze and an identity crisis).[8] The artist novel genre that Llamazares and Caso adopt and transform in *El cielo de Madrid* and *El mundo visto desde el cielo* proves very adaptable to the model of the novela del desencanto that has been so commercially successful in the decades that bookend the twentieth century. Lozano Mijares attributes this success to readers' ability to identify with the novels' protagonists and, in turn, learn about themselves as they read about the lives of others.[9] The Transition and post-Transition periods saw readers turn to literature less for social or political solidarity and more for personal growth, and for this reason novelas del desencanto tend to be undemanding, plot-driven books that feature highly private and emotional narratives.

In the contemporary novels studied here the narration of memory works to uphold official state policies of the Transition and post-Transition eras, especially the wholehearted embrace of neoliberalism. Their use of memory differs from the novels published during the 1960s and 1970s that Herzberger studies, which use individual memories of the past to create oppositional narratives that contest the Franco regime's monolithic, state-sanctioned versions of history. Andreas Huyssen sees the literary focus on the individual, and the individual's private emotions, in today's cultural climate as a humanizing subversion of neoliberalism's calculating systemization. Huyssen speaks of the contemporary tendency toward "obsessive self-musealization" that serves as a way for those looking back on their lives to "claim some anchoring space" in a chaotic world.[10] He suggests that the popularity of memoir writing and confessional literature today reflects an urge for self-preservation in the face of the "planned obsolescence of consumer society."[11] And yet, as Rachel Greenwald Smith asserts in her book *Affect and American Literature in the Age of Neoliberalism*, individualization is both key to capitalism and intensified by neoliberalism, so the focus on the individual and his or her personal emotions does not necessarily subvert market-oriented thinking at all.[12] In fact, Walter Benn Michaels considers these "individualized" (or, to use Lozano Mijares's language, "reprivatized") texts, such as the "novel of identity" and the memoir, to be "the neoliberal genres par excellence."[13] These novels and memoirs, which offer readers "self-realization through intimate contact with an other," are popular and salable precisely because readers understand this perceived intimacy as a sign of authenticity.[14]

Novelists of memory strive to establish an emotional and often ethical connection with their readers, and it is precisely this connection that leads Smith to characterize their books as "neoliberal novels." For her, the notion of emotional connection differentiates the "liberal novel" from the "neoliberal novel." Readers in the neoliberal era read for different reasons and with new systems of valuation of the novel that "conform to an economic matrix of investment and return" in which there is a productive or edifying outcome derived from the consumption of literature.[15] The neoliberal novel, then, presents itself as one of the many kinds of "investments" readers can make in themselves. It offers those readers the chance for self-improvement through reading, and for alliance, emotional identification, and growth.[16] In the artist novel, the opportunity for readers to identify with the artist figures—who in Caso's and Llamazares's texts are represented in many ways as largely "normal" people with artistic professions—situates the late twentieth-century manifestation of the genre within the parameters of Spanish postmodernism, especially as it is expressed in the novela del desencanto, but it marks a departure from the traditional artist novel and consequently reconfigures the genre for the age of late capitalism.

At least through the mid-twentieth century, the artist novel was a site for depicting exceptionality. The (almost always male) artist protagonist inspired interest because the novelists provided access to the greatness of the genius's mind, with the intention of leaving the reader awed or inspired by the difference in the artist's experience of the world from the common person's. Francisco Calvo Serraller explains that artist novels have long tended to represent artists as "los creadores más radicalmente herméticos, dotados de una identidad indescifrable por partida doble, pues no sólo resultan opacos hacia fuera, sino también hacia adentro" (the most radically hermetic creators, gifted with a doubly inscrutable identity, for they seem unintelligible not only to others but also to themselves).[17] In Spain, very few artist novels were published in what Smith characterizes as the "liberal" era of the novel, largely due to the dominance of social realism in the Franco period. According to Smith, the liberal novel depends on "the belief that people hold hidden interiors" that can be examined, turned inside out, and revealed for the reader's enjoyment.[18] It tends to focus on the "interior life of a discrete individual" without necessarily providing the same emotional connection the neoliberal novel will offer later.[19] The charismatic myth that informed many representations of artists—the perceived opacity of character, the heroic struggle to balance idealism and the making of art for its own sake with the world of desires, the radical pursuit of autonomy virtually inaccessible in the real world—made the artist an ideal protagonist for liberal novelists in other parts of the world.

The artist has become a subject of interest in the neoliberal novel for completely different reasons, though the root of his value as a protagonist still lies in a belief in his creative autonomy. Today, the artist appeals to the neoliberal novelist not for his or her heroism, separateness, and opacity, but rather as a potential paradigm of authenticity, of originality and self-definition, a model to which nonartist readers can relate and aspire. The clichéd belief that creative work is noble, self-expressive, and more gratifying than "normal" work persists, despite the complex sorts of identity work in which real creative workers engage. In *Literature and the Creative Economy*, Sarah Brouillette argues that even when an author's or artist's work is commercial or middlebrow, its value depends on the creator's perceived uniqueness or the idea that the work was generated by a distinctive individual. However, the emphasis on a singular creator often mystifies the realities of making an artistic product, obscuring the network of people whose labor brings a work of art or literature into being and before an audience.[20] Most artists do not stand apart from the economy but instead find ways to produce works with meaning and social impact from within the confines of capitalism; at the same time, *appearing* to deny commercial necessity is often key to that success.[21] The appearance of resisting incorporation into capitalist cultural markets is, to some degree, expected and actually increases the artist's value because his or her "special position vis-à-vis capitalist value has been structured into the field."[22] For a reading public interested in authenticity and identity work, in optimization and making projects of themselves, in investing in learning and promoting authenticity in the name of increased productivity and happiness, the artist novel today can offer an opportunity to connect with characters whose resistance to the market in pursuit of their "passion" makes them appear inspiring and authentic.

The association of artists with the concept of *difference* has a long history that becomes apparent with even a cursory review of artist novel tradition, whose roots in western Europe date back to the late eighteenth century. The artist novel emerged at a time when, in the face of the disappearance of the "universal" ideal of beauty, creators began to represent an individually subjective view of the world. The art-buying public had changed, and while artists were now freer to engage in self-expression, the liberation from traditional patrons like the court and the church provoked crises of legitimation.[23] As time went on, the artist came to be considered a "culture hero" in some circles for his struggle to endure as an author of handmade work in an increasingly mechanized world. Bernard Smith explains: "It was in this survival situation that he survived into the industrial society as a new mutation of a culture-hero, in order . . . to sustain an old-fashioned, but human, mode of production in an increasingly inhuman, inorganic situation."[24] The artist was understood to stand apart and inhabit a space that was uniquely and authentically representative of the human experience because of its ostensible distance from commerce and technology. While the artist may not be considered a hero today, the idea of his or her labor as separate from the rest of the "inhuman, inorganic" world has persisted and now serves as a model for many other kinds of work. As Brouillette has shown, the work of artists, defined as "free, unique, and individual," contrasts with "dishonorable" work that is routine and impersonal, often associated with the service industry.[25]

The artist's work is perceived not only as separate from the rest of the market economy but also as "oppositional" to it. Artist protagonists like the ones in these novels who aspire to work in elite fields of cultural production, must at least appear to resent the commodification of their work; they must project an image of their own "freedom" from commercial markets if they hope to eventually profit from those same markets. Brouillette observes that readers of literature today are "themselves inclined to disavow instrumental goals as secondary to, or as inhibitors of, immaterial goods like self-knowledge, authenticity, originality, and happiness," so the artist character's disavowal of his or her own instrumentalization by capital presents a point of identification for even nonartist readers.[26] The Spanish literary representations of artists studied here superficially resemble the heroes of the romantically inflected Künstlerroman of the late nineteenth and early twentieth centuries. The easily recognizable characteristics of the artistic personality are, paradoxically, those used to signal artist characters' originality and capacity to identify (and express) their irreducibly "true" selves, uncontaminated by the dictates of society or commerce. Brouillette convincingly argues that many of the characteristics that mark artists' supposed rejection of commodification are actually also *effects* of commodification because they underscore social notions of uniqueness or genius that make the work valuable in the cultural marketplace.[27]

In this chapter, I argue that Caso and Llamazares deftly blend the artist novel with the novel of memory to create texts that typify a particularly neoliberal re-imagining of the Künstlerroman in which the artist does not have to heroically and completely deny commercial necessity to be authentic, but rather finds some measure of autonomy within the capitalist markets now considered an enduring reality in Spain. The detailed, first-person recounting of the artists' lives in *El cielo de Madrid* and *El mundo visto desde el cielo* places special emphasis on the artists' bohemian beginnings and disinterested pursuits in the immediate post-dictatorial era. This is a way for the authors to embed markers of their protagonists' quest for autonomy that signals their conscious distance from market-oriented pursuits that form part of the socially produced category of "artist." The artist protagonists begin their careers with a strong, coherent sense of self, but as their careers progress, they grow disillusioned with the myths about creative identity and labor, their narrative voices take on an open-ended, malleable quality, and they look back on their younger incarnations as naïve and misaligned with the realities of artistic practice as they have experienced it. In both novels, the narrators' present-day lives are characterized by successful creative careers and "privatized" love in the form of stable family ties (or the desire for them). The acceptance of the protagonists' role as fathers is a crucial component in each novel; the birth of Carlos's son in *El cielo de Madrid* allows him to justify "selling out" to the cultural industry so that he can act as a breadwinner, while Julio ends *El cielo de Madrid* filled with regret for having abandoned his daughter, Aline, twelve years earlier in order to devote himself to his art.[28] In both cases, the protagonists find that to fully realize their authentic identities they must connect with others, especially their partners and children. They show us that the artist's own individualism, as Brouillette states, "was never entirely incompatible with the individualization of goals in bourgeois modernity."[29] The highly individual gratification found in family life and economic stability combines with a nominal devotion to disinterested art-making as they pursue economic success to depict a satisfying search for an "authentic" self to an equally individualistic neoliberal readership.

Caso and Llamazares take very different routes to arrive at the same core concept: that there is value in seeking meaningful modes of self-expression from within the limits of capitalism. Both of these novels were published in what Mitchum Huehls and Rachel Greenwald Smith call the "ontological phase" of neoliberalism in the Western world, meaning that the values of neoliberalism necessarily permeate and inform them.[30] In a particularly Spanish context, the novels can also be understood as products of the Culture of the Transition, or the CT; they accept a free market economy as natural and durable and demonstrate no "radical" impulse to chart an anticapitalist path often associated with the artistic lifestyle.[31] *El mundo visto desde el cielo* and *El cielo de Madrid* are explorations, not just of the possibility for artists to achieve autonomy today, but of autonomy's very desirability.

---

*El mundo visto desde el cielo* is Angeles Caso's third novel, published in 1997, and the one she has claimed "tiene más relación con ella misma" (is most related to her own life).[32] She admitted that she could have chosen a writer as the novel's protagonist, but in addition to the fact that "ya se ha hecho muchas veces" (that's been done so many times), she wanted to choose a painter because it let her "ahondar en el mundo de la sensualidad y de colores" (delve into the world of sensuousness and colors).[33] On the cover of its 2011 mass-market paperback edition, the novel is described as the story of "la pasión creadora y la falsa apariencia del amor" (the passion for creating and the false appearance of love). This rather insipid tagline undercuts Caso's complex representation of the artistic profession and its associated emotions. It does, however, emphasize Planeta's marketing strategy by appealing to readers interested in those artistic stereotypes. The novel is narrated in the form of a monologue in which Julio, a wealthy and famous Asturian painter, takes stock of his professional and personal life while seated before a completed painting on which he has spent the past twelve years of his life. Julio created this painting because he hoped to "pintar un cuadro con todas esas cosas que parecían resumir [sus] afectos" (paint a painting that brings together all the things that are dear to [him]) that would be his definitive masterpiece after a prolonged creative slump occasioned by the suffocating presence of his partner, Aurea, and their infant daughter, Aline.[34] In the novel's first pages, Caso sets up a "once lost but now found" narrative that echoes the ethos of the nineteenth- and early twentieth-century Künstlerroman. Julio recalls his fervent belief that with Aurea and Aline's departure he would recover his lost energy that had been sapped by relating to others who demanded so much of his time: "Supe que, al fin, volvería a pintar. . . . Yo era el Resucitado, aquel que ha estado a punto de ahogarse y logra sacar la cabeza del agua." (I knew that, finally, I would paint again. . . . I was the resurrected one, the person who had been about to drown and was now able to get his head above water.)[35] Yet, there is a stark contrast between the way Julio imagined his future and his present reality, staring at a painting for which he gave up everything and that now means nothing to him. Instead of feeling excited and overwhelmed by the glory of his masterwork, Julio describes himself as "un gilipollas que trata de enfocar sus ojos deslumbrados para mirar un cuadro enorme y ajeno" (a jackass who tries to focus his bleary eyes to see this enormous and foreign painting), which is nothing more than "grandes manchas de colores luminosos y descarados" (large blotches of luminous and insolent color).[36] This disconnect between what he hoped to feel and what he does, as well as his inability to see himself reflected in his own work, provokes Julio's nostalgic and regret-filled monologue of recollection, addressed to the daughter he has not seen in twelve years.

The act of remembering in this novel is intimately tied to identity formation. Julio recognizes that it is with memory, which he describes as unjust and fragile, that we all "tratamos de construirnos un ser" (try to build an idea of ourselves).[37] The painting, *El mundo visto desde el cielo 2* (*The World Seen from the Sky 2*), with which he has tried to construct a sense of self, has disappointed him because it is far too static to accurately represent the dynamism of his life. With the painting, Julio attempted to remove his memories from the flow of time, to claim anchoring space in this immobile representation of himself, but by the time the painting is finished and Julio is recounting his story, he is more adrift than ever. The nonlinearity of the narration and the dynamism of the ways that memories are recalled and recounted show that the "I" who narrates them is still in the process of revising his understanding of himself, a process in which the reader necessarily becomes an active participant. For example, within the novel's first twenty-five pages, Julio's stream of consciousness leaps from a recollection of a trip to Brazil with Aurea that ended their relationship, to his decision to leave the Paris art scene years before he met Aurea, and then to the way his father instilled a love of art in him at a young age. Sometimes Julio's memories are sparked by objects, like a drawing he made of his father when he was young, a photo of the mother who abandoned him when he was a baby, or a porcelain dragon figurine that belonged to his nanny, Prudencia. As Herzberger notes, protagonists in the novel of memory often turn to physical objects to set loose a chain of remembrances, as the objects themselves are depicted as "inert and lifeless until they are awakened to meaning by memory and narration."[38] At other times, certain memories are discovered embedded within Julio's other memories. For example, a reminiscence of Julio's dealer making an unexpected visit to his house in Asturias holds within it the memory of his own artistic passion in childhood. All of these memories are interspersed with direct address to his daughter, in which Julio comments from his current vantage point on the ways he acted, thought, and related to others in the past, often wishing that he could have done things differently.

Julio finds that the experiential sensations of the past are impossible to relive in the present, but their recollection is essential to Julio's *understanding* of his past. He complains that it is nearly impossible to recover intense feelings like love or pain in the present: "Después de acordarlo, el dolor insensato no da dolor, no. Da cierta vergüenza." (When you remember it, that kind of foolish pain doesn't actually make you feel pain, no. It makes you sort of embarrassed.)[39] By creating a protagonist who does not feel in real time, but one who recalls and intellectualizes feeling and thus sees his past with critical distance, Caso also re-imagines the artist novel. Julio's memories may resemble the plot of a traditional Künstlerroman, but his critical distance from the events he narrates allows him to cast his behavior and beliefs as foolish or naïve. His youthful desires to "ser mejor pintor aún, acercarme a la perfección, parecerme a Dios" (be an even better painter, get close to perfection, be like God) inspired him to cruelly reject his first love, Pilar, but those desires now seem foolish and shortsighted, not to mention histrionic.[40] Julio's view of himself, which is reflected in his painting, is not of a heroic man who sacrificed everything for the worthy cause of art, but is instead a "patético diosecillo, víctima de su obsesión" (a pathetic little god, victim of his own obsession).[41] Caso's protagonist inverts the charismatic myth in other ways, too. Julio, for example, often recalls the disdain he felt for his Parisian dealer, Jean-Luc, whom he describes as almost cartoonishly fiendish, imagining him with fox-like claws and greedy eyes, ready to prey upon Julio's painting for personal profit, selling his Spanishness in Paris as a fetishistic token.[42] However, now, Julio tells Aline, "he llegado a recordar con cariño a Jean-Luc y su piso de la rue Royale" (I've come to remember Jean-Luc and his apartment on the Rue Royale fondly).[43] What was once fierce disdain for the commodification of art, as one would expect in a Künstlerroman, softens to a fond nostalgia, reflecting the values of a different age.

Perhaps Julio's most important realization from his current vantage point, however, is that, on some level, he regrets leaving his daughter, as he admits in one of his direct addresses to Aline: "También muchas noches te echo de menos a ti. . . . [T]e juro que te echo de menos, que he imaginado mil veces los cambios de tu cara, el color de tu pelo." (There are many nights I also miss you. . . . I swear that I miss you, that I've imagined the changes in your face, the color of your hair thousands of times.)[44] If his story had been narrated chronologically, ending with Aline and Aurea's departure, he may have appeared triumphant or heroic for sacrificing love and family for art as a great and noble cause. However, in the act of narrating his memories, Julio is given the space to reflect on his actions and realize the importance of the relationships he eschewed in the name of being a "real" artist. By writing Julio's story as a novel of memory, Caso has the opportunity to give her readers the best of both worlds: in Julio's recollections, an artist novel in the style of the nineteenth-century Künstlerroman, and in Julio's present-day address, the contemporary revision and rejection of an anachronistic existence, which offers neoliberal readers the opportunity to identify with the artist humanized by his nostalgia and his regret.

The narration of Julio's youthful heedlessness in the name of art reveals that the monolithic voice of myth—in this case, the charismatic myth of the artist that Julio had internalized as his truth—is a defining factor in his view of himself as an artist. Julio berates his dealer, even abandons his child, without a second thought because such actions are consistent with what he understands an artist to be. Recalling his past from the present, however, leads Julio to question everything, evidenced by his observation toward the end of the novel that his entire narration has been, as he says, an attempt to "explicar por qué me he pasado doce años pintando este cuadro, por qué os abandoné, por qué mi cobardía y el despecho de Aurea me han impedido volver a verte, atreverme a llamar, a preguntar por ti" (explain why I spent the past twelve years painting this painting, why I left you both, why my cowardice and my spitefulness toward Aurea kept me from seeing you, from calling, from asking about you).[45] Faced with a painting whose greatness was supposed to justify his egoism but now seems senseless and ridiculous instead, he is prompted to question the very basis of the myth upon which he built his understanding of himself and of the world around him.

Julio's rejection of Aurea is a way for Caso to represent his supposedly noble dismissal of the "interested" world in all its forms: the ostensibly suffocating ties of love and family that keep him from creating; the desire for material profit represented by her name, which roughly translates to "golden,"; and even the academic consecration epitomized by Aurea's doctoral thesis on his work. The incompatibility of art and love that Caso depicts has a long history in the artist novel tradition. As Maurice Beebe notes in his influential mid-century study of the Künstlerroman, the male artist protagonist rarely finds both emotional and professional fulfillment because art is depicted as a jealous and tyrannical mistress.[46] When the adolescent Julio ends the relationship with his first love, Pilar, it is because he is confronted with a manifestation of artistic genius that makes him regret his own misaligned priorities, devoting himself to love at the expense of his art. Goya's *The Drowning Dog*, seen on a visit to the Prado one afternoon, moves him: "Me eché a llorar a gritos. Amargas lágrimas por el arte perdido." (I burst into tears. Bitter tears for the art I had denied myself.)[47] The importance of Goya's pathetic dog as the catalyst of this realization is revealed later when Aurea, who will lead to an even more splendid downfall, offers to be "la perra de [su] pintura" (the slave to [his] painting).[48] Rejecting Pilar, and later rejecting Aurea, is depicted not as a rational choice, but rather as an existential need: "No era un asunto de elección, de preferencia, o de voluntad. No me había sido otorgado ese privilegio. . . . Lo mío era un problema . . . de voz, esa voz de loco dentro de mí que me empujaba a dejarlo todo y pintar." (It wasn't a matter of choice, preference, or will. I hadn't been granted that power to choose. . . . My problem was one . . . of voice, that crazy voice inside me that pushed me to give up everything and paint.)[49] This attitude evokes the Byronic artist of the Romantic period who stood heroically alone in the world. The myth of the artist in which Julio grounds his actions gives him faith that he has acted in accordance with his highest self. In short, he understands himself as a fundamentally different *kind* of person by virtue of his profession and thus defends decisions that those around him perceive as cruel and hurtful.

In a novel about artistic authenticity, this representation of romantic relationships is not surprising. As Brouillette notes, the "expressive individual" has been understood as one for whom self-expression and the autonomy to carry it out are paramount. Artistic identity has long been connected to an "insistent break with bourgeois mores," often represented by "official," and especially matrimonial, relationships.[50] The sense that daily life is burdensome to a person who wishes to dedicate himself to creative pursuits is immediately clear in Caso's novel, when Julio describes Aurea and Aline's departure as freedom from "una cena equilibrada, tus llantos insoportables, el olor permanente a colonia de niño y caca de niño y leche de niño" (a balanced dinner, [Aline's] insufferable crying, the ever-present smell of baby oil and baby poop and baby milk).[51] Julio sees himself as someone almost genetically averse to a baby's strict schedule or the timetable of family dinners. Instead, he imagines a life dictated only by his desire to paint—sleeping in his studio, drinking whisky, and eating frozen pizza, without a care for how it will affect those around him. The shedding of family ties gives Julio the sense that he is living authentically as an artist, though this feeling proves to be temporary.

Julio also aims for artistic authenticity by disdaining the marketing and promotion of his work, embracing a completely anticommercial and antibourgeois attitude. Brouillette argues that the creation of works that represent inner strife or subjective, personal experience helped consolidate the notion of the artist as antibourgeois.[52] In *El mundo visto desde el cielo*, Julio recalls that the work that launched his career, a painting titled *Antimaternidad* (*Anti-motherhood*), capitalized on his own trauma, which stemmed from his mother's desertion of the family when he was a baby: "Al menos pude pensar que el abandono de mi madre me había servido para iniciar mi carrera triunfante" (At least I could think that my mother's abandonment had served to get my triumphant career off the ground).[53] Despite acknowledging his career as "triumphant," Julio also recalls the ways in which he disdained fame: rejecting a prestigious prize he has been offered, refusing to present his work at Documenta, and snubbing his Parisian contacts because they are not friends but "intereses" (people of interest).[54] However, Julio continues to profit from the work he sells with what seems like little compunction. In a scene near the end of the novel, Aurea secretly invites Jean-Luc to see Julio's most recent work; Julio is unsatisfied with the image of flowering trees because he has painted it in accordance with Aurea's desires rather than his own, and the piece feels out of place in his larger oeuvre. Despite Jean-Luc's praises, Julio is furious that Aurea, now in her role as an academic interested in his legacy, and Jean-Luc, interested only in money, have conspired to take over his work. Julio insults them and flees to the mountain behind the house to, as he puts it, "recuperar yo mis propias almas perdidas en el verdor que se iba expandiendo en torno a mí" (recover my own soul lost in the greenishness that was spreading out all around me).[55] Yet when he returns from indulging his tantrum, he is surprised that Jean-Luc has not taken the painting to sell, saying, "Pensé que estaba claro que se lo podía llevar" (I thought it was clear he could take it).[56]

Julio reveals the tension experienced by those artists living inside Rafael Reig's "culture bubble" (discussed in the introduction) who are faced with conflicting desires to remain pure and to profit. In his recollections, Julio can effectively do both. Despite all his posturing, Julio is aware that he cannot actually permit Jean-Luc to stop selling his work. He and Aurea, he reasons, are able to "vivir bien con el dinero que había ganado en años anteriores y con el que aún ganaba cada vez que . . . Jean-Luc sacaba uno de mis cuadros de la trastienda de su galería y se lo colocaba a algún incauto" (live well off the money that I'd made in previous years and that I still made every time . . . Jean-Luc took one of my paintings out of the back room and sold it off to some unsuspecting sap).[57] However, as he reconstructs his identity through narration of his past he romanticizes his failures more than his successes. In a direct address to Aline, Julio disdains the fame he has achieved as he exclaims that being famous is a curse. Of course, he believed himself a genius, but fame and fortune were never the goal.[58] Failure, or at least lack of recognition, is an easier reality to inhabit, he explains: "En el fracaso puedes guardar la esperanza. . . . En el fracaso puedes parapetarte, armarte de ira, echarle la culpa al mundo." (When you're a failure you can hold on to hope. . . . When you're a failure, you can take shelter, arm yourself with rage, blame the world.)[59] In other words, the lack of recognition allows him to perform the "artist against the world" identity that he was so drawn to in his youth, without the contradictions that an embrace or performance of this identity occasions in the successful or consecrated artist. From Julio's perspective, fame turns a dynamic artist full of limitless possibility into a static, even lifeless, object: "La fama . . . te convierte en estatua" (Fame . . . turns you into a statue).[60] When he was still nothing to no one, it was easy to imagine a myth-fueled, romantic future; he tells Aline that "la nada es consoladora" (nothingness is comforting).[61] Caso capitalizes on the stereotypes associated with artistic work and personality—Julio glorifies and romanticizes failure throughout the retelling of his life and only rarely alludes to the real material benefits that he derives from his success. The external markers of artistic autonomy—disdain for the market, scorn toward his dealer, the rejection of honors—correspond to the recognizable social category "artist," and it is clear that Julio still longs for a time when he could believe in them in good faith. However, given that *El mundo visto desde el cielo* is an artist novel for the neoliberal age, the protagonist's (at least partial) repentance for the egocentrism that led him to abandon his family in favor of total absorption in his work mediates the typical stereotypes and offers readers an opportunity to identify with Julio.

Julio disdains celebrity for the way it "mummifies" him or reduces him to something easily received and even consumed by others, but from his present vantage point, surveying the painting to which he has devoted the past twelve years of his life, he sees that the way he has tried to capture his own life on the canvas has had the same stultifying effect. The moments Julio deems most perfect were those that seemed eternal, uncoupled from the passage of time. For example, at the beginning of his relationship with Aurea when he was most in love, he remembers thinking that his life was complete, "un cuadro perfecto, prolongándose el tiempo inmutable e infinito" (a perfect painting, time seemed to stretch out immutably and infinitely).[62] In more general terms, he tells Aline that a perfect life could only exist "fuera del tiempo" (outside of time), where there is no disillusion with the past or even hope for the future.[63] The title of Julio's painting, *El mundo visto desde el cielo 2*, refers to the height from which movement and dynamism become imperceptible. Julio's disillusionment with both his painting and his life is related to his own inability to stop time through his spatial representation. He once believed that in "los cuadros miserables que pintamos y en las irreales novelas que escribimos" (the miserable paintings we create and in the unrealistic novels we write), he could enjoy some semblance of "dominio sobre el tiempo" (dominance over time), but by trying to exert that control through his art, by trying to freeze moments in time in his paintings, Julio's work becomes static, affected, and stunted, even further removed from the elusive timelessness he longs for.[64]

Herzberger argues that memory novels with plots like this one fragment composition by rejecting a chronological retelling of the protagonist's life and by "reconfiguring the design of followability" precisely to remind the reader that the past is not static and resists easy control.[65] Julio's fragmented narration disrupts his (and the reader's) sense of time, as well as his sense of a coherent self. It confirms Herzberger's affirmation that the novel of memory "asserts the impossibility of narrative assertion."[66] Julio's attempts to define himself have failed both visually and verbally. Even his decision to destroy his own creation is thwarted in the novel's final pages. Just as he prepares to burn his painting, thick rain clouds gather and he asks rhetorically, "¿Tú crees que será posible encender un fuego bajo este chaparrón? Ya te decía yo que siempre andábamos haciendo el ridículo." (Do you think it will be possible to start a fire in this downpour? Like I said, we're always making fools of ourselves.)[67]

Ultimately, after taking stock of his life and career, Julio is left feeling that his total dedication to his art, aligned with the charismatic myth that fueled his youthful dreams, has left him with nothing. He is even reduced to questioning whether making art is worthwhile when it no longer has the possibility to heal or fulfill its creator, much less those who view it. Reckoning with the work he has produced leads to a personal reckoning as well. George Hagman describes the artist's aesthetic experience with his own work in terms of a love affair, which often involves an "unsettling recognition of the other as a real person with flaws and limitations (especially to one's own fantasies). Thus the reparation of art and love is not easy or safe; rather, it is often tragic and incomplete."[68] Julio's disillusionment with his work creates a profound anxiety about his own sense of self. After twelve years of solitude and selfish dedication to his craft, which he feels have amounted to nothing, he is more adrift than ever before.

The only solution lies in the human relationships he has always disdained. In the final pages of the novel, he remembers Aurea's last words to him, screamed in anger as she left: "¿Quién te crees? ¿Dios? Todos necesitamos a los demás. . . . Todos. Hasta tú." (Who do you think you are? God? Everyone needs other people. . . . Everyone. Even you.)[69] This revelation is the key to understanding *El mundo visto desde el cielo* as a neoliberal novel in the terms that Rachel Greenwald Smith proposes. Precisely because it is an artist novel, *El mundo visto desde el cielo* deals in some of the "dramatic revelation of inner emotional life" that Smith attributes to the neoliberal novel's predecessor, the liberal novel.[70] However, the dramatic revelation of facets of Julio's inner life—his unrelenting compulsion to create or his supreme egocentrism, for example—is tempered by his ultimate realization that it is only through attachment to other people that he can be fully himself, both as an artist and as a human being.[71]

---

The most salient difference between *El mundo visto desde el cielo* and *El cielo de Madrid*, by Julio Llamazares, is that the latter represents a "successful" search for identity that culminates in the establishment of the nuclear family of the sort that the painter Julio rejected. Carlos, Llamazares's protagonist, has a more consolidated sense of self and purpose that is reflected in the novel's form. Llamazares's novel progresses in an extremely linear and compartmentalized fashion that contrasts starkly with Caso's text, whose scattered memories reflect Julio's own search for meaning and self-definition. Carlos's story in *El cielo de Madrid* is told chronologically and divided into four distinct phases, marked in homage to Dante's *Divine Comedy*: the limbo of Carlos's bohemian beginnings, the hell of his integration into the cultural industry and the consolidation of his fame, the purgatory of his self-imposed exile from the city, and finally the "heaven" of fatherhood and domestic coupledom.[72] In contrast with Julio, who through his painting has tried to capture his life in one particular static moment, Carlos attains "conciencia de ser un río [él mismo]" (consciousness of being a river [himself]), constantly evolving and open to change even when it is painful.[73] Like *El mundo visto desde el cielo, El cielo de Madrid* is narrated as a retrospective monologue, but with fewer digressions, less nostalgia for the romantic, anticapitalist position-takings of bohemian youth, and no sense of regret or mourning for what could have been. Like Julio, Carlos addresses a listener who cannot respond to or contest his story: his newborn son, just a few hours old. Carlos explains to the boy in one of the novel's final pages the purpose of his story: "Para que sepas quién fue tu padre, cuál fue su vida y su trayectoria, qué hay detrás de su pintura y de su obra. Te lo cuento ahora, que no me escuchas, porque cuando me escuches, ya no sabré decírtelo." (So you know who your father was, what his life and his trajectory were like, what's behind his painting and his work. I'm telling you now, when you can't listen to me, because when you can, I won't know how to tell you.)[74] While Julio recounts his fragmented tale to a daughter he has already known and left behind, a casualty of a past that he regrets but cannot change, Carlos delivers his linear story neatly into the future, to a son with whom he is just beginning a relationship. Julio rejects emotional connection and suffers; Carlos embraces it and thrives. Though Carlos was once plagued by "un vacío infinito que crecía día a día en [su] interior" (an inner emptiness that was growing day by day inside [him]), the affective links between himself, his nameless partner, and their infant son allow him to reach his own personal "cielo" (paradise).[75]

Although the protagonists in Caso's and Llamazares's novels find themselves in very different situations in their respective narrative presents, the retellings of their artistic careers share some significant similarities. Like Julio, Carlos uses his narration to revise and rectify moments in his past. For example, recalling one of his first exhibitions in Madrid, Carlos describes the clients of the gallery and potential buyers of his work as "gente que yo despreciaba entonces" (people I used to disdain back then).[76] He recalls breaking up with a girlfriend in the name of rejecting "una estabilidad que yo entonces desprecié, en aras de la libertad" (a stability that I looked down on back then, for the sake of freedom).[77] Now that he has found the person with whom he admits to wanting to spend the rest of his life, and given that he supports his family with the money he makes from those gallerygoers' purchases, Carlos sees his youthful posturing as foolish. Even so, his retelling, like Julio's, does not emphasize a cozy relationship with the art market. Throughout the novel, Carlos continually contrasts himself to his friend Mario, a novelist who has successfully dedicated his life to writing best sellers. He also differentiates himself from his friend Suso, who aspires to be a "pure" writer, but has never published anything. Carlos sees himself between those two poles: he shares Suso's *desire* for purity, though not the wherewithal to see it through, and he shares Mario's need for income to pay the rent and put food on the table. In the middling position Carlos inhabits between them, Llamazares generates sympathy for him. He is more relatable than Suso, who gives "lecciones de bohemia" (lessons in being bohemian); continues "alimentándose de su nihilismo y su leyenda" (living off his nihilism and legends) and supporting himself with his parents' money; and considers failure to be the "best novel of all."[78] But Carlos is not as openly profit-seeking as Mario, who arrived in Madrid with "un deseo de triunfar cuanto antes" (a desire to be successful as quickly as possible) and, given his hope to be a best-selling author and his openness to being valorized by the literary market, feels little need to appear too disinterested.[79] This artist protagonist of the contemporary Künstlerroman, like many a reader of the neoliberal novel, does not reject outright the possibility of seeking both a meaningful mode of self-expression and a comfortable lifestyle within capitalist parameters.

Another key difference between Caso's and Llamazares's novels is that Llamazares much more concretely situates his artist novel in historical time. Carlos arrives in Madrid in a highly significant year, 1975, meaning his own artistic career begins with Franco's death and runs parallel to the transition to democracy. By situating his creative protagonist in Madrid of the early Transition, Llamazares necessarily brings to mind the social and cultural context of the movida madrileña. Carlos remembers Madrid at the time of his arrival as a place that "no tenía ningún límite" (had no limits): "En Madrid, todo estaba permitido, al menos para nosotros" (In Madrid, everything was allowed, or at least it was for us).[80] The movida developed as a countercultural youth movement in the climate of euphoria that followed Franco's death and was part of the cultural renaissance that had been widely anticipated with the fall of the dictatorship. The demand for cultural products was high, and with less censorship and greater economic prosperity among the general public, artistic expression took on new forms and offered artists opportunities that had not been seen in decades, especially those outside of traditional fields like painting and literature. It is into this milieu that Carlos and his friends integrate when they arrive in Madrid, which appears to them as "una especie de puerto franco en el que se vivían ya los nuevos tiempos que se avecinaban" (a sort of open port in which the impending new era was already being lived).[81] As Hamilton Stapell explains, the local government of Madrid, headed up at the time by Mayor Enrique Tierno Galván, took a strong interest in the movida because of its plurality and inclusivity, but also because it promoted cultural participation over political mobilization, which, during the transition to democracy, "might have led to polarization and social unrest."[82]

Carlos makes clear that young people like him also preferred cultural participation to political mobilization. He recalls that he and his friends had a political consciousness, "[Pero] anteponíamos la vida y el arte a la política. Cuestión que no provocaba no pocas ni pequeñas discusiones con los que habían hecho de ésta prácticamente una religión" ([But] we put art and life before politics. This was something that provoked great and frequent disputes with those who had made politics a sort of religion).[83] Thankful for a movement that encouraged democratic and civic participation but skirted politics, Tierno Galván's administration helped fund the cultural arm of the movida through the sponsorship and promotion of exhibitions, cultural magazines, and the like.[84] Stapell asserts that there was a great deal of synergy between different disciplines and venues during the movida era that allowed work to be shared. He cites, to name two examples, the founding in 1982 of ARCO (Feria Internacional de Arte Contemporáneo), Madrid's most prestigious art fair, and art coverage in *El País*, which circulated names and ideas.[85] Both cause Carlos's career to take off in the novel: he is featured in a report on "new Spanish painting" in *El País* that turns him into an object of interest among the other newspapers as well, and, later, his participation in ARCO transforms his "éxito modesto" (modest success) into "éxito fulgurante" (stunning success).[86]

These shifts happen for Carlos after several years in Madrid and coincide with what can be considered the end of the movida. When Tierno Galván died in 1986, the new municipal administration took a different approach and ended the kind of government sponsorship of regional projects that Tierno Galván had championed. Madrid's government settled more in line with the national Spanish Socialist Workers' Party (PSOE) and its "Europeanizing" trends.[87] Given that "Europeanization" was based on embracing free markets and fostering prosperity, state sponsorship of artists was reduced, and private cultural "industries" were encouraged to fill the void. This is evidenced by the fact that, as Stapell explains, total spending on culture by the city of Madrid decreased by 30 percent between 1986 and 1987.[88] This change was met with little resistance, for "the capital passed from 'punk' to 'yuppie,' as everyone aspired to be a financier instead of an artist."[89] While Carlos and his friends retain their artistic dreams, the shift away from the bohemian days of the early Transition gives way to marked professionalization, coinciding with the trends experienced more broadly in Madrid. In fact, Carlos directly compares his and his friends' evolution to that of the city. By the end of the 1980s, he notes, "Ni yo era el mismo de aquella época, ni mis amigos seguían siendo los que eran, ni Madrid era ya tampoco la misma ciudad de entonces. Como nosotros, había cambiado profundamente, empujada por el ritmo de su modernización." (I wasn't the same person I had been back then, my friends weren't the people they had been, and neither was Madrid the same city it was then. Like us, Madrid had undergone a profound transformation, pushed by the rhythm of its modernization.)[90] In the late 1980s, culture began to be put to work for economic growth, especially as cultural industries claimed to offer great possibilities for employment. At the same time, Carlos and his friends were becoming creative professionals, leaving behind their communal living and turning their dreams of being artists into jobs.

In Carlos's recollection of his past, the Dantean term chosen for each phase of his career assigns value to that phase and also helps justify and confirm his position in the narrative present, which he thinks of as his "cielo," or paradise. The movida era, depicted in the section titled "Limbo," is represented with some nostalgia, a bohemian age of community and art that is innocent and painfully beautiful, unable to be recaptured. Carlos's dismissal of this stage in his life as simple naïveté is significant, for until he reaches his "heaven" at the end of the text, he longs to return to "limbo" and recover its communal and hopeful spirit. It becomes clear, though, that, like youth itself, this phase was always transitory and not a place to which one could return. The structure of the first section, different from the other three, confirms this notion. Carlos's memory of his days in "limbo" does not immerse the reader in the joy of those moments firsthand. Rather, he begins by remembering the day he realized, much to his own chagrin, that this phase was ending. It is 1985, and Carlos is seated in El Limbo, a bar in which he and his friends have spent many of their nights, remembering with great nostalgia their first years in Madrid. Those years have drawn definitively to a close, largely for reasons of their individual economic success and subsequent alienation from one another. Carlos fears accepting change and remembers a premonition that once he left the bar that night everything would change. Longing for the safety of sameness, he is comforted by a painting on the bar's ceiling, which looks like a night sky, complete with stars and an ever-waning moon. The repeated association of the unchanging but artificial sky with Carlos's state of limbo suggests that what he desires at this stage is artificial, too. Madrid's actual sky outside the confines of the bar offers even greater possibilities. Llamazares has noted that, for him, the "cielo" of the novel's title "simboliza los sueños y las ilusiones de Carlos y de todos sus amigos" (symbolizes the dreams and hopes of Carlos and all of his friends).[91] Leaving behind the limiting sky of El Limbo, which is a mere simulacrum of reality, means embracing possibilities for their lives and careers that are unforeseeable in the moment.

Not surprisingly, in the "El Limbo" section of the text, Carlos also recalls and subsequently revises the belief he and his friends shared about what it meant to be an artist, which was largely characterized by romantic anticapitalism. He describes this attitude as an "aesthetic anarchism" that was theoretical, not practical: "Un anarquismo teórico que bebía en las fuentes más radicales, las del romanticismo puro, pero que, en la mayoría de los casos, el mío, sin ir más lejos, se traducía simplemente . . . en una actitud estudiada y adoptada muchas veces a propósito" (A theoretical anarchism that drank from the most radical founts, those of pure romanticism, but that, in the majority of cases, like my own, could be translated simply . . . to a studied attitude that we purposefully adopted).[92] Although it was "[una actitud] que nosotros creíamos sincera todavía en aquel momento" ([an attitude] we still believed to be sincere in that moment), Carlos says time has taught him that he does not need to reject love and stability or look down on all the buyers of his work.[93] In other words, he has learned that there are other models for artistic comportment that feel equally valid. As his fame and net worth grow, Carlos continues to look back nostalgically at Limbo as a golden age. At the time of the narration, however, he recognizes that the person he was in Limbo was not an authentic manifestation of self to which he should strive to return but rather a performance of certain commonly accepted external markers of "autonomy." It will be Carlos's own nostalgic remembrances (which often deliberately overlook the precariousness of a time when he was always struggling to pay the rent) that will aggrandize his period in Limbo until the era swells to almost utopic proportions in his memory. When he starts to become famous as an artist, Carlos acknowledges it is hard to explain to those who want to gain the wealth and status he has achieved that all he wants now is to "regresar al limbo, ahora que, según todos, habías alcanzado el cielo" (return to limbo, now that, according to everyone else, [he'd] reached heaven).[94]

After he begrudgingly moves past the communal and bohemian lifestyle of the movida years, Carlos attempts different ways of finding the version of himself that feels most sincere. While he admits that material success and celebrity status bring him both economic and sexual benefits, a large part of the second section, titled "Hell," is dedicated to explaining all the reasons why he is not drawn to the art world. Carlos attempts to define himself as an authentic artist precisely by distancing himself from professionalization. This entire section reads as a critique of what Luis Moreno-Caballud describes as the "fame and name" paradigm that characterized the CT, in which new cultural industries "were creating a kind of cultural 'star-system' to stimulate sales."[95] Moreno-Caballud does not see artists as innocent parties taken advantage of by big media groups. He instead implicates artists in the "fame and name" game because they cultivate and capitalize on "the individualism that was latent in the tradition of aesthetic modernity (to the detriment of its civic potential)."[96] In the novel, Carlos contrasts himself with the other "star" painters at his gallery, known individually for their very marketable personalities. The gallery owners encourage Carlos to "cambiar de imagen" (change his look), for that look "es importantísima y más para los artistas" (is incredibly important and then some for artists).[97] In the retelling of his story, Carlos emphasizes all the ways he tried to distance himself from these mandates in order to demonstrate that he had only bought into the art world's games to a certain degree, unlike his best-selling friend Mario, for example, who "tomaba completamente en serio aquel mundo" (took that world totally seriously).[98]

Carlos's refusal to give in to what Moreno-Caballud calls the "degraded individualism" of the CT leads him instead to seek refuge in a different kind of mythified eccentricity. In the section Llamazares titles "Purgatory," Carlos tries to find solace in Miraflores, a tiny town in the mountains where he rents a chalet and lives for three years.[99] Carlos's belief that he will recapture his "true self" in isolation—and then translate that truth to canvas—is yet another manifestation of the marketable myth of artistic authenticity. The notion that an artist's individuality, expressed pictorially on his canvases, is worth buying comes from the belief that the artist is capable of distancing himself "del flujo de los significados cotidianos" (from the flow of daily meanings), a distance that will reveal some great truths about the self or the world.[100] This is what Carlos hopes will happen when he takes refuge in Miraflores, but instead it becomes a "duro purgatorio personal" (difficult personal purgatory).[101] When he is divested of emotional connections, it becomes even more difficult for him to create, and he calls himself "un hombre aterido y lleno de soledad que era incapaz de pintar en paz" (a paralyzed and lonely man incapable of painting in peace).[102] However, his retreat is perceived by those in Madrid as a strategy to cultivate an elusive aura around himself and his work, and his desirability as an artist actually increases as he develops "una aureola de misterio que derivaba precisamente de [su] silencio" (a halo of mystery that derived precisely from [his] silence).[103] This quasi-monastic departure from the world also demonstrates that Carlos needs others on both a personal and an artistic level; it is his loneliness that forces him back to Madrid and thus sets him up to find fulfillment in relationships.

Carlos reveals very little about the mother of his child or the new life they have built together upon his return to Madrid. The final section of the book, "Paradise," is just eight pages long, significantly shorter than the other three. Llamazares explains its length this way: "Dedicar otras ochenta páginas a contar que regresa a Madrid y que vuelve a encontrarse con sus amigos ya no tiene interés. . . . Al encontrarse consigo mismo, había aprendido que el cielo no está en las grandes ilusiones y en el éxito, sino en encontrar un lugar propio en el mundo, tener una persona que te quiera, llevar una vida más o menos agradable." (To dedicate another eighty pages to saying that he comes back to Madrid and sees his friends again wouldn't be interesting. . . . When he found himself, he learned that heaven is not in great aspirations and in success, but rather in finding your own place in the world, a person who loves you, building a life that's generally pleasant.)[104] This is a striking statement to describe an artist protagonist, even one in the contemporary artist novel, for it appears to be a capitulation to the bourgeois values the artist has traditionally and performatively disdained. París-Huesca reads the ending of Llamazares's novel as a portrait of a generation that came of age in the transition to democracy, one that has been "vencida por el sistema que mueve al individuo a encontrar la felicidad a través de la estabilidad económica y afectiva, anulando cualquier posibilidad de que los valores que proyectaron en la Transición puedan triunfar en esta sociedad capitalista" (defeated by a system that encourages the individual to find happiness in economic and emotional stability, annulling any possibility that the values projected onto the Transition could triumph in a capitalist society).[105] In some ways, Carlos exemplifies the ethos (if not the external trappings) of what David Brooks calls a "bourgeois-bohemian," or Bobo: a person "with one foot in the bohemian world of creativity and another in the bourgeois realm of ambition and worldly success."[106] For the Bobo, creative capacity is maximized when economic constraints are minimal, so there is no shame in pursuing financial stability through a successful artistic career. In fact, this has become so common it is now the norm. Brouillette also observes that many believe that the artist's authenticity is no longer threatened by the "possibility that her inner bourgeois will be revealed" and that the "wish to do creative work . . . is perfectly reconcilable with a desire to live in prosperity."[107]

*El cielo de Madrid* is ambivalent, however, because the market continues to be depicted as something that can annihilate the artist's uniqueness. Carlos suggests this when he complains that creating work for the gallery, especially when he is still in debt and must produce at a rapid pace, turns him into a copyist of himself rather than a unique creator. However, once Carlos has consolidated himself as an artist, he is able to say that he is no longer "searching for success" and that "la realización de [su trabajo] es su verdadero éxito" (bringing [his work] into being is true success), picking up once again the language and tropes that allow him to appear self-actualized to the reader.[108] The women artist protagonists discussed in chapter 2, who produce their own work and struggle to make a living from it, would, perhaps, argue with Carlos on this point, for it is precisely his economic stability that allows him to make such assertions about the true meaning of success. The average reader in a neoliberal society like Spain's is likely to value Carlos's ostensible disavowal of instrumental goals. He still appears to be resisting his own valorization by the market at the same time that he profits from it. Llamazares engages the same strategies of condescension that highlight his autonomy when he presents his public self, saying in an interview that he writes only for himself, not "para excitar a nadie, ni para entretener a nadie" (to excite anyone or to entertain anyone).[109] While the novel may not be autobiographical, in this, Llamazares and his protagonist resemble each other.

Llamazares's novel is valuable and marketable to readers who want to connect emotionally to Carlos's search for self, the realization of his authenticity, and his newfound happiness. The love shared between Carlos and his friends in their bohemian community is replaced by a less communal and decidedly more neoliberal love, located in the family, along with a more restricted sense of social responsibility. This artist novel awakens readers' interest not simply because its protagonist is represented as exceptional, but because it offers what Rachel Greenwald Smith suggests the neoliberal reader is looking for: "identification, a sense of alliance, and emotional enrichment."[110] The reader can expect to be rewarded for the time invested in the book with a sense of connection to a character who, theoretically, chooses family over profit and solidifies a sense of self in the process. Carlos's critique of certain standardized cultural practices, especially those that belong to the large-scale field of cultural production, proves to be quite amenable to capitalist incorporation within the novel as his distance from Madrid increases his work's value, but also outside of it as the novel is marketed as a "search for happiness" that culminates in casting off the false paradise of fame and fortune.

---

Blending the genres of the memory novel and the artist novel allows Caso and Llamazares to reconfigure the latter for the post-Transition era in which capitalist reality is enduring and full-throated romantic anticapitalism is anachronistic. The retrospective first-person narration addressed to an interlocutor who is unable to contest the narrative gives each artist protagonist total control over his own story and allows for the most advantageous retelling to justify or explain his circumstances in the narrative present. The very fact that these artists feel compelled to validate their career and life choices and explain their success is indicative of their need to continue publicly performing at least some level of disinterestedness. As Mark Banks reminds us, "the demand from the public for original products generated by concrete and named individuals" means that artists' ability to make careers out of their talents lies in emphasizing their authenticity and uniqueness as creators.[111] They do this by performing (consciously or not) some of the traits essential to the myth of the artist—the same one that undergirded the Romantic-inspired artist novel. But in different ways, the novels by Caso and Llamazares reveal that commitment to art and meaningful self-expression (which we should not cynically dismiss as impossible to achieve) can and often must co-exist alongside the decidedly commonplace values of economic stability, emotional well-being, and a dedication to family.[112] It is possible to read Caso's novel as containing the seeds of more radical or militant possibilities for art to break with capitalism, but neither of these novels suggests that such a rupture from commerce will take place any time soon. In this way, they both uphold the CT ideology that tacitly supports and even promotes democratic party politics and capitalist free markets.

Again, the artist protagonists in *El mundo visto desde el cielo* and *El cielo de Madrid* are not interesting to readers for their exceptionality. Rather, these novels, both clear examples in form and content of the "reprivatized " Spanish novel of the post-Transition, are successful insofar as they allow the reader to identify with the artist who finds his "paradise" (or who believes he could have found it) within the family unit. Having lived the dictates of an anachronistic myth, Julio is left with a scattered and fragmented sense of self, reflected clearly in the novel's narrative fragmentation, while Carlos has allowed himself and his ideas about what it means to be an artist to evolve over time, ultimately leading him to his personal paradise—a family. Julio's intransigence is reflected in his static painting, while Carlos's adaptability manifests in his conception of himself as a river, ever changing and open to the flow of time. The way both artist protagonists minimize the substantial profits they have made from the art world increases the reader's perception of their authenticity as artists. However, the failure to recognize those profits also hides the fact that they are freer to express themselves "authentically" when they are relieved of economic necessity. Living on their accrued profits, Julio can spend twelve years on one painting (only to burn it later) and Carlos can retreat from Madrid for three years, maintaining his home in the city and his chalet in Miraflores. The women artist protagonists discussed in chapter 2 never attain a level of success that would allow them to hide their connections to the market. The market never has the chance to annihilate the women's creativity, for they struggle to find buyers for their work, a problem the men of these novels never face. The stark difference between the weight of fame these men struggle to bear and the inability of the women to succeed at all highlights the (male) economic privilege that allows Julio and Carlos the opportunity to succeed and disavow their success, to have families and continue to be taken seriously as artists, and to appeal to readers as both authentic and relatable.

CHAPTER 2

# The Postfeminist Turn in the Artist Novel by Women

## THE CASE OF ALMUDENA GRANDES, CLARA USÓN, AND NIEVES HERRERO

In one of the first studies ever published on artist novels by and about women, Linda Huf asserts that books about women artists share so many similarities with one another and differ so greatly from those written by men that they should be considered as having their own unique tradition.[1] When Huf published her book in 1983, the study of women's artist novels was just beginning in earnest, running parallel to the rise of feminist art history in much of the West.[2] More than a decade earlier, Linda Nochlin had famously answered her own question—"Why have there been no great women artists?"—by placing blame with "our institutions and our education" rather than "our stars, our hormones, our menstrual cycles, or our empty internal spaces."[3] For Nochlin, women's lack of artistic canonization could be attributed to the "myth of the Great Artist," a myth about "genius and atemporal, mysterious power" that has always been gendered male and that has refused to take into account the social and economic conditions in which great art has been produced.[4] Though there were disparate models of narrating the artist hero's experience in novels by and about men, the individualistic nature of the artist was a guiding thread throughout. From the bohemian, "art as experience" mentality to the monastic ivory tower existence, the emphasis on unfettered individualism was incompatible with the concept of woman as selfless nurturer dedicating herself to the care and service of others.[5] While men's artist novels tend to grapple with the conflict between art and life, many women's artist novels are driven by the question of how to simultaneously inhabit the conflicting identities of "woman" and "artist."

Many of the artist novels written by western European and North American women in the nineteenth and twentieth centuries focus on the myriad structural constraints that kept women from succeeding as artists. These novels challenge the belief, widely held into the twentieth century, that women were biologically incapable of creating art, and they detail the practical and material impediments to a woman's artistic career, challenges that range from maternal and domestic responsibilities to the lack of a dedicated workspace and inadequate access to professional training. Rachel Blau DuPlessis extrapolates a feminist conclusion from these fictional representations of the constraints on the woman artist, asserting that "the figure of the female artist encodes the conflict between any empowered woman and the barriers to her achievement."[6] For the protagonists of nineteenth- and twentieth-century women's artist novels, it is a countercultural choice to forgo family, domesticity, and love in order to devote themselves to creating. Art is invested with liberating potential, and the women of these novels achieve feminist goals (even if they are never named as such) by aesthetic means.[7] As Roberta White notes, the choice to imagine entirely fictional female painters in artist novels, rather than create fictionalized versions of real painters with historically recorded lives, allows the imaginary protagonist to be "a projection of the author's idea of art and women's claims to a place in the world of art."[8] The creation of fictional but *possible* worlds in which a woman could feasibly transcend the many barriers between her and the opportunity to make art and perhaps even become a practicing professional artist made women's artist novels radical expressions of hope.

The artist novels by Spanish women studied in this chapter—Almudena Grandes's *Castillos de cartón* (2004), Nieves Herrero's *Todo fue nada* (2005), and Clara Usón's *Corazón de napalm* (2009)—were published in an era in which many women no longer saw a need for feminism because they perceived that the structural constraints that once gave rise to conflict in women's artist novels had disappeared with the transition to democracy. This belief is emblematic of a late twentieth- and early twenty-first-century postfeminist culture characterized by greater gender parity in education, the proliferation of media representations of women in pop culture who see themselves as empowered, and the dismantling of both the notion of "woman" as a unified subject and "patriarchy" as a site of critique.[9] Yvonne Tasker and Diane Negra define postfeminism as a broad "set of assumptions, widely disseminated within popular media forms, having to do with the 'pastness' of feminism, whether that supposed pastness is merely noted, mourned, or celebrated."[10] Even as postfeminism acknowledges some of feminism's gains, it also actively distances itself from the feminist politics of the past: "[Postfeminism] involves an 'othering' of feminism . . . , its construction as extreme, difficult, and unpleasurable."[11] The antagonism toward a feminist politics of collective empowerment—rejected by many young women for whom the term *feminist* is synonymous with *victim*—goes hand in hand with what Angela McRobbie has dubbed "female individualism." For McRobbie, this is the notion that young women should now "consider themselves free to compete in education and work as privileged subjects of the 'new meritocracy.'"[12] In other words, thanks to feminist gains, the belief holds, the labor market no longer sees gender. By extension, if the best person for the job will get it, the only impediments to a woman's success are her own individual failures or lack of initiative. This postfeminist dogma has important repercussions for the women's artist novel. The twenty-first-century artist protagonists seem to have no obvious barriers to their success: they are unmarried and childless and have access to professional training and studio space in which to work.

While these women face few of the domestic conflicts that plagued their fictional predecessors, not one of the protagonists in the novels by Grandes, Herrero, and Usón becomes a successful, practicing artist. Why, in an era in which all paths seem open to them, do these characters fail?

---

In Spain, the ratification of the 1978 constitution seemed to offer a glimmer of hope for equality in many spheres as women were granted legal parity with men for the first time since the Second Republic in the 1930s. As repression dissipated through the 1980s, in Spain men and women alike embraced an "anything is possible" attitude that, as Yaw Agawu-Kakraba observes, theoretically "enabled the expression of hidden wishes and a free cultural life."[13] However, many Spaniards experienced a growing sense of disenchantment in the Transition and post-Transition years, especially those who had hoped for a broader social acceptance of feminism with the death of Franco. Given that the Transition did not radically break with the past but rather slowly and incompletely substituted Franco-era institutions with liberal democratic ones, the codified and institutionalized gender roles underlying Francoist culture and policies were not eradicated overnight, if at all, and feminist politics never truly reached mainstream acceptance.[14] According to a report by *El País* in 2013, just 1.7 percent of women in Spain identified themselves as feminists, and many actively spoke out against the label.[15] This number of self-identified feminists is shockingly small. For contrast, in an omnibus poll conducted in 2013 by the *Huffington Post*, 23 percent of U.S. women embraced the label, as did 16 percent of men.[16] In twenty-first-century Spain, as in many other Western cultures, discourses of female empowerment stand in as substitutes for feminism. Christina Scharff explains that "young women are positioned as the beneficiaries of late modern conditions," and the media emphasis on "flexible, presentable and capable female workers" confirms this notion.[17] In post-dictatorial Spain, the victories for women's rights in the 1978 constitution contributed to a marked lack of urgency to achieve feminist goals and even led women to question the relevance of feminism itself.

One of the dominant narratives in postfeminist books and films emphasizes the ways women's labor in the professional sphere has changed. The protagonists of these texts, many of whom work as "media professionals," are often single and preoccupied with finding work-life balance (between dating, professional obligations and advancement, social lives, and, for many, one day having children; that is, achieving the holy grail of "having it all").[18] The language of personal choice, and consequently of personal responsibility, comes to dominate the discourse of these postfeminist protagonists, and their professional success is ostensibly made possible by a free market economy that does not discriminate. Tasker and Negra explain, citing Thomas Frank's concept of "market populism," that in contemporary narratives the market is often invoked to remind women of the prevailing culture of social egalitarianism and opportunity. "Market populism," they observe, attributes the deeds and choices of biased and fallible people to the ostensibly objective market: "Markets were serving all tastes; they were humiliating the pretentious; they were permitting good art to triumph over bad; they were extinguishing discrimination; they were making everyone rich."[19] In Spain's new climate of neoliberalism, characterized by acquisition and individualism, women's economic success (at least relative to the past) and their ability to see themselves as consumers came to signal their liberation.

But what happens when the woman aspiring to professional success in a postfeminist culture is an artist? As chapter 1 showed, many of the stereotypes surrounding artistic identity found in narrative and in the real world have been gendered male and depend on a performance of economic disavowal. The conditions for producing art, the power relations that determine its cultural valorization, and, consequently, the representational paradigm for artists in literature have always favored men, but postfeminist narratives discourage highlighting these structural injustices because they would rather cast women as the managers of their own lives and inequality as the product of personal failures.[20] In this way, as it rejects feminism for its supposedly pessimistic focus on constraints, postfeminism normalizes "new patterns of exclusion and demographic propriety."[21] Nevertheless, the markers of *femaleness* and *femininity* continue to circumscribe women's lives and determine their possibilities. If it is true that women's greatest opportunity for success in a neoliberal and postfeminist context is contingent on finding their market niche, it becomes more difficult for women to embrace the traditional "autonomous" artist label that depends on distance from the economy.

In this chapter, I explore how this representational paradigm of women's labor in postfeminist novels changes when the protagonists are artists. The novels by Usón, Grandes, and Herrero detail the aspirations of three young painters who never become Great Artists and have stopped hoping they will. All three novels are narrated retrospectively and nostalgically, and this backward-looking narration suggests that their protagonists see their careers as finished before they have begun. They accept small lives—painting commercial paintings under a false name, working in an auction house, watching the men around them triumph—with some bitterness but mostly resignation. The women's lack of success in these novels reflects real statistics—despite the fact that more than half of the students who graduated with fine arts degrees in Spain in the 1990s were women, by 2010 they still made up only about 30 percent of all the country's working artists.[22] The hopelessness and resignation that permeate these artist novels represent the real-life predicament of many women artists in a neoliberal post-Transition Spain—neither able to embrace the ruthless individualism and disdain for the market that have been the hallmark of the mythified male Great Artist nor able to find and embrace the economic success that signals liberation for their postfeminist peers.

In terms of the space women occupy in it, the publishing world bears striking similarities to the art world. As Christine Henseler has demonstrated in her book *Contemporary Spanish Women's Narrative and the Publishing Industry*, the increased recognition that women writers began to achieve in the 1990s literary boom came at a price. Henseler argues that the rapidly commercializing literary market in the post-Transition period gave "women's literature a place to establish itself."[23] Women were publishing more and receiving more media attention than ever before even as they were still battling "the discriminatory practices of a traditionally male-dominated literary field."[24] The claiming of spots on best-seller lists, interviews with cultural supplements (often accompanied by highly stylized photos), submissions to high-profile literary prizes, and even the featuring of women authors in academic articles and books like this one allowed more and more women authors to make inroads in the industry and earn a living from their writing.[25] Commercially, women authors' work was more visible, but it is precisely that visibility that raises suspicion in an industry that operates economically but still requires symbolic disavowal of the economy (or at least the performance of it) for the author to acquire cultural capital. Henseler refers to the women writers born in the 1960s and 1970s as the "contaminated" generation, standing in stark contrast to the "cultured" women writers of the Franco era.[26] Usón, Grandes, and Herrero, all born around 1960, belong to this group of market-contaminated authors whose "life experiences . . . parallel the development of the modern book market" and who are "most often associated with the 'selling out' of the cultural industry."[27] Just as women's important but partial gains in the workforce have been taken as a sign of gender parity, the increased presence of women on the Spanish literary scene has led some to believe that women now *dominate* it. Even though the numbers do not corroborate this assertion, some male authors have even complained that it is easier for women writers to succeed today than it is for men, that they "explotan su sexo para vender" (exploit their sex to sell) and take advantage of "women's literature" as a marketable trend.[28] And yet, commercial success does not lead to canonization or consecration, and it surely does not give women Great Artist status. As Silvia Bermúdez observes, as of 2002, there was just one female member of the Real Academia Española—Ana María Matute, a darling of that "cultured" generation of women writers who were theoretically untainted by free market success. For Bermúdez, this indicates that "it would be absurd to believe that a normalization process has been achieved by women authors in regard to prestige and cultural value" just because they have entered the public sphere of authorship in greater numbers.[29]

Women authors often use creative protagonists who work in the plastic arts to make direct autobiographical references less obvious. These artist characters serve as models to help women grapple with the creative conflicts of their day. Why, then, do Grandes, Herrero, and Usón's artist protagonists offer such a bleak vision of the possible lives open to young, female creative professionals in Spain today when their authors, all commercially successful and highly visible, have benefited so greatly from the changes in the Spanish literary market?[30] The recognition by both the public and creative industry professionals that these authors certainly understand to be a requirement of success is precisely what their protagonists never get despite their training and their talent. As a result, these artist protagonists never have to struggle with the burden of fame that weighs on the male protagonists in the novels studied in chapter 1; there is no moral dilemma rooted in reconciling artistic identity with success, so the women protagonists of these twenty-first-century novels feel less compunction about desiring profit. The postfeminist nature of these novels lies in the protagonists' freedom to choose their professions, their lifestyles, and their romantic partners, but these choices do not lead to self-actualization or success. It would be an exaggeration to call any of these texts fervently anti-feminist. Yet, in order to feel empathy for these women, whose belief in the neoliberal doctrines of personal choice and responsibility do not lead to their fulfillment, readers must subscribe to a feminist politics that recognizes women's collective, structural disadvantages in the art world, disadvantages that still persist today. Given that such a small number of Spaniards identify as feminists, especially among the non-academic readers to whom the novels are meant to appeal, such a reading is far from guaranteed. Though the struggles faced by these novels' protagonists may signal to an academic feminist reader the continued need for structural and institutional change, the commercial success of the novels themselves also means they are part of an influential postfeminist popular culture that helps to shape women's beliefs about what they can expect from their lives, both professionally and personally. As McRobbie asserts, "Relations of power are indeed made and remade within texts of enjoyment and rituals of relaxation and abandonment."[31] For McRobbie, this means that these commercially successful texts and films are "vital to the construction of a new 'gender regime,'" namely, one that teaches women to believe that discourses of individual empowerment—professional, personal, sexual—can successfully come to replace any kind of feminist politics.[32]

Through their protagonists' respective failures, the authors of each of the three novels explore a different side of the question, What does it take to be a successful woman artist today? In *Todo fue nada*, with its mother-daughter plot, Herrero asserts the generational differences that supposedly make it easier for women to create today, despite the fact that the younger woman is less successful by virtually all metrics. The protagonist, Carmen, uses the rhetoric of feminism to highlight the conditions that kept her mother from achieving greatness, but her own aspirations for her artistic career remain unrealized despite her knowledge of the obstacles. Both *Todo fue nada* and *Castillos de cartón* measure women's empowerment in sexual terms. Grandes focuses primarily on the shift of a young artist from a sexual object to a desiring subject, a frustrated attempt that does not empower or bring her the freedom she seeks. In Usón's *Corazón de napalm*, women's empowerment is measured differently, not solely in terms of sex but in terms of economic freedom that the protagonist hopes to achieve in this text through successfully selling her work on the art market. The novel wrestles with the inherent incompatibility of the notion of a neoliberal womanhood defined by economic self-sufficiency with a charismatic understanding of artistic activity that discourages economic interest.

All three of the women artist characters explored in the following pages can be described as "conflicted actors" who inhabit multiple subject positions.[33] They make more or less conscious choices about their living situations and career paths as artists, but they are also still influenced on some level by roles considered "natural" for women and by culturally inscribed notions of creativity and femininity. It is precisely their conflicts that mark these characters as postfeminist, conflicts that can each be boiled down to the fundamental clash between a lived experience of a patriarchal culture's pervasive and ongoing misogyny and the effects of decades of "raised" popular feminist consciousness that has led some to believe that structural injustice has been overcome. What is more, this already conflicted understanding of what it means to be a woman in twenty-first-century Spain collides head-on with the notion of the male-inflected charismatic myth of the artist, leading each protagonist to a state of profound disorientation.

---

Nieves Herrero's 2005 novel *Todo fue nada* was marketed as a tale of women's empowerment. The young and aspiring artist's relationship with a Great Artist supposedly provides her the opportunity for self-reliance and self-management in the form of "las claves para afrontar su futuro con independencia y valentía" (the keys to face her future with independence and bravery), as the publisher's website declares. The publisher explicitly promoted Herrero's work as "literatura femenina" (women's literature).[34] This is noteworthy because, as Akiko Tsuchiya has asserted, female authors in Spain have responded to the label "women's literature" in two primary ways: either by rejecting any attention to gender difference or by appropriating "gender-inflected notions to serve their own ends," ends that are largely economic and promotional.[35] *Todo fue nada* is certainly "gender aware," in that it appears conscious of existing inequalities, but, as Scharff notes, the gender awareness with which many young women have grown up today does not always translate into support for or even acknowledgment of a need for feminism.[36] Similarly, the protagonist's own trajectory in *Todo fue nada* does not reflect an empowering feminist message despite its "girl power" rhetoric. This is not uncommon, for as Tsuchiya has observed, the use of the labels "feminine" or even "feminist" for popular women's works often indicates "the extent to which market forces have led [female authors like Almundena Grandes and Lucia Etxebarria] to consciously package these concepts for consumption by their readers," but often says little about the authors' actual attitudes toward women's issues and gender more generally.[37] The popular feminist rhetoric that Herrero's artist novel embraces on the surface does not translate to a feminist message when this novel is read against the grain.

Ediciones Martínez Roca promoted *Todo fue nada* by suggesting that painting is central to the story but also to Carmen's supposed empowerment. Carmen, a twenty-year-old art student, attempts to vindicate her recently deceased mother, who was a painter and art professor. Of the three novels I study in this chapter, Herrero's most dramatically and explicitly emphasizes the generational differences between mother and daughter in terms of the possibilities open to them and the choices they make within those possibilities. *Todo fue nada* is a postfeminist rendering of a trope common in women's artist novels that DuPlessis identifies as the "emergent daughter" trope: a woman steps into the role of artist as a "thwarted mother bequeaths her ambition to the child."[38] Interestingly, Carmen's mother, Lourdes, *was* successful by many accounts. Before her death, she established herself as a successful painter of large-scale nude portraits, supplemented and stabilized her income working as a university art professor, and appeared to have been happily married. Carmen's posthumous assessment of her mother changes when she learns that Lourdes had a tumultuous extramarital love affair with a famous painter, one that she eventually broke off because of her commitment to her husband and child. In Lourdes's failure to follow her passion, Carmen sees a great tragedy, and she recasts her mother's life in terms of her degree of sexual and personal liberation rather than in terms of her accomplishments as an artist.

Lourdes's artistic and professional success suggests to Carmen that equality between men and women in the world of work has long since been achieved, so that it is normal to the point of being unremarkable. Carmen instead interprets her mother's accomplishments with a postfeminist sensibility, one that understands women's success in terms of "individualized self-definition and privatized self-expression exemplified in the celebration of lifestyle and consumption choices."[39] It is this aspiration to self-definition that the emergent daughter, Carmen, will inherit.

In a passage from one of Lourdes's diaries, bequeathed to Carmen after her mother's death, Herrero dramatizes the differences between mother and daughter, highlighting the circumscription of the one and the ostensible freedom of the other. When Lourdes's lover, Santiago Bari, entreats her to run away with him and establish a studio in Berlin, she reminds him that she cannot give herself to art in the way he can because of her maternal responsibilities: "No es tan sencilla como piensas. Tengo una hija, no se te olvide. Romper lazos sin hacer daño resulta imposible." (It's not as easy as you think. Don't forget that I have a daughter. Breaking ties painlessly will be impossible.)[40] Lourdes writes in a later entry that Bari's life is characterized by a lack of restrictions: "No tiene ninguna atadura, es un ser libre. Yo no. Nunca lo he sido." (He has nothing holding him back, he's a free man. I'm not free. I never have been.)[41] Carmen extrapolates from her mother's story a larger conclusion about the historical conditions of women's art making that she couches in feminist rhetoric. In a conversation with Bari (her mother's lover and later her own), she laments the injustice that art history has imposed on women: "¿Te has fijado . . . en que no hay mujeres que destaquen tanto como Picasso, Velázquez, o el mismo Goya?" (Have you ever noticed . . . that there are no women who stand out like Picasso, Velázquez, or even Goya?).[42] She cites artists like Judith Leyster and Angelica Kauffman and exclaims, "[Por siglos] los hombres siempre os habéis interpuesto en nuestras carreras. Por eso, nos vemos obligadas a elegir entre nuestra profesión o nuestra familia." ([For centuries] men have always gotten in the way of our careers. That's why we find ourselves obligated to choose between our profession and our family.)[43] Though Carmen has no children and no relationship to stop her from pursuing her own artistic career, she uses the first-person plural to include herself among those women who have been victimized by the need to choose, which demonstrates her desire to take up the cause for her mother. She vows to Bari that she will never find herself in her mother's position: "No existe el hombre que me aparte de mi pasión por la pintura" (There is no man who could pull me away from my passion for painting).[44]

And yet Carmen never demonstrates the unbridled passion for painting she describes, and it appears that her own artistic career is stalled. The lack of historical precedent for women Great Artists that Carmen cites might be understood as a justification for this paralysis. Carmen expresses her greatest fear as such: "Yo tengo pánico a no trascender, a que mi obra no la conozca nadie" (I'm terrified of not being remembered, that no one will see my work).[45] As Laura Freixas asserts, creating art that one does not think will not be recognized, rewarded, or appreciated "es una heroicidad que pocos—y cada vez menos—están dispuestos a asumir; pero si lo hacen, es porque saben que van a 'resucitar'" (is a heroism that few—and increasingly fewer—are prepared to take on; but if they do, it's because they know they will be "resurrected").[46] The artists whose work has been celebrated later in life or even posthumously have, in large part, been men, Freixas notes, and so women have even less incentive to create art if they feel it will be recognized neither in their lifetimes nor after their deaths. This fear of irrelevance might help explain why Carmen has felt paralyzed in her ambition to become a painter. Carmen's mother's life of moderate sales and supplemental income from her work as a professor has little in common with the life of the Great Artist (represented by Bari) to which Carmen aspires. Lourdes's story becomes for Carmen a cautionary tale—a path to be avoided at all costs: "Quería que la historia no se repitiera, que rompiera con la tradición femenina de hacer siempre lo conveniente y nunca lo deseado." (I did not want history to repeat itself; I wanted to break with the feminine tradition to do what is appropriate and never the things one desires.)[47]

Carmen's attitude toward her mother's life reflects the postfeminist shift in orientation—"from 'living for others' to 'living a life of one's own'"—that Shelley Budgeon notes has allowed women to "enter as full participants into a late modern culture of the self that endorses self-invention, autonomy and personal responsibility."[48] According to Budgeon, this shift has changed and raised the stakes for articulating "successful femininity," which now "involves living a tension between exercising the traditional feminine mode of relationality and the exhibition of individualized agency previously associated with masculinity."[49] Carmen seems to wish that her mother had been able to adopt more of those individualistic masculine traits that in Bari rise to the level of caricature. Bari openly describes himself as "el egoísmo personificado" (selfishness personified) and believes that artists are not suited for life "en pareja" (coupled up).[50] Bari has all the characteristics of the Great Artist hero: a vocational calling rooted in childhood, a contempt for the old guard, and resentment toward "todo lo que huele a comercial" (everything that reeks of the commercial) despite the fact that his art has made him extremely wealthy.[51] He is also blind to the structural constraints that hold women like Lourdes back and separate them from men like him, as is evident when he asks her why she does not believe she can actually have it all: "¿Quién ha engañado a las mujeres? ¿Por qué no tenéis procesado en vuestra mente que la responsabilidad no está reñida con la búsqueda de vuestra propia felicidad?" (Who told women these lies? Why can't you figure out that responsibilities and the search for happiness are not in conflict with one another?)[52] Bari's belief, which Carmen appears to share by the end of the novel, is that her mother did not take enough responsibility for her own happiness. This is the wrong Carmen must right as she takes up her mother's quest.

The novel's purported feminist credentials, displayed both by the characters' rhetoric and by the promotional materials for the novel, are undercut by Carmen's actions. Her assessment of her mother's career might suggest that in order to vindicate Lourdes, Carmen would eschew restrictive relationships and establish a deeper connection to her mother through a dedication to art, similar to the one Bari has displayed in his own career. However, like her mother, she falls in love with Bari and enters into an all-consuming sexual relationship that leaves her with no time or desire to paint. She is not the early twentieth-century emergent daughter character who rejects the heterosexual romance plot for a "matrisexual bond."[53] Rather, the novel celebrates Carmen's lifestyle choice, exemplified by a "transgressive" sexual relationship with a man older than her father, as an essential part of her own self-definition, what she calls the "difícil camino de ser uno mismo" (the difficult journey toward becoming one's self).[54] The identity that Carmen constructs for herself reflects what Rosalind Gill calls a "new femininity," typical of postfeminism, "organized around sexual confidence and autonomy."[55] However, it does not take the (academic feminist) reader long to see that Carmen's new identity does not hold much liberating potential. In the end, she acquiesces to her father's demand that she desist in her relationship with Bari and gives in to the desires of the men in her life while discarding her own. Even more telling, however, is her tacit renunciation of painting.

The final scene of the novel does not find Carmen a consecrated artist, or even an artist on the road to success. Rather, it places her alone in her living room, watching Santiago Bari on television. Bari continues to triumph. He has added to his already substantial wealth and secured his consecration, evidenced by "una exposición antológica sobre su pintura [que] ha superado todas las previsiones de los organizadores [en el MOMA (Museum of Modern Art)]" (a noteworthy retrospective [that] has surpassed all the expectations of the [MOMA] organizers).[56] Though Carmen has done nothing to help advance Bari's career and has left her own to languish, the narrator describes her reaction to seeing the news report on Bari as a feeling of "great satisfaction." Her clamorous cries for women's equality in art—notably made before she begins a sexual relationship with Bari—are nowhere to be found. That version of feminism seems to have proved too extreme and hectoring to see through. Deborah S. Rosenfelt asserts that postfeminist novels often retain the vision of injustice typical of feminist novels, and even a longing to replace it, but the recognition of oppression or victimization does not lead to "stages of awakening consciousness to active resistance," nor does it lead to "victory or transformation."[57] The empowerment Carmen feels lies in her personal and sexual choices, not in her transcendence of the limitations on her sex, largely because those social limitations are presented as having already been overcome. Carmen does not recognize the injustice of Bari's failure to acknowledge her mother's domestic and maternal labor as labor, nor does she see a problem with idealizing the masculine vision of the Great Artist. *Todo fue nada*, published and promoted as "women's literature," capitalizes on a gender-inflected, even feminist-sounding, rhetoric and combines it with stereotypical notions related to artists' freedom and difference to produce a novel with the trappings of a story of women's empowerment. Ultimately, though, this novel is postfeminist at its core—taking feminist gains for granted and equating sexual liberation with total liberation.

---

The theme of sexual liberation as a sign of empowerment also appears in Almudena Grandes's artist novel *Castillos de cartón*. Grandes made a name for herself in the arena of erotic fiction. Her first novel, *Las edades de Lulú*, was marketed as "high-brow" erotica in Tusquets's La Sonrisa Vertical (Vertical Smile) series.[58] Grandes, one of those authors of the generation Henseler describes as "contaminated" by market connections, experienced great economic success with her first novel. Bermúdez argues, however, that she gained symbolic capital by "leaving behind the field of erotic literature and by becoming, supposedly, a 'serious' novelist in 1991 with *Te llamaré Viernes* [*I Will Call You Friday*]."[59] Bermúdez claims that Grandes used the commercial genre of erotic literature to establish herself and then took the name recognition her polemical novel generated to gain access to more prestigious presses.[60] Her protagonist in *Castillos de cartón*, the college-aged María José, dreams of being a successful artist, but like Carmen in *Todo fue nada*, she ends the novel having given up painting entirely. Grandes has explained that she chose to represent artist characters in her novel because "su experiencia es parecida a la de los escritores" (their experience is similar to that of writers), noting that though she personally has not experienced great failures on the literary market, "no se puede comprender el éxito si no se tiene muy presente la perspectiva del fracaso" (you cannot understand success unless you are very aware of what it looks like to fail).[61] According to Grandes, all of her protagonists—María José and her lovers Marcos and Jaime, all three artists—fail in different ways, but a closer look reveals that even their failure is not equal; María José loses more than anyone else, including her very desire to paint.

*Castillos de cartón* (2004), Grandes's sixth novel, is narrated by María José when she has reached adulthood and given up her dreams of being a painter to work in an auction house. The majority of the novel, however, is set in late movida-era Madrid, which María José describes in terms of its promise and possibility: "Estábamos en 1984, teníamos veinte años, Madrid tenía veinte años, España tenía veinte años y todo estaba en su sitio, un pasado oscuro, un presente luminoso." (It was 1984, we were twenty years old, Madrid was twenty years old, Spain was twenty years old, and everything had fallen into place, a dark past, a bright present.)[62] Just as in *Todo fue nada*, a contrast is established between a darker time when things were more difficult, especially for women, and a present in which anything feels possible. While Herrero accomplishes this through a mother-daughter relationship that exposes generational differences, Grandes uses the end of Franco-era repression and references to the movida to establish the relative liberty of her young female protagonist. María José's ultimate failure as an artist, as well as the failure of her nontraditional relationship with Marcos and Jaime, reveals the failure of the Transition and the betrayal of its promises to women. Grandes says that young María José's Spain is "un país amable y progresista, que caminaba hacia adelante que reía y quería ser feliz" (a nice and progressive country, one that was moving forward, that laughed and wanted to be happy), one that has nothing in common with "este páramo roñoso que tenemos ahora" (this filthy wasteland we live in now).[63] The radical freedom the Transition promised—reflected in the novel by both the free expression of art and the ménage à trois between the artists—was ephemeral, if it ever existed at all. While *Castillos de cartón* can certainly be read in terms of disillusionment with Spanish politics and society, it is also worth observing how Grandes represents the power dynamics between men and women artists in the supposedly liberated days of the early Transition.

It is not only Spain that shifts from a dark past to a bright and promising present but also María José herself. A flashback to her Catholic schoolgirl days in the novel's first section, titled *El arte* (Art), depicts a lesson she learned early about how her sex could circumscribe her possibilities for creating art. In this memory, the young María José proudly submits to her art teacher an original drawing inspired by a doll she hated. Considering the doll too saccharine, María José transformed it in her own rendering so that it "inspiraba un desagrado que estaba a medio camino entre la repugnancia y las ganas de llorar" (inspired a kind of disgust that was somewhere between revolting and tear-jerking).[64] Her teacher, a nun, chastises her for turning in "una porquería" (trash), and María José quickly learns that certain kinds of art are out of bounds for "good" girls, noting: "Nunca repetí aquella lámina, pero comprendí enseguida que me había equivocado. . . . Aproveché la primera ocasión para volver a pintar un paisaje verde." (I never handed in anything like that again, but I understood right away that I had made a mistake. . . . I took advantage of the first opportunity I had to go back to painting a green landscape.)[65] With her innocuous landscapes, María José can publicly appear as a "nice girl" who paints pretty pictures; in private she continues to paint things she enjoys—things the nun might deem frightening or disgusting. María José calls herself a double agent, "pintando cosas diferentes para mí y para los demás" (painting different things for myself and for others).[66] This strategy is effective for María José; by staying in the socially approved lane for her sex, she wins schoolwide art contests and, with them, adult approval. Her own chagrin at having caved to these social pressures haunts María José into her young adulthood, and when she arrives at college, she begins to cast off the cultural restrictions that until then had kept her safe from reproach. The university environment does prove more liberated, and her series of paintings of children with Down syndrome quickly becomes her signature theme that "miradas menos prejuciosas y más conscientes valoraron muy deprisa" (less judgmental and more informed gazes appreciated right away).[67]

In order to combat the paralyzing doubt she continues to feel, Jose adopts a set of countercultural attitudes and practices that she hopes will mark her as different, as an artist. She changes her name, going by "Jose" because "María José Sánchez García [era] un nombre fácil de olvidar [(was) an easy name to forget]," and starts drinking cognac in the morning and smoking cigarettes she dislikes because it seems like something that artists do.[68] But these actions also suggest a before and after, a liberation of the woman's subjectivity that allows her also to enter without fear into a romantic relationship with two men, the ultimate marker of her resistance, difference, and empowerment, which comes to dominate the rest of the novel. As Gill has noted, the postfeminist era brought with it a notable "resexualization" of women's bodies in media and popular texts, as well as their "sexual subjectification."[69] In novels like *Castillos de cartón* or *Las edades de Lulú* before it, the representation of women's desiring subjecthood is often seen as a positive change, a sign of empowerment. Though some read these desiring protagonists as "autonomous feminist subject[s]," Gill questions the belief that sexual subjecthood alone makes them the "assertive liberated subject[s] of the feminist imaginary."[70] As we have seen, the postfeminist orientation puts women's self-expression in place of politics, suggesting that any choice a woman makes is feminist because a woman has made it. In *Castillos de cartón*, it is certainly the young Jose's sexual exploration, rather than her artistic expression or professional success, that signals this time in her life as one of possibility and empowerment.

A closer look at the relationship between Jose and her partners, Marcos and Jaime, reveals a deeply embedded "retro-sexism." The defining feature of the relationship, especially as it nears its end, is that Jose remains in a dominated position even as she participates in a socially transgressive act. Jaime is extroverted and confident, an excellent copyist with little original imagination, and less objectively attractive but sexually seductive. Marcos, by contrast, is more attractive but less confident and sexually impotent but the far better artist of the two men. Marcos's talent leaves Jose demoralized: "Yo nunca llegaría a tanto" (I'd never be as good as he was).[71] Jose has already begun to doubt her own capacities as an artist when she meets Jaime and Marcos, but she romanticizes them as the artists she could never be, making herself more insecure than ever about her own abilities. What is more, the unspoken battle for dominance in art between the two men expresses itself in a struggle for dominance in the bedroom, too, with Jose as the prize to be won. When Marcos overcomes his sexual impotence near the novel's end—a change that corresponds to his stunning success on the gallery circuit—Jaime responds angrily and jealously as a tacit war for superiority ensues, played out within the confines of the romantic relationship. It becomes clear that Jose's choice to participate in an unconventional relationship in many ways masks the extent to which she is cowed and submissive in that relationship, in thrall to men like so many women in conventional relationships before her. Agawu-Kakraba notes that in the Transition period, the enacting of "subversive" or liberated lifestyles and sexual practices signaled an emancipation with respect to the Franco era but did not change the fundamental belief systems of the society in which those supposedly subversive practices were embedded.[72] Once the trappings of emancipation were stripped away, it was evident that the patriarchal conditioning to which women like Jose had been submitted all their lives had not melted away overnight.

Grandes has said that she chose artist protagonists for her novel because "el talento es un eje de poder; el otro es el amor y el sexo" (talent is an axis of power; the other is love and sex).[73] Jaime triumphs in the realm of sex while Marcos triumphs in the realm of art, and Jose is victorious in neither. The respective failures of Marcos, Jaime, and Jose do not make them equal, as Grandes has alleged, because even if Jose's male counterparts are unable to sustain success because of their lack of originality (in Jaime's case) or their emotional fragility (in Marco's case), Jose never achieves any artistic success in the first place. In large part, she gives up painting because she is committed to protecting the egos of the men she loves. This is especially true of Jaime, whom she is afraid to eclipse and alienate. Marcos sees the truth that Jose cannot: "A veces, hasta pienso que has dejado de trabajar por eso, porque te importa más conservarlo [a Jaime] que pintar, porque prefieres que te chupe la sangre a demostrarle que eres mejor que él" (Sometimes I think that's why you stopped working, because keeping [Jaime] by your side means more to you than painting, because you'd rather he suck the life from you than prove you're better than he is).[74] Even though Jose is without the traditional burdens of marriage and motherhood, her relationship with Jaime is one of self-effacement and sacrifice that is not unlike Lourdes's marriage in *Todo fue nada*. Jose, too, lives a life for others rather than a life for herself.

While Marcos becomes "uno de los pintores más caros de su generación" (one of the most sought-after painters of his generation) and "un pintor grande de verdad" (a truly great painter), Jose's talent languishes, and this loss is presented as a choice.[75] Marcos tells Jose: "Ibas muy bien, pero te paraste, y sabías que iba a ocurrir, que te ibas a parar" (You were on the right track, but you stopped yourself, and you knew it was going to happen, that you'd stop).[76] Jose's failure as an artist is part of a narrative of empowerment based on autonomy and personal choice. As Budgeon notes, these narratives deny the structural constraints on women and lead to "fundamental misrecognition of the causes of social disadvantage [which] are seen to reside in the ability or motivation of individuals to make 'good' choices."[77] Jose learned early that the art with which she most identifies is not appropriate for girls, and she trained herself to hide because reactions to her work awoke a sense of inferiority. This led her to trust herself less, and that internalized lack of trust reveals itself as she doubts her own abilities even in the face of praise from teachers and other students.

Jose's power as an artist—one first measured by school contests and her teachers' approval—comes from effacing herself and conforming. Her attempts to cast off those years of conditioning are met with some internal resistance, and that resistance, which eventually translates into paralysis, is seen as a personal failure on Jose's part. This is especially true when she is compared to Jaime, who is bursting with confidence despite the mediocre quality of his work, or to Marcos, who is unconfident but supremely talented in a way Jose does not seem to be. It is not surprising, then, that Jose would try to access power by becoming an object of both Jaime's and Marcos's desire. As Gill notes, women's "choice" to become sex objects endows them "with the status of active subjecthood," which suits their otherwise "'liberated' interests."[78] And yet Jose's sexual subjecthood does not translate into self-actualization or professional success as an artist.

Grandes has said that she considers her artist protagonists tragically heroic because Jose, Jaime, and Marcos all "quisieron pegarle un mordisco demasiado grande a la vida" (wanted to take too big a bite out of life).[79] However, Jose seems to want little more than what Grandes herself has achieved: a successful career as an artist. Grandes believes that her generation, the young adults who began their lives and careers in the early days of the Transition, like Jose, Marcos, and Jaime, were the ones "elegidos para la gloria" (chosen for glory), who thought progress after Franco's death would be linear and straightforward.[80] The Spanish cultural milieu did not support that progress in the way they dreamed, and men and women alike suffered the disappointment of falling short of glory, but in *Castillos de cartón* those disappointments are still drawn along gendered lines. Rather than asserting women's capacity to triumph in post-Franco Spain, the novel glorifies a typically male charismatic artist—the brooding, solitary genius embodied by Marcos—whose "failure" takes the form of suicide when the weight of his fame, which resembles the experience of the artist protagonists in chapter 1, becomes too much to bear. Marcos is overcome by celebrity and wealth that Jose can only dream of from her desk at the auction house. Her own glorification of the male genius ends up being self-destructive. As Margaret Boden asserts, if one believes that creativity is reserved only for a select few, then one "cannot sensibly hope that perseverance, or education, will enable them to join the creative elite."[81] Jose is unable to see herself as a successful artist who lives out her dreams, and the "laws of normality" take over her life and confine her to a bourgeois existence complete with an unhappy marriage and a dispassionate nine-to-five job, suggesting that despite all the progress made in the arena of women's rights, "normalcy" for women still does not include artistic success.

---

Clara Usón also captures the lack of parity between men and women in literary and artistic realms in her 2009 novel *Corazón de napalm*. After *El asesino tímido* (2018) won the twenty-sixth annual Premio de la Literatura Sor Juana Inés de la Cruz, a prize awarded each year to a woman writer in Spanish by the International Book Fair of Guadalajara, Mexico, Usón said that though she was pleased to have won, "ojalá llegue un día que no haga falta un premio de literatura femenina, porque las mujeres hayamos alcanzado la absoluta igualdad en todos los sentidos" (hopefully there will come a day in which a prize for women's literature won't be necessary, because women will have achieved absolute equality in every sense).[82] Despite the widespread achievement of equal rights with men in a legal sense, women still do not have equal opportunities in publishing and art worlds dominated economically and symbolically by men. Usón, as well as her painter protagonist, Marta, see that women's opportunities for success lie in their access to the market. In an interview Usón gave shortly after the publication of *Corazón de napalm*, she explained that she identified with Marta's desire to support herself financially by making art, explaining: "Ahora mismo como escritora, mi mayor preocupación es el número de libros vendidos, algo impensable cuando di mis primeros pasos. Tanto vendes, tanto vales. Hay que saber venderse. Somos un producto." (Right now as a writer, my greatest concern is the number of books sold, something unthinkable when I was getting started. Your worth depends on how much you sell. You have to know how to sell yourself. We are a product.)[83] Much more than *Todo fue nada* or *Castillos de cartón*, *Corazón de napalm* openly broaches the subject of women's relationship to the art market, and Usón's identification with Marta suggests that the novel reflects her understanding of the literary market that she herself must navigate. A pattern begins to emerge: in *Corazón de napalm* another woman with talent, professional training, and no domestic impediments narrates retrospectively the career she gave up and the hope she lost. *Corazón de napalm* is the story of a woman who learns that her art is not respected unless she conforms to certain expectations of her sex, which still exist despite the belief that the market has leveled the playing field. Because of the instability and uncertainty inherent in such a world, not to mention the burdens of personal responsibility and self-management, the novel takes its postfeminist turn as Marta embraces the fantasy of patriarchal protection by becoming a wife and mother, giving up her career in the process.

*Corazón de napalm*, winner of the 2009 Premio Biblioteca Breve, narrates two parallel stories set in different historical moments. The story of Marta's artistic career takes place in 2006 and is narrated in the even-numbered chapters, while the odd-numbered chapters tell the story of fourteen-year-old Fede, who is an aspiring punk and a fan of Sid Vicious and is hopelessly in love with his mother. Fede's charming but tragic story is set in 1984 and culminates when he accidentally kills a baby he has kidnapped in the hope of getting enough ransom money to buy his mother, Carmen, the medication she needs to manage her AIDS. Carmen, knowing that her days are numbered, takes the blame and goes to prison in Fede's stead, where she eventually dies by suicide. The stories converge after fourteen chapters, when the reader learns that Marta's lover and prospective fiancé Juan is none other than the grown-up Fede, who now goes by his given name. Fede/Juan reaches adulthood believing that his mother died in prison of her disease, and through a strange turn of events, it is Marta who eventually reveals to him the truth of Carmen's suicide. Overcome with guilt, Juan also kills himself, leaving Marta to cope not only with her failures as an artist and a woman but also with the burden of her own guilt.[84]

The opening of the novel encounters Marta in a state of profound frustration with her career. She does not name specific instances of failure to sell her work or break out on the gallery scene, but she hopes the "marchantes y galeristas de Madrid descubrieran [su] escondido talento, esa oportunidad que con tanta frecuencia había brindado a los galeristas catalanes y que éstos, temerariamente, habían rechazado" (dealer and gallery owners in Madrid will discover [her] hidden talent, that chance [she'd] so frequently offered to Catalan gallery owners and that they, hastily, had rejected).[85] Marta's brief and early reflections on her own failures and her critique of the system in which she has tried to participate set the tone for the other artistic projects she will take on over the course of the novel. First, she expresses annoyance with the belief that one is only considered an artist when one is paid for artistic practice, something that, so far, has eluded her. Second, she critiques what she calls the "culto insensato a la originalidad" (foolish cult of originality) that has haunted her entire career.[86] Marta's comments reflect a frustration with a market in which visible expressions of originality and autonomy are foundational to success, for her own aspirations lie elsewhere. Marta's true desire is to be a world-class copyist. Her artistic dream is to re-create her favorite Diego Velázquez painting and to display it next to the original, in the hopes that visitors to the exhibition would prefer her new version. She hears her imagined viewer's surprised exclamation in her head: "'Prefiero el de Marta Valdés, tiene más calidad.'" ("I prefer Marta Valdés's. It's higher quality.")[87] As Marta complains, she can only be recognized as an artist if she makes money by selling her art and the only way to sell art is to create a singular piece that can be associated with her name. In short, Marta protests a specific cultural construction and value system for creativity, what Luis Moreno-Caballud refers to as the "fame and name" paradigm that was central to the Culture of the Transition, or CT, in Spain. He posits that "culture" is considered that which "can 'put a name' on supposedly exceptional individuals in whom all the value of aesthetic creation . . . is concentrated[, which] facilitates the monetization of cultural value."[88] Marta's economic necessity means that she has no choice but to participate in this system if she wishes to make the money that is required to live and that would allow her the economic freedom to pursue her own project as a copyist.

Marta's only attempt to establish herself as a famous (and wealthy) artist is a total failure before it even gets off the ground. After losing her job as a guide in the Prado Museum for berating a patron, Marta has run low on funds, and she is in desperate need of a formula that would let her "conseguir mucho dinero con rapidez" (make a lot of money quickly).[89] Marta imagines the remedy to her financial woes might lie in conceptual art, "una inmensa tomadura de pelo . . . pero una buena manera de ganar dinero" (a total joke . . . but a great way to make money).[90] Inspired by the financial success of artists like Damien Hirst, Marta's economic insecurity forces her to turn toward a market sector that she believes might hold the most promise of economic return. Marta convinces herself that all she needs to do is find a provocative or shocking new idea to transpose to a visual medium so that she can "embaucar a un coleccionista . . . y persuadirle de que [su] proyecto (el que fuere) era genial" (swindle a collector . . . and persuade him that [her] project (whatever it ended up being) was fantastic).[91] The idea comes to her one day as she sees her goddaughter playing dress up with a plastic rat—Marta decides that her conceptual art masterpiece will be a taxidermied rat nativity. Her murine manger scene will be "un espectáculo sorprendente, y sobre todo, repulsivo, muy asqueroso" (a shocking spectacle, and above all, repulsive, truly disgusting).[92] This idea, Marta believes, will lend itself to multiple levels of critical analysis and interpretation, scandalize the religious establishment ("¡Cómo se pondrá la iglesia!" [What will the church say!]), and, most importantly, bring in a huge sum of money.[93]

Marta's decision to consciously make lucrative art is reminiscent of the choice many Spanish women authors make to adapt their work to fit the profitable genre of women's literature. However, her failure is related to her inability to understand that, despite the inseparable relationship of market demands and art, those demands do not standardize artistic output. There is no formula that will lead to her immediate and unquestioned success. On a more practical level, however, Marta finds another, arguably gendered, obstacle to her realization as a conceptual artist. The first obstacle comes when Marta realizes she does not have the stomach to kill the rats for her nativity scene herself. She hires some neighborhood hoodlums to do the dirty work for her, but a miscommunication leads to their bringing her the rats very much alive. As she watches the rats writhe in the bag, Marta is overcome with guilt and cannot bring herself to slaughter them. She releases them; they scurry away with her conceptual art dreams in tow, and Marta blames herself for her failure by comparing herself to Hirst, known for his work with dead animals: "[A él] no le había temblado la voz cuando encargó a un pescador que le consiguiera un tiburón muerto, y una vez tomada la decisión, no se retractó. El sí que era un artista y no yo." ([His] voice didn't tremble when he ordered a fisherman to get him a dead shark, and once he'd made the decision, there was no going back. He was a real artist and I wasn't.)[94] The guilt Marta feels about killing the rats reminds her of a typically feminine problem: that her artistic goal presents a conflict between caring for and about others (four-legged ones, in this case) and succeeding as an artist. She envies Hirst's selfishness, his willingness to allow a living creature to die for his own fame, and perhaps also his ability to marshal the services of those around him for his creative ends. In the face of her failure to exhibit the kind of ruthless self-interest she imagines necessary for the creation of financially successful art, Marta stops trying. She does not desist because potential buyers or dealers have turned her away, but because she struggles to see herself as the Damien Hirst figure she thinks she needs to be. Marta cannot hunt her own rats or perform the physical labor associated with this project, and she ends up convinced she is not the woman for the job. In fact, she comes to believe that her failure to produce the rat nativity means she is not worthy of being an artist at all.

Though she struggles to make a name for herself, Marta has some success in the art world when she takes on subordinate roles or adopts a new identity. Freixas observes in her analysis of *Corazón de napalm* that Marta is never able to become the painter she hopes to be but instead "sólo es aprobada en tanto que subalterna o impostora" (is only approved of as long as she is an entry-level employee or an impostor).[95] Her work as a studio assistant for the famed Valencian painter Maristany brings her little more than bitterness. Marta calls her job that of "una pintora asalariada" (a salaried painter), and though it meets her economic needs, it is not what she imagined for herself when she was a "pintora en ciernes llena de proyectos e ilusiones" (a budding painter full of plans and dreams).[96] As Marta contemplates a Maristany retrospective at MACBA filled with paintings she executed, she cannot help but feel resentment at the thought that her labor "quedaba enterrado bajo su firma" (remained buried under his signature).[97] In this moment, Marta sees herself as a cultural handmaiden, fulfilling a socially sanctioned role for women that gets her paid but leaves her personally unsatisfied. Her work with Maristany also teaches Marta how hard it is to gain a foothold in the art world, where names and reputation mean so much. The old painter has years of fame and a vast fortune behind him, and his name carries weight that Marta fears hers never will. When she compares herself to Maristany, Marta cannot help but think, in contrast to his almost magical signature: "Lo que firmo yo como Marta Valdés será arrojado a un contenedor por mis futuros herederos, si llego a tenerlos" (What I sign as Marta Valdés will be thrown in a bin by my future heirs, if I ever have any).[98] After Maristany dies, Marta leaves her job because she refuses to go along with his young widow's plan to forge posthumous paintings in her husband's name. Though Marta gives up a stable income, she also gives herself the freedom to seek out recognition for her works in her own name, but, as we have seen, for Marta this is easier said than done. At the end of the novel, and despite her eventual market success, the name "Marta Valdés" does, indeed, remain unknown.

Marta only achieves success on the art market when she conforms in a different way to a stereotypical version of women's art. She takes the advice of a male friend—a painter himself, with much more success on the gallery circuit—who tells her that contemporary Chinese art is selling well. In what begins as a joke, Marta paints a series of "falsos cuadros chinos o parodias chinescas, con un toque pornográfico" (fake Chinese paintings or chinoiserie parodies, with a pornographic touch).[99] She is the first to express her surprise when they sell for over six thousand euros each on Charles Saatchi's online gallery, where she uses the assumed name Wu Chao. As Freixas points out, Marta's friend Juan Carlos, who seemed no great fan of her "serious" artistic attempts, reacts with glee when he sees her Chinese parodies: "Se entusiasma cuando lo que ella le presenta es una obra menor, *kitsch*, marginal, erótica y exótica" (He is very enthusiastic when she brings him work that is minor, kitsch, marginal, erotic, and exotic).[100] The words Freixas applies to refer to Marta's Chinese paintings are the same ones that have long been used to ghettoize women's literature. Marta is rewarded for creating paintings that conform to the stereotypes associated with women's art. Her dealer, Turpin, who showed no interest in her paintings signed Marta Valdés, is excited by the controversy and publicity her work could generate, telling her, "Cuánto más ruido mejor; más interés despertarás y más subirá tu cotización" (The more noise we make with this the better; you'll generate more interest and your value will go up).[101] As Freixas observes, the fact that Turpin is interested in potential controversy and in Wu Chao's hermetic but sexy image reminds the reader of the debate generated around women's literature—namely, are women selling quality work, or are they selling a highly marketable, stylized image of themselves? Freixas writes: "[Un arte o una literatura femenina] se nos muestran como engañosos, pues no parten de una realidad 'espontánea' alguna, sino de su trucaje, de una impostura interesada"

([Feminine art and literature] seem deceptive to us, since they do not come from women's "spontaneous" reality, but rather they are rigged to be successful; they are an interested imposture).[102] Whatever artistic merit there is in Marta's work is lost in the noise of the aggressive marketing campaign that surrounds it; her paintings sell not because of their inherent value or because of the value of her name, but because they were rigged to have an impact.

The choice of the name Wu Chao also highlights the notion that women are capitalizing on their sex and their image to sell books. According to Marta, Wu Chao was a Chinese courtesan who later became the concubine of a seventh-century emperor. She brutally eliminated her competition until she landed herself in a position of ultimate power as the absolute ruler of China. Marta adopts the name of a woman who began by "selling out," literally trading her body to gain a foothold in the world she wanted to rule, a notion that is often associated with women's art and literature. Henseler observes that the so-called prostitution of Spain, the idea that the country "had sold out lofty ideas for love of material comforts," coincides unabashedly "with the literary opportunities, level of production, and visibility of women writers."[103] This echoes in the text when Marta responds to her mother's surprise at her newfound wealth from the sale of the erotic paintings, saying: "[Mi madre] sospecha que me estoy prostituyendo" ([My mother] suspects I've become a prostitute).[104] Though women often need the market to establish themselves as artists, critics decry their attachment to market values, a complaint that is tied to charismatic notions of disinterestedness that are still key to the art world's functioning. Marta reflects the contradiction that Usón believes lies in every female author: "Cuando pienso en los best-sellers, pienso, qué horror, venden muchísimo, pero quizá me gustaría tener esa posición y forrarme" (When I think about best sellers, I think, how awful, they sell so many copies, but perhaps I'd actually like to find myself in that position and get rich).[105] The money Marta makes from her kitschy erotic paintings gives her the opportunity to take time to create something for herself—a painting of her ex-lover Juan, as a child with his mother. The novel gives no indication that the painting, or others like it, will sell or that Marta's stint as Wu Chao will have important ramifications for her career as the artist named Marta Valdés.

For Almudena Grandes, the publication of a best-selling erotic novel may have paved the way for her later work as a "serious" artist, but Marta's work as Wu Chao has garnered for her no name recognition, though it could be argued that her success and the interest it generates help Marta see herself as capable of being a professional artist. Though Marta has returned to painting for and as herself (at least in private), the novel ends with a bleak reflection on the fate of all art. Marta takes comfort in the idea that in a distant future the earth will be destroyed: "[La Tierra] se fundirá con [el Sol] y desaparecerá y con ella, todos esos libros y obras de arte que tildamos de eternos: yo no pasaré a la eternidad, pero Picasso tampoco" ([The earth] will be swallowed up by [the sun] and will disappear and with it all of those books and artworks that we call timeless: my work won't be immortalized, but neither will Picasso's).[106] It is only the belief that no one will be remembered that comforts Marta about what she assumes will be her own lack of transcendence.

The story of Marta's artistic trajectory reveals the instability that accompanies her choice of profession, even in early twenty-first-century Spain, where she should be poised to succeed. However, in many novels written in the postfeminist era, there exists what Tasker and Negra call a "deep uncertainty about existing options for women," which combines with an "idealized, essentialized femininity that symbolically evades or transcends institutional and social problem spots."[107] After Marta loses her job with Maristany and her conceptual art plan backfires, she starts to consider yet another option for her life: marriage and children. The independence she once valued as a necessity for artistic life turns to anxiety about being alone in the face of her professional failures. Suddenly, the fantasy of patriarchal protection offers a respite from the economic and emotional vulnerability she feels. When her boyfriend Juan—a financially stable, bourgeois judge—proposes marriage, Marta breathes a sigh of relief: "Lo primero que pensé fue 'ya era hora.' . . . [Y]a había alcanzado la provecta edad de treinta y cinco años y nadie me había hecho proposiciones" (The first thing I thought was "it's about time." . . . I had reached the ancient age of thirty-five and no one had proposed to me).[108] In addition to reflecting postfeminism's age consciousness and preoccupation with temporality, Marta's reaction demonstrates that despite a liberated lifestyle that corresponds as much to her age as to her profession, she retains a traditional belief system that considers heterosexual marriage the ultimate marker of "success."

In Marta's relationship with Juan, she invokes a specter of feminism in order to reject it. She acknowledges that having children would mean that her "carrera pictórica habría de sufrir un parón" (artistic career would come to a screeching halt) and that even contemplating motherhood is almost unthinkable: "Hay ciertas cosas que una mujer con ínfulas de bohemia no se atreve a pensar a sabiendas" (There are some things that a woman who thinks she's a bohemian doesn't think knowingly).[109] Marta does not explicitly name feminist struggles or politics, but she implies that the once uncomplicated, even automatic desire for a "traditional" home has grown fraught with a complicated calculus around what it means to be a woman, a wife, a professional, a mother.[110] Marta's thoughts about children reveal a critique of feminism as too extreme, a confining rather than liberating force that makes women feel guilty for turning away from careers and toward heterosexual coupledom. As McRobbie notes, the invoking and subsequent undoing of feminism reassures women that it is acceptable to "move beyond feminism to a more comfortable zone where women are now free to choose for themselves."[111] When no other options seem viable to Marta and her success as an artist is in doubt, this traditional path, which she once disdained, becomes more and more appealing for its clearly defined parameters and attendant financial security.

For Marta, accepting a more traditional femininity feels like a reprieve. It allows her to cast off a mask, to abandon the pose of the committed, disinterested artist: "Me gustaba decir, por contraposición al común de los mortales, diligentes soldados de los ejércitos de hormigas que integran en la sociedad, siempre bullendo, atareados, en torno al hormiguero, que era cigarra que vivía al día comprometida sólo con mi arte. Era una pose; lo que yo sabía, y no decía a nadie, era que algún día me casaría y mi marido se ocuparía de velar por mi porvenir y asegurar mi bienestar económico." (I used to like to say, in contrast to those mere mortals, diligent soldiers in the ant armies that make up society, always so busily bustling around the anthill, that I was a cicada that lived dedicated to my art. It was an act; what I knew, and what I didn't tell anyone, was that one day I'd get married and my husband would be the one to worry about my future and ensure that I was taken care of financially.)[112] In this passage (which Marta pronounces before gaining her success as Wu Chao), both feminism and the charismatic myth are tacitly invoked to demonstrate how they have restricted conventional desires, namely, marriage and motherhood. Feminism has taught Marta that she should provide for herself rather than depending on a man to take care of her—something she has tried to do by teaching art at a girls' school, drawing caricatures of tourists on the Rambla, and working as a guide at the Prado, in addition to her attempts to make money by capitalizing on the "hotness" of conceptual art. However, the work that she does to ensure her own survival keeps her from devoting herself entirely (and disinterestedly) to her art. McRobbie observes that in postfeminist texts, it is common for women to feel a sense of relief as they "escape this censorious politics [of feminism] and freely enjoy what has been disapproved of."[113] Indeed, when Marta speaks about the consequences of having children and the postponement or termination of her artistic career, she feels neither sadness nor regret. Rather, she explains, "de forma inesperada, me alivió" (in some unexpected way, I felt relieved).[114] Within Marta continue to exist conflicting voices that one day might make her resigned to a "decoroso y burgués futuro de ama de casa y madre de familia" (proper, bourgeois future as a housewife and mother) and the next inspire her to recover her "ínfulas artísticas" (artistic airs), two positions that clearly cannot exist together.[115] Marta's path demonstrates that in the post-Franco, postfeminist era, women are struggling to make a place for themselves in an art world that still values the autonomy inherent to the myth of the charismatic male artist. Marta is only recognized as an artist when she conforms to certain expectations of her sex, but the novel distinctly avoids any politicized understanding of these dynamics. In her failure, Marta sees only herself, her choices, her inability to live up to the image of what she believes an artist should be, rather than the structural deficits of the art world.

In the end, neither Marta's aspiration to become a copyist nor her desire to get married is realized. Her engagement to Juan eventually crumbles when she realizes that the relationship mirrors her artistic career in some unsettling ways. As an artist, Marta is only successful when she works as a stand-in (for Maristany) or as an impostor (as Wu Chao), so when she sees a photo of Juan's mother, to whom Marta bears a striking resemblance, she realizes that her role in the relationship has also been that of a surrogate. Marta has helped Juan fulfill the Oedipal fantasy described in the earlier chapters; if she had not looked so much like his dead mother, it is unlikely that Juan would have chosen her. In art as in love, no one seems interested in Marta Valdés as Marta Valdés. As a surrogate Carmen, she can be Juan's lover; as a ghost-painter, she can taste consecration; as an invented Chinese painter, she can profit, but as Marta Valdés, her life feels unstable and uncertain, without love, glory, or gold. Freixas reads in Marta's struggles the same problem "con el que se enfrentan todas las mujeres que acceden a la creación artística, lo que explica sus carreras vacilantes, a saber quienes detentan el poder no se lo traspasan" (that all women creatives face, which explains their shaky careers, as they know that those who unjustly hold power will not give it up), but it takes a reader with a particular feminist disposition to read a systemic critique in *Corazón de napalm* because, in the mind-set typical of postfeminism, the novel casts Marta's failures in love and in work as personal ones.[116] However, Usón, in her interview for the 2018 Sor Juana Prize, admitted that her feminist perspectives have changed with age: "A medida que me hago más mayor me vuelvo más feminista" (The older I get, the more of a feminist I become).[117] Perhaps years of working in an art world that still discriminates against women have changed Usón's mind about the need for attention to the structural constraints that continue to demand prizes and special promotion for women, who, contrary to popular belief, still have not reached a state of parity with men.

---

*Todo fue nada*, *Castillos de cartón*, and *Corazón de napalm* all demonstrate how the postfeminist preoccupation with female professional success is reconfigured in the context of the art world. Like other postfeminist novels, the works by Herrero, Grandes, and Usón take for granted that equality for women has been achieved on some level in all workplaces. The fact that some women have succeeded and been loudly celebrated in the worlds of art and literature is taken as a sign that parity has been achieved and even that women have gained a majority in artistic and literary fields. Though no one denies the novels' female protagonists chances to succeed outright because of their sex, and they are ostensibly granted equal access to training and professional opportunities, it is not hard to see that all the men around them are more successful than they are. The postfeminist notion that women's success can be measured by their participation in the labor market, as well as by their ability to be seen and see themselves as consumers, also underlies these novels. However, judging women's professional value in terms of economic gains and market visibility gets more complicated when the women are artists. As Freixas has observed, the more women triumph in terms of "lo comercial y mediático" (the commercial and the celebrity scene), the more they fail in terms of "la calidad y el prestigio" (quality and prestige).[118] The women's disadvantage in the art world is rarely named as specifically gendered. The nun's critique of María José's drawing is only implicitly gendered. The Catalan gallery owners do not reject Marta's work by telling her that they do not want women's paintings. But, when these stories of women's art making are compared to men's, like those discussed in chapter 1, the difference is striking. In all of these novels, as women struggle to access the symbolic capital (the prestige that might, in the long term, produce economic returns), they must also work in the short term for the commercial success that will allow them to survive, diminishing their talent and potential for achieving quality and prestige in the process. Both Grandes and Usón have made explicit connections between their artistic protagonists and the literary world they inhabit, and their novels give voice to the disparity that continues to exist between male and female creative professionals in practical terms as well as in their opportunities for imagining possible lives and identities for themselves.

Interestingly, however, the acknowledgment of disparity does not translate into an activist stance or an outspoken advocacy for women artists. Rather, in postfeminist style, the authors depict protagonists who search for individual solutions to a collective problem. The lifestyle choices in *Todo fue nada* and the embrace of sexual subjecthood in *Castillos de cartón* are examples of women's attempts to empower themselves on their own terms. *Corazón de napalm* presents the quest for empowerment itself to require too much self-management and sees the promise of relief in an embrace of the traditional feminine roles of mother and wife. Postfeminist novels like these matter precisely because they join with other elements of postfeminist culture—one that stands in contrast to a feminist *politics* and that has no politics of its own—to shape young women's notions of possible lives and careers. Artist novels by women had long been aspirational tools for imagining a liberated future for both authors and their readers, but these artist novels do not help readers imagine a future in which their work can be shared, in which they might make a living as artists, or in which they might be able to successfully balance life and work. Instead, they depict a world in which women are individually responsible for their success, a responsibility often experienced as a burden that ends up being too great to bear.

Finally, these novels also reveal Spanish women's ambivalent relationship to the literary market, where they are at once highly visible and marginalized or made invisible. The authors of these novels capitalize on market niches, such as the "girl power" discourse of *Todo fue nada* or the erotic angle of *Castillos de cartón*. They also establish themselves through prizes; Usón was awarded thirty thousand euros with the Premio Biblioteca Breve she won for *Corazón de napalm*. These authors understand that making art is complex and requires dual commitments to art and commercial necessity that complicate the concept of being an "autonomous" producer of art. In their novels, this tenuous, often unsuccessful balance that women artists must strike between art and the market is completely depoliticized. As successful practitioners of this delicate balancing act, these authors must recognize that the literary market in a country like Spain, where few people identify as feminist, will not receive militantly feminist tracts with open arms, so this postfeminist depoliticizing may very well respond to the authors' own need (and desire) to profit. The women artist protagonists' trajectories are, in any case, quite different from those of their male counterparts explored in chapter 1. For them, there is no retreat to an ivory tower, no bemoaning the burden of fame. Rather, for the women artists, art and life are still very much mixed. Their existence in the world as women continues to circumscribe their possibilities to exist as artists.

CHAPTER 3

# The Art Historian as Neoliberal Subject in Lourdes Ortiz's *Las manos de Velázquez* and Paloma Díaz-Mas's *El sueño de Venecia*

The rise of the artist novel in post-Transition Spain was accompanied by a parallel proliferation of novels about related facets of the art world, including museum curators, dealers, and art historians. Though the primary focus of this book is the artist novel proper, post-Transition novels about art historians—often classifiable within the genre of the campus novel—are strikingly similar to artist novels in their depiction of cultural work. Artist novels and campus novels both feature the work of those whose day-to-day activities do not seem to be the stuff of literature. Robert F. Scott frames the question this way: "Ask any university lecturer and he'll tell you his day is no more exciting than that of the average bookkeeper. So why can't novelists resist him?"[1] Why does the recounting of professors' work appeal broadly to both academics and nonacademics alike?[2] A similar question could be asked about artists, whose average daily activities do not provide many sources of intrigue. Like the artist novels studied in chapters 1 and 2, Lourdes Ortiz's *Las manos de Velázquez* (2006) and the final chapter of Paloma Díaz-Mas's *El sueño de Venecia* (1992) discussed here explore myths about artistic *and* academic labor. As unique permutations of the campus novel, they elegantly render the practices of and changing myths about academic labor in the humanities in an era of neoliberalism. Like the art world in the artist novel, the university is represented as a place that operates by its own rules, and the work that takes place in both of these worlds is constituted as special in comparison to that which goes on outside of it.

Thomas Discenna explains that the modern university was founded on an idea of "culture" that is predicated on the denial of the labor of those who work within it. He notes that whether "culture" is understood anthropologically or as an ideal represented by arts and letters, it is positioned as something that stands outside commerce; it is a space where "the commodity does not yet rule."[3] By establishing that "culture" stands apart from the market, the work of university professors—but also artists, writers, and other "cultural" workers—can be denied as labor. The campus novel exists as a genre, Discenna argues, precisely because the work that goes on in the university is perceived to be strange or special and, for that reason, interesting.[4] Like the artist protagonist, most academic characters are depicted as being unsuited for or incapable of survival in the "real" world of work. With their art historian protagonists whose work centers on the seventeenth century in Spain, Díaz-Mas and Ortiz employ the techniques, including narrative self-reflexivity and intertextuality, of what Linda Hutcheon calls "historiographic metafiction." Works of historiographic metafiction draw attention to the subjective experience of the writer of historical discourse, often through the figure of a writing protagonist, to encourage the reader to consider the context and conditions in which the writing was produced.[5] These techniques not only differentiate the novels by Ortiz and Díaz-Mas from the traditional campus novel (often centered on the experience of a literature professor) but also provide an opportunity for the authors to critique the deleterious effects of neoliberalism on the university and its employees.

*Las manos de Velázquez* is a campus novel that focuses less on campus politics and more on the nature of time as it is experienced in academia. As Elaine Showalter notes in *Faculty Towers*, her book about campus novels, professorial time is uniquely structured, seeming both "overloaded day to day and painfully drawn out and Beckettish year to year."[6] Ortiz's novel, centered on the life and work of a neurotic and insecure middle-aged art historian named Teodoro, captures as few campus novels do the "peculiar mix of the quotidian and minute task with the daunting awareness of eternity."[7] The narration of Teodoro's life oscillates between two poles: the frustrations and occasional successes or breakthroughs of his research on early modern painting that he hopes will leave a lasting impact on the field and the constant reminders of his own mortality as he worries that his much younger wife, Mónica, is enjoying her life more thoroughly than he is (in her nonacademic career) and tiring of him and his obsession with Velázquez. As an art historian by trade, Ortiz not only understands intimately the life of a professor but also has a deep understanding of early modern painting, on display in ekphrastic passages and excerpts from Teodoro's book.[8]

*Las manos de Velázquez* and *El sueño de Venecia* both represent the changes to professorial labor that have occurred in recent decades. While the former does this through process, the latter achieves it through a representation of the product. *El sueño de Venecia* is not a campus novel per se, but the novel's final chapter, titled "Memoria," is written as a parody of academic discourse in the form of an art historical essay. There is no explicit depiction of the campus where the work takes place or even a focus on the professor or his or her life. Díaz-Mas's novel instead invites more active collaboration from the reader, inviting greater understanding of the professor's human experience precisely through its lack of representation in the text. *El sueño de Venecia* is composed of five chapters, each set in a different era and parodying a literary genre popular at the time, beginning with the picaresque novel, passing through the eighteenth-century epistolary novel, the nineteenth-century realist novel, and the twentieth-century novel of memory written by women, finally ending with the parody of an academic paper. The guiding thread between these disparate chapters is a seventeenth-century wedding portrait of an unlikely couple—Gracia de Mendoza, a Jewish sex worker, and her husband Pablillos, an orphan *pícaro* nearly fifteen years her junior. The portrait changes hands over time, and the novel depicts its willful misinterpretation, physical damage, and manipulation in the form of repaintings, one that transforms Gracia into the Virgin Mary. It finally lands in the art historian's hands in the novel's final pages upon being discovered fastened to the underside of a table in a private residence. The art historian's interpretation of the painting uses available data to arrive at very different conclusions than those laid out in the preceding chapters about the painting's creation and deformation over time, ultimately misidentifying the central figure and actively negating the identity of its actual subjects. The narrators of each of the first four sections of the novel is explicitly unreliable, and the final chapter invites the reader to question the accuracy of the art historian's ostensibly objective research, not because this novel aspires to tell historical "truth" but because, like much postmodern fiction, it "questions *whose* truth gets told."[9] The reader is ultimately tasked with making sense of the professor's historiographical interpretation of the painting, which invites consideration of the conditions under which the research has been produced.

The effect of neoliberalism's encroachment on the university in both of these texts is historical writing that suffers because the environment is not one that permits creativity to flower. While these authors critique the impact of neoliberal practices on scholarship and on human lives, their proposed solution is a model of work that looks a lot like the one enshrined by the myth of the charismatic artist—one characterized by flexibility, personal passion, and self-management (rather than management by a university administrator)—a model that is equally problematic for the way that it has been co-opted by managers in nonartistic professions and wielded to extract even more control and working hours from their employees. This model also denies and devalues professorial labor by treating the work as a "passion," by blurring the lines between leisure and work to such an extent that the professors, like the artists in chapters 1 and 2, are expected to work disinterestedly doing things they enjoy.

Just as the rise of neoliberalism and changes in the art world challenged the charismatic myth of the artist and the representation of artists in literature, neoliberalism's implantation in the university system in the West in the 1980s and beyond occasioned a shift in the mythology surrounding the academic profession. The academic's "prior romance," according to Stephen J. Ball, was based on idealized notions of learning for its own sake and a sense of disinterestedness not unlike the kind demanded of the charismatic artist. The "new romance," he asserts, is one in which "the enterprising academic is the central figure."[10] It is rooted in self-promotion and the performance of productivity, in which the highest aspiration is to a machinelike rhythm of publishable output, uninterrupted by physical or mental illness, emotion, or other unforeseen manifestations of humanness. Like the artist novel, then, the contemporary campus novel hinges on a defining tension between the needs of the mind and the needs of the flesh.[11] Showalter cites this dilemma as a common thread between many academic novels, naming it as the "constant dialectic between competitiveness and idealism—or, scholarship as a means to an end or as an end in itself."[12]

I have already demonstrated the ways that, for fictional artists, creative pursuits stand in opposition to the rest of human experience in all its forms; male artists debate whether they can have fame and family and still consider themselves authentic artists, while women artists strive to make their lives and identities as women mesh with the identity of "artist." A similar opposition rises for academic protagonists, who must decide whether to commit themselves to disinterested, noble intellectual exploration or be distracted by the world—represented by sex and love, but also by the allure of professional honors, status, and fame. The desire for and inaccessibility of academic superstardom is exacerbated in the climate of neoliberal productivity, in which professors strive for tenure or to maintain their positions. Even those who never become superstars must work to make themselves "calculable rather than memorable" in their human dimensions.[13] As Sally Dalton-Brown observes, this striving is at the heart of a dilemma that can be considered a common convention of the campus novel.[14] The publish-or-perish imperative represents the life of interested desires, reflected by status-seeking and competition, which clashes with the idealized "life of the mind" that supposedly characterizes academic existence.[15]

Outside of Spain, campus novels centered on the experience of faculty, which Showalter calls *Professorromane,* have offered a "spiritual, political, and psychological guide to the profession" for the past fifty years.[16] Though campus or academic novels existed before the twentieth century, many scholars identify the 1950s as a defining moment for this genre in the United States.[17] Leigh Claire La Berge notes that the growth of master of fine arts (MFA) programs brought more professional writers into the American university, and they began to shift the campus novel toward the faculty experience and away from the student experience.[18] Given the boom in MFA programs, it was also no surprise that after the 1950s the campus novel began to commonly feature an English or a creative writing professor as its protagonist. Almost never depicted as inspiring or heroic in any way, the academic (nearly always male) has been commonly represented as "stifling in his own environment," so much so that this notion became a defining feature of the genre.[19] The world of the academy in the campus novel, much like the corporate art world in the artist novel, does not allow creativity or intellectual work to flourish and is dominated by politics. In this world, the naïve professorial protagonist flounders, especially when pitted against enterprising and ruthless colleagues. This environment, a contaminated place that forces its inhabitants to abandon their ideals, not only fosters competition between academics but also invites a painful comparison of one's output and lifestyle to "internalized expectations of brilliance."[20] Finally, the academic's own disempowerment is often expressed through sexual predation, as he commonly finds himself embroiled in relationships with students or colleagues that underscore his naïveté.[21] The campus novels of the United States in the second half of the twentieth century shared these characteristics consistently enough that Dalton-Brown has argued that the genre is defined by "remarkable sameness."[22]

At the same time these changes were happening across the Atlantic, both within the university and in the fiction written about it, the university in Spain during the Franco dictatorship became what Susana Gil-Albarellos calls "un campo inexpugnable" (an impenetrable camp) not particularly suited for narrativization.[23] While Spanish novels from the Franco era, like Carmen Laforet's *Nada* or Luis Martín-Santos's *Tiempo de silencio*, offer portraits of student experience, novels about professorial experience did not emerge in significant numbers in Spain until after the end of the dictatorship, and the genre never consolidated in quite the same way that it did in the English-speaking world. However, the effects of the American campus novel on the Spanish one should not be understated. As Matthew J. Marr has observed, the recent Spanish campus novel often features "a Peninsular traveler [to the United States], . . . often a visiting professor of Spanish."[24] By writing campus novels that are also classifiable as travel literature, authors like Javier Cercas, Josefina Aldecoa, and Antonio Muñoz Molina often "critique those characteristics and excesses of Peninsular culture which exacerbate its recession from the fore as an imperial power."[25] The novels by Ortiz and Díaz-Mas break with this trend of academic travel literature by setting their novels in Spain and focusing on Spanish history and issues.

Dalton-Brown asserts that the campus novel can be a "highly thoughtful genre" if it is able to "struggle against its own template."[26] Ortiz's and Díaz-Mas's use of art historian protagonists and the techniques of historiographic metafiction create unique permutations that transcend generic boundaries and push the limits of this narrative form. *Las manos de Velázquez* and *El sueño de Venecia* immediately differentiate themselves from the typical campus novel because of their focus on history instead of language or literature, facilitated by their art historian protagonists. The self-reflexivity of both novels as literary artifacts also extends to their self-conscious treatment of history and historiography as narrative. They are overtly and diegetically self-aware texts, to situate them within Hutcheon's typology of metafiction, which means they are explicitly "conscious of their own narrative processes."[27] The self-awareness of each text looks different, but each of them has at its core a recognition of its own fictionality and an overt consciousness of its use of language. Hutcheon notes that by playing with "ways of ordering" and by emphasizing the relationship between the reader and the text as it is created, the reader of "overtly narcissistic" metafiction is forced to "learn how he makes sense of this literary world [and] his own real one."[28] The awareness of their existence as texts also problematizes the claims to historical veracity advanced by the art historian in each novel, which consolidates the notion that our knowledge of the past is always circumscribed by textuality.[29] Both of these novels emphasize their protagonists' relationship to the archival material at their disposal. By highlighting the writing process, as Ortiz does, or by revealing, through parody, certain linguistic codes that govern that process, as Díaz-Mas does, the authors remind readers that just as the texts they read are constructions, so, too, are the traces of the past that constitute the archive on which historical writing (and the whole notion of history) depends.

In *Las manos de Velázquez*, Ortiz thematizes the process of writing an academic book. The focalization of the narration through the writing protagonist emphasizes the process of selection, ordering, and other emplotting techniques shared by writers of both fiction and history. As Hutcheon puts it, historiographic metafiction "represents a challenging of the (related) conventional forms of fiction and history through its acknowledgment of their inescapable textuality."[30] Teodoro lays bare the conventions of fiction writing through his denial of them; he is constantly trying to prove to himself that the book he is writing is *not* a novel. This denial has two effects: it explicitly draws attention to fiction's narrative codes, and it also points to the rather narrow stylistic scope of academic writing. Teodoro's anxiety about his writing drives the plot, but it also emphasizes a common concern of metafiction: the limits of language to both express feeling and communicate fact.[31] Writing is depicted in this novel as a very human experience, seen in both Teodoro's compositional process and his disillusionment with the existing academic research on Velázquez that has been unable to capture the painter holistically. Hutcheon observes that metafictional texts transform the process of writing "into part of the shared pleasure of reading," though Ortiz's text makes clear that this process of creation is, in fact, a mix of shared pleasure and profound anxiety about attempting to express personal or historical "truths."[32]

Díaz-Mas's *El sueño de Venecia* does not feature a protagonist in the process of writing. Rather, the novel is a diachronic exploration, through parody, of literary genres from the seventeenth century to the present that highlights the unreliability of the five unique narrators of each chapter. Hutcheon asserts that parody is always a form of diegetic metafiction, as it invites an examination of difference and similarity that requires the reader to recognize the codes of the parodied texts to determine a new code that can lead to a more open reading, therefore combining elements from both the fore- and backgrounded texts.[33] Unlike *Las manos de Velázquez*, which uses historiographic metafiction to focus on the inadequacy of words, *El sueño de Venecia* takes a different approach, instead prioritizing the "power and potency of words, their ability to create a world more real than the empirical one of our experience."[34] The art historical essay parodied in the fifth chapter highlights its own textuality and is devoid of any sense of "objectivity," pure mimesis, or innocent representation of facts. The structure of the novel, which includes literary narrators in the first four chapters, invites the reader to see the professor who authors the essay in the final chapter as a *narrator*, too, not some unbiased, disembodied voice that represents fact. The emphasis on the essay's textuality and narration by a person who is unnamed and unseen but obviously just as interested in creating a particular narrative as Teodoro in *Las manos de Velázquez* reminds the reader of the textuality of the archive itself. In this case, the archive, used to determine the provenance and history of the painting in *El sueño de Venecia*, was written by people conditioned into racist and sexist worldviews that excluded relevant information as evidence, which leads to a distorted contemporary interpretation of the painting—a testament to the power of words to create worlds that do not necessarily respond to those that existed empirically.

The intertextual nature of both *El sueño de Venecia* and *Las manos de Velázquez*—and, Hutcheon argues, all historiographic metafiction—also problematizes the romantic notion of the unique and individual creator, the myth with which all of these novels grapple. In dialogue with Jean-François Lyotard, Hutcheon notes that the position of the writer as "original creator, proprietor, and entrepreneur of his or her story" is a capitalist position that can be used as a marketing technique to attract readers. Overt intertextuality, on the other hand, is a reminder that "no one ever manages to be the first to narrate anything, to be the origin of even his or her own narrative."[35] In other words, these texts reveal the codes that authors use to make their narratives—whether fictional or historical—intelligible to readers. *Las manos de Velázquez* and *El sueño de Venecia*, as historical and (meta)fictional narratives, at once undermine the reader's ability to see the fictional text as having a single or unique origin and problematize the idea of simple causality in the historical arena.[36]

As Samuel Amago notes, all self-reflexive texts highlight the narrator's relationship to the construction of the narrative as well as to "the reader's role in the process of making meaning."[37] Amago's book *True Lies* reveals the richness of the metafictional tradition in contemporary Spanish fiction and asserts that this postmodern metafiction "functions as a celebration of literary difference and subjectivity [and as] an important critical reassessment of the historiographical enterprise."[38] In both Ortiz's and Díaz-Mas's novels, the same textual self-consciousness that reveals the text to be a linguistic construct also allows for the incorporation of the academic narrators' very human experiences into the literary text.[39] The explicit connection of human experience and text invites the critical examination of the construction and interpretation of academic and historiographic texts written inside the confines of the novel. Tearing down the walls that traditionally separate the reader from the text can also lead to a critical representation of the context—namely, that of the corporatizing university, including the pressures of "performativity" and competition—in which it was written.

While the notion of competition between scholars is common in campus novels, in the case of *Las manos de Velázquez* and *El sueño de Venecia*, the competitiveness that characterizes contemporary "audit culture" has an impact on the way history is transmitted and understood.[40] For Ortiz's protagonist, Teodoro, and the unnamed art historian of *El sueño de Venecia*'s final chapter, the relationship to their peers and predecessors becomes a source of dramatic tension as both attempt to define the novelty of their own assertions. Their quest for originality turns into a hunt for complexity and difference that each researcher strives to be the first to see. Art historian James Elkins asserts that such quests for difference cannot be removed from the context of the contemporary neoliberal university, as today's scholars in the humanities must write more to find, keep, or improve their jobs, and these "real world" factors have effectively changed the way art historians look at pictures.[41] The quest for newness drives the plot of both novels. Teodoro strives to write a monograph about Velázquez that does not repeat the same tired stories about the painter's life. The art historian of *El sueño de Venecia* uses the essay that constitutes chapter 5 to refute a prior scholar's claim that the woman in the painting is, in fact, Gracia de Mendoza and to instead name it as a different portrait that has long been missing. Paradoxically, however, the attempts of the professors to gain symbolic power through novelty actually require them to forsake the very originality they seek. Dalton-Brown asserts that the academic protagonist of the campus novel often uses "whatever stratagems one can to secure one's academic territory."[42] But that does not mean that anything goes in pursuit of that conquest; like art, scholarship must conform to socially constructed parameters to be recognized as such. Both Teodoro and *El sueño de Venecia*'s art historian respond to a demand to fall in line stylistically and thematically with orthodox academic practices and writing styles, either renouncing more original hypotheses, as in Díaz-Mas's novel, or embracing them at the risk of their failing to be recognized, as Teodoro does in *Las manos de Velázquez.*

What is more, the emphasis on "performativity," the linking of "effort, values, purposes, and self-understanding to measures and comparisons of output," also has an impact on the art historian character's personal life.[43] In *El sueño de Venecia*, Díaz-Mas limits the depiction of the art historian to his or her words on the page. This narrator with no name and no personal backstory is the ultimate parody of the ideal, enterprising professor whose life outside of work is irrelevant and invisible. Ortiz, by contrast, depicts Teodoro's sense of alienation from himself, which is provoked by a punishing workload and a sacrificial ethos that push him to his breaking point. This humanized vision of the professor and the self-reflexive depiction of his writing process help the reader understand that even the pictorial "facts" that Teodoro describes are narratives. As James Heffernan reminds us, art historical texts offer "stories designed by an interpreter who is cast as the verbal representative of visual art" and that that interpreter is unavoidably influenced by his interested desire—in pursuit of legacy, publication, career advancement, or all three—to produce novel scholarship.[44] The study of the past is interesting or attractive not only for disinterested reasons but also for the ways in which it may allow the historian to advance in a capitalist society.[45] David Becerra Mayor has observed this tendency in some contemporary novels about the Spanish Civil War (many of them classifiable as historiographic metafiction as well), in which historian protagonists begin the text in a state of frustration with either their work or their personal life, a frustration that "en ningún caso se atribuye a las propias deficiencias de la sociedad capitalista, sino a su falta de virtud o talento" (under no circumstance is attributed to the deficiencies of capitalist society, but to their own lack of worth or talent).[46] Historical memory and the writing of history, then, is presented in a utilitarian way, used for resolving the "frustraciones individuales" (individual frustrations) of the researchers.[47] The focus in Ortiz's and Díaz-Mas's novels is on the more distant Spanish past, but a similar fate befalls their protagonists.

The historiographic metafictional techniques used in these campus novel variants highlight the textuality of historical discourse and demand of the reader an assessment of the conditions in which that work was produced. They reveal the pressures and realities of the university in the neoliberal age, and the constraints and limitations those realities place on academic labor. Ortiz's novel in particular emphasizes how the model of labor adopted in this context is one that mirrors the artist's work in the sense that it requires a strong degree of self-management and often leads to the total erosion of boundaries between life and work. The neoliberal university can capitalize on the "passion" of those who work within it to extract more labor from them for no additional pay, but only if there is buy-in from both sides. While passionate and subjective work might seem like the antidote to capitalist calculation and systemization, these texts show that this model can be highly valuable to capitalism as well.

---

Even if *El sueño de Venecia* cannot be strictly characterized as a campus novel, it does depict the results of professorial labor through a parody of the product rather than a representation of the process or environment in which the work is produced. The techniques associated with historiographic metafiction—namely, parody and intertextuality—allow the reader to construct a "second meaning" through the recognition of differences between two codified discourses (the text being read and the texts being parodied).[48] The parody of academic discourse in *El sueño de Venecia* signals the textuality of history to identify the limitations of discursive forms of knowledge. By drawing information about the painting in question from textual archival sources, the art historian effectively confirms the historical subjects' continued marginalization and erasure from the historical record. The gaps in the archival material are filled with intertextual and equally discursive early modern story forms, which lead the art historian to a conclusion that perpetuates stereotypes and denies the existence of the subjects the reader came to know in the first chapter. Ultimately, the parody leads to a revelation not of absolute truth but rather of a disclosure of who controls the historical narrative.

In the first chapter of *El sueño de Venecia*, a fourteen-year-old orphan, Pablillos, narrates the story of his life, which culminates in his marriage to the beautiful Jewish courtesan Gracia de Mendoza. In an obvious parody of *Lazarillo de Tormes*, the chapter is written as a persuasive letter to an anonymous authority figure about the plethora of masters with whom Pablillos has developed loving bonds, leading to his place at "la cumbre de toda buena fortuna" (the summit of all good fortune).[49] The chapter does not detail the kind of painful and abusive relationships Lazarillo experiences in the anonymous sixteenth-century source text. Instead, Pablillos describes the nurturing relationships he developed with masters who belong to marginalized sectors of Spanish society: an Italian immigrant painter, a cross-dressing gay man, and the Jewish sex worker who becomes his wife. The parodic "second meaning," which is permitted to the reader able to identify the difference between the events of the chapter and the background source that informs them, venerates and vindicates those who were not officially or socially recognized as members of Spanish society in the sixteenth century, represented by Pablillos's kind masters. The chapter celebrates the way these characters inhabit liminal interstices in a repressive Counter-Reformation society, defying commonly held stereotypes about the period.

The first chapter concludes with the creation of Pablillos and Gracia's wedding portrait, which becomes the novel's guiding thread.[50] Zaide, a freed slave not allowed to legally exercise his artistic vocation, paints Pablillos and Gracia as if they were Spanish nobility, that is, wealthy and *limpios de sangre* (of pure blood). The painting defies all social conventions and hides the truth of Gracia's highly unconventional life behind noble dress and the composition of the painting. Though it is not revealed in the first chapter, it seems likely that Gracia was born into a family of the minor aristocracy with the name Ana de Alfarache, a moniker she would eventually renounce. The archival record of her existence would likely be greater had she not disowned her family and embraced her new life as a courtesan, but as it stands, few textual traces of her life as Gracia are saved in the official record for posterity. Her portrait, with its representation of an aspirational identity, is the exception. It is this "text" that will arrive in the art historian's hands in the final chapter, having been misinterpreted, cut in two, and repainted in the centuries since its creation.

Much has been written about the ways that Díaz-Mas's novel reveals the elisions and ellipses inherent to historiography. Reyes Coll-Tellechea, for example, describes *El sueño de Venecia* as a novel about "cómo se elaboran, se cuentan, y se revisan las historias y la historia" (how stories and history are produced, told, and revised).[51] Through the painting's restoration, detailed in the final chapter, the art historian attempts to strip it to its essence by literally removing painted layers of the past and then uses discourse to textually represent the painting in the essay we read. Jessica Folkart has observed that in each chapter of the novel, the history of the painting and its subjects is reconstructed "según el discurso dominante de distintas épocas de la historia y la literatura españolas, problematizando las identidades definidas por los discursos para cuestionar su validez" (according to the dominant discourse of different eras in Spanish history and literature, problematizing the identities defined by those discourses in order to question their validity).[52] The highly textual nature of the past allows for a reflection on the narrativization of history in historiographical writing and, consequently, on the importance of recognizing the historiographic narrator's implied enunciative situation that has proved crucial to the novel's previous chapters. In the final chapter, the art historian's forceful and ostensibly conclusive language effectively alerts the reader to the *illusion* of transparency and objectivity in historical writing.

Though it seems dangerous to use the word *truth* to refer to any of the highly subjective stories told by the host of "interested" narrators in *El sueño de Venecia*, the first chapter stands as the reality against which the reader can measure the art historian's final claims for their veracity in the final chapter. The art historian gets maddeningly close, even naming and then discarding the hypothesis that the woman in the painting is Gracia de Mendoza, known courtesan and favorite of Philip IV. The reliance on the archive prompts the rejection of this conclusion in order to advance an interpretation that better aligns with the art historian's professional ends. The removal of the adolescent Pablillos from the painting in the nineteenth century when it was cut in two means that only a disembodied hand remains poised on Gracia's shoulder, which the art historian believes to have belonged to a young woman based on its delicacy and size. The archive appears to confirm this interpretation when it is discovered that a seventeenth-century painting by a Sevillian follower of Diego Velázquez, the fictional Bartolomé de Zabala, of two young women appears in an inventory but has been presumed lost. The art historian, basing the claim on the belief that the painting in question once represented two women, believes to have uncovered the missing painting of the inventory. This hypothesis is furthered by the remaining letter "Z" of the signature, taken to be the "Z" of Zabala rather than of the freed slave Zaide's name, which never entered the historical record. All of this "evidence" allows the art historian to identify the woman in the painting as doña Rufina de Alfarache, sister to Ana before her transformation to Gracia de Mendoza, whose hand once rested on her shoulder. A study of the Alfarache family tree reveals a not uncommon obsession with purity of blood, which leads the art historian to conclude that no daughter of the Alfarache family in the age of the Counter-Reformation would ever take the risks that Ana did by forfeiting her given name and going by a highly conspicuous Jewish name instead. The essay concludes that it would have been "una muestra de cinismo impensable—según los tiempos que corrían—que adoptase precisamente ese nombre marcado para establecerse en la Corte y ejercer el viejo oficio" (a show of unthinkable cynicism—for the time—to adopt that specific and conspicuous name to set herself up in the court and practice the world's oldest profession).[53] The art historian's interpretation is indeed plausible, but if the first chapter's recounting is to be believed, it is also untrue. As Robert Spires observes, the readers of Díaz-Mas's fiction know much more than the "final narrator with his or her arsenal of erudition and technology."[54] However, the art historian only has available the information that has physically survived into the twentieth century: the painting itself, the inventory, the Alfarache family tree, the extant works of Bartolomé de Zabala, and the story, preserved through letters, of Ana de Alfarache's fall from grace that, ironically, transformed her *into* Gracia. The interpretation of the final chapter underlines both the inevitable textuality of knowledge about the past and the narrativization process inherent to historiographic writing.

Harry Berger Jr. explains that it is possible for art historians like him to use archival data to "confirm or fill out interpretations" about the lives and behavior of the sitters in early modern portraiture, but while this is to some degree a natural and expected part of the art historian's work, at times the data from the archive can take on a censuring role, excluding certain kinds of information from consideration and ultimately transforming the image into an "allegory of the archive."[55] The archive, which typically excludes marginal figures like Zaide and Gracia because of their race, gender, station, or profession, cannot be trusted to provide access to the whole story, and yet, in Díaz-Mas's parody, the art historian's blind faith is entirely invested in the archive. Once the art historian has determined "con casi total certeza" (with almost total certainty) the identity of the woman in the portrait, it remains to justify the painting's physical manipulation, which removed the second figure (whom the readers know to be Pablillos) from the canvas. To do this, the art historian supports the archival evidence with another kind of discourse: early modern story forms. Díaz-Mas represents both the "textualized remains of history," in the form of archival material, and narrative patterns drawn intertextually from seventeenth-century honor dramas as responsible for re-inforcing stereotypes and frustrating attempts to depict alternative versions of the past.[56]

Though the reader has learned in the third chapter that the painting of Gracia was cut in half in the nineteenth century by her distant descendant Alvaro upon his departure for Cuba, this detail is not registered in any of the archival material to which the art historian has access.[57] The interpretation upon which the art historian eventually settles is dramatic and even literary. Using letters and records from the period to deduce that the youngest Alfarache daughter, Ana, was impregnated and later protected by a Spanish nobleman, the art historian assumes that her fall from grace led to her sister's reclusion in a convent, where she could hide from her shame. Her humiliated father, having lost two daughters, was left with no choice but to "eliminar el doloroso recuerdo" (eliminate the painful memory), cutting the painting in two to remove the image of his disgraced child and preserve the memory of the other.[58] The art historian's fanciful explanation can be explained in Hayden White's term *encodation*, or the tendency to make sense of strange or inexplicable historical events like this one by using "culturally provided categories such as . . . story forms."[59] The use of story forms allows for a familiarization of strangeness because the reader "has been shown how the data conform to an *icon* of a comprehensible finished process, a plot structure with which he is familiar, as part of his cultural endowment."[60] However, in the case of *El sueño de Venecia*, the novel's self-reflexivity works to render problematic this process of familiarization, as the reader recognizes that while this interpretation may conform to familiar patterns, it is not consistent with the information the novel has already provided. This disconnect complicates our belief in a naïve or tidy representation of the past.

The parody of the academic essay, which produces a coherent narrative that is plausible in its familiarity, leads the reader to question who controls the discourse, or, put another way, whose truth is being told. It is here that the context in which the art historian works, one that is not named but implied in the parody, becomes imperative to understanding the professional demands that this interpretation fills. The voice that ultimately speaks for the portrait in *El sueño de Venecia* takes control of the painting's story for interested reasons. The narrative voice of the essay explains that this supposed discovery of the missing Zabala painting makes it possible to "cubrir una laguna en el catálogo de obras perdidas del artista sevillano" (fill a gap in the catalogue of lost works by the Sevillian artist).[61] It is easy for this line to get buried in a chapter dominated by historical data and forceful argumentative language, but it reveals the art historian's interested motives for advancing this particular interpretation. Another (ostensibly foreign) scholar has already proposed that Gracia de Mendoza and Ana de Alfarache are the same person, none other than "[la] amante del mismo Felipe IV y protegida de la mejor nobleza madrileña" (Philip IV's lover and the favorite of the highest nobility of Madrid), but the art historian calls that hypothesis "completamente descabellada" (totally absurd).[62]

The tenacious insistence on the veracity of the counterargument—that the woman in the painting is Ana's sister, Rufina, that this once lost painting is a true discovery—is what allows this art historian to textually mark the research of this essay as different, important, and therefore worthy of publication. Just like original visual art, academic writing must also make clear the "imprint of the system of positions in relation to which [its] originality is defined."[63] If we agree with Spires that the interpretations of the painting in each chapter of *El sueño de Venecia* reveal "much more about the period than [they do] about the artifact," then the implied voice of the university professor in the final chapter demonstrates the effects of neoliberalism on academic life and work.[64] The "academic capitalism" of the

Spanish university, underpinned by the notion of performativity that requires tracking and carefully managing one's output, creates the conditions in which the unnamed scholar likely produces the essay that concludes *El sueño de Venecia*.[65]

The unfolding of *El sueño de Venecia* suggests that understanding Spanish history requires a measure of creativity and flexibility. However, the "publish or perish" mentality of the university system restricts the time and mental space scholars have to consider alternative interpretations or to think outside the safely pre-established schema of the discipline. The first chapter's representation of the strange, liminal space that Gracia creates in her home, one that defies stereotypes about the period, would be difficult for any contemporary historian to faithfully reconstruct. Through its strangeness, however, Díaz-Mas highlights the importance of acknowledging the limitations of discursively inscribed knowledge about the past, as well as the potency of words to create worlds that seem more real than the ones actually lived and experienced in the past.[66] This has especially important repercussions in the hands of someone like the art historian, whose writing contributes to the "official" discourse. The misinterpretation of the painting and consequent erasure of marginalized subjects from this historical record can be understood, then, in two overlapping ways. The novel's self-reflexivity underscores the intertextual nature of the erroneous narrative; the art historian must draw on both the textualized traces of the past in the form of archival material and the early modern story forms to fill the gaps in the archival material. Telling the "original" (as in unpublished) story of the painting boosts the art historian's career prospects. The desire to mark the work as new not only leads to the denial of Gracia, Pablillos, and Zaide's agency in the staging and creation of the portrait but also consolidates the obliteration of their voices and perspectives from the historical record. Díaz-Mas modifies the dilemma common to the campus novel that places the academic in a position to choose between the life of the mind and status-oriented or commercial desires. Here, the choice is between a more accurate and diverse representation of Spanish history and career advancement, and the art historian chooses the latter.

---

*El sueño de Venecia* highlights the effects of the corporate university on scholarship; *Las manos de Velázquez* emphasizes its effects on the scholar himself. Ortiz gives greater weight to the campus novel's typical dilemma—the "life of the mind" versus a life of desires—that Díaz-Mas's final chapter merely implies. Teodoro has stagnated in his professional and personal life. Dalton-Brown notes that the scholar "stifling in his own environment" is a mainstay of the campus novel genre, whose authors often center plots on a "battle to stay in academe or escape."[67] Though in some ways *Las manos de Velázquez* is an unorthodox campus novel, in this respect, Ortiz stays true to the genre. For Teodoro, the battle between the mind and the flesh plays out at both institutional and domestic levels. His struggle at home is in the lack of time and quality of attention he has to invest in his relationships, particularly with his young wife, Mónica. The story of a student's seduction by a professor (or vice versa) that characterizes many campus novels here serves only as background. The capitulation to desire occurred years ago when Teodoro met Mónica, then a graduate student in his department's program, and left his first wife to marry her. It is Mónica's desire for a richly lived life that creates tension for Teodoro, for while he recognizes her refusal to be a typical "faculty wife," he does not know how to set the boundaries between his life and work that would allow them to build the partnership she wants.

The battle to stay in academia or to leave it is also waged at the level of scholarship, as Teodoro fights, first, with the paucity of the information the archive can offer for his investigative ends and, second, with what he considers to be the narrow limits of scholarship deemed acceptable by academe. Ortiz employs historiographic metafictional techniques, especially intertextuality and overt self-reflexivity about the process of writing history, to describe Teodoro's struggle to write a definitive monograph about

Velázquez, which emphasizes the limited parameters of acceptable scholarly work. The novel's sophisticated oscillation between narrative points of view allows Ortiz to represent Teodoro's perspective, seen from both within and without, as his own expectations for his work clash with his actual production. He finds the facts of Velázquez's life a challenge to convey linguistically in his writing, but he also finds words are unable to accurately articulate his own feelings. Teodoro's tortured reflections on the inadequacy of words mirror the insufficiency of the archival sources to present a complete picture of the painter. At the same time, they expose Teodoro's insecurity about the effectiveness of his own writing. This frustration can be read as a consequence of the neoliberal emphasis on personal responsibility, which refuses to take into account the structural factors that define and complicate "success."

The self-reflexivity of *Las manos de Velázquez* has the effect of making apparent certain conventions of fiction and, like all metafiction, reminds the reader of fiction's constructedness. In a work of historiographic metafiction such as this one, emphasizing history and fiction as linguistic constructs serves to complicate the claim that history's power derives from objective truth and shows that, just like fiction, its true force is actually rooted in verisimilitude.[68] Teodoro's insistence on distancing his own academic book from a work of fiction is one of the ways Ortiz highlights linguistic constructedness and the conventionalization of the narrative forms of both fiction and historiography. For example, in the novel's opening pages, Teodoro laments the lack of information contained in the historical record about Velázquez's personality. He wants to "atrapar el alma, fundirse con el pintor, oír sus latidos, sus miedos, sus satisfacciones" (trap his soul, become one with the painter, hear his heartbeats, his fears, his satisfactions), but doing so would require that he proceed based on intuition.[69] Such subjective analysis would lead him perilously close to nonacademic work. He thinks: "Pero las intuiciones son . . . ficción. Y no voy a escribir una novela." (But intuitions are . . . fiction. And I'm not going to write a novel.)[70] The only way to access Velázquez's thoughts and emotions is to take the stance of an omniscient and diegetic narrator, but, as Alan Robinson notes, the historian is by default a heterodiegetic narrator, a voice removed from the world in which the story takes place.[71]

Teodoro's ontological status as a character of fiction and his dialogue with empirical historical sources allows this work of historiographic metafiction to inhabit historical and literary planes simultaneously, situated as it is "within historical discourse [but] without surrendering its autonomy as fiction."[72] Teodoro often reflects on the power he grants himself as a narrator—for example, imagining dialogues between Velázquez and those around him. In an invented conversation between the painter and Philip IV, after the latter requested he bring back nudes prohibited by the Inquisition from his collecting trips to Italy, Teodoro envisions and transcribes Philip IV's directives: "Vete a Italia y busca para mí, tráeme esculturas delicadas, sugerentes, picaronas. . . . Compra para tu rey, que él se merece un palacio a su altura." (Go to Italy and search for me, bring me delicate, suggestive, naughty sculptures. . . . Buy for your king, who deserves a palace worthy of him.)[73] However, after Ortiz installs these conventions of fiction, she subverts them by reminding the reader how Teodoro's academic book should differ. After reading his imagined conversations, which for all their plausibility are not documentable fact, the narrator declares: "No estaría mal un párrafo así. Pero no es una novela lo que está haciendo. No es ficción." (A paragraph like that wouldn't be bad. But he's not writing a novel. It's not fiction.)[74] Ortiz then offers a paragraph that describes the same period and experience—that of Velázquez as a collector for the king—in the "frases cortas y simples, sin connotaciones subjetivas, sin recovecos" (short and simple sentences, without subjective connotations, without hidden meanings) that academic writing demands.[75] Adapting to those conventions leaves Teodoro feeling utterly unsatisfied, however. He is convinced that there has to be more to the story than can be said using the scholarly language that constrains him.

Teodoro's vacillations between his attraction to the conventions of fiction and his commitment to historiography also leaves space for Ortiz to comment on history's relationship to fiction, exemplified by its emplotment and narrativizing of information. In the first chapter, Teodoro exclaims that "los datos no dicen nada" (facts don't say anything), so Teodoro molds those facts to fit a "unifying form."[76] As Hayden White maintains, the historian's task is to encode "the facts contained in the chronicle as components of specific *kinds* of plot structures."[77] Teodoro creates a cohesive narrative whole from the facts drawn from the archive and previously published historical tracts, as well as from the painted works themselves. The bibliography that Ortiz includes at the end of the novel directly invites intertextual comparisons between the "new" text of the novel and the source texts. This asks readers to recognize the background elements on which the text is based, as well as their role in the creation of the fictive universe of the novel. A narrative voice that seems to belong to Ortiz herself explains that the books listed in the bibliography are provided for the "lector atento" (attentive reader) who may wish to "confirmar o rebatir con criterio las tesis de Teodoro" (confirm or refute Teodoro's theses with discernment).[78] While a straightforward work of historical fiction may have relied on the same sources to plausibly re-create past worlds, Ortiz's naming of her sources and invitation to the reader to engage with them reveal this novel as intensely self-conscious about that process.

These sources offer Teodoro knowledge about the past, but knowledge and understanding are not one and the same. *Understanding*, he believes, comes through a different kind of exploration, one that belongs more properly to fiction and that would allow him to inhabit Velázquez's mind and give voice to his presumptive feelings. In the novel, paintings by Velázquez and his contemporaries serve as additional historical intertexts in the form of ekphrases.[79] Through his interpretations of these paintings, Teodoro tries to move beyond his mere knowledge of the past and arrive at a true understanding, but they also lead him to a better understanding of himself. The ekphrases that appear in Ortiz's novel are dialogic and autoreflexive, and according to Valerie Robillard's scale of interactions between artwork and text, they create "semantic and ideological tension" between the seventeenth-century paintings and the contemporary novel, reflecting and problematizing the connection between them.[80] The desire to access the painter's feelings, like anger or tenderness, leads Teodoro to the paintings themselves, not to the archival material or the academic writing of his predecessors. However, invested as he is in his work, the paintings also mirror his own feelings and emotions, which are denied to him by his punishing workload. Nearly every ekphrastic passage blends temporal registers and makes apparent the ideological tensions between the original work as it was conceived and Teodoro's contemporary interpretation of it. At the same time, it allows the reader to construct a second meaning from the differences appreciable between the original and new work.

For example, an appraisal of Velázquez's painting of Aesop allows Teodoro insight into his first failed marriage and the way his ex-wife might have felt as a result of his actions. He describes a "rostro amargado y al mismo tiempo digno, cargado de reproches que se enfrenta al espectador, juzgándolo, condenándolo desde una pobreza, un desaliño y un cansancio del que sabe y soporta" (face that is embittered and dignified at the same time, laden with reproach that confronts the viewer, judging him, condemning him from a poverty, an untidiness, and a fatigue of one who knows and puts up with much).[81] Teodoro, tired of his predecessors' "fórmulas manidas para que todo encaje" (hackneyed methods that force everything to fit), finds that Aesop's gaze is not a clownish satire, as some have seen it, but rather a powerful rebuke, which can only be apprehended if the viewer is attuned to the painting's underlying emotion.[82] Teodoro can identify the dignified suffering and judgmental appraisal because he sees his ex-wife's gaze radiating from Aesop's eyes. He feels her "cansancio y decepción" (tiredness and disappointment) but also her sarcastic contemplation of his marriage to his new young wife.[83] A similar process takes place when his strained relationship with his adult daughter, Magdalena, is explored through ekphrastic descriptions of seventeenth-century paintings of Mary Magdalene or when after having an affair he considers an appropriate punishment for himself by contemplating Velázquez's painting of the severe-looking nun, Madre Jerónima de la Fuente. The cumulative effect of these ekphrases, which pepper the text, is to remind the reader of the way that the historian makes sense of the world, bringing to bear not only textualized traces of the past but also his own subjective experiences.

Teodoro's imaginative ekphrases also make Velázquez's personality accessible to Ortiz's readers. Isabelle Touton has observed that, after the 1990s, literary representations of famous figures from the early modern period in Spain tended toward "la valoración afectiva del individuo en su vida privada y en sus pulsiones más íntimas, y por consiguiente, su humanidad" (the emotional valuation of the individual's private life and his [or her] most intimate impulses, and consequently his [or her] humanity).[84] Often, when Teodoro's mind begins to wander away from the hard facts and into the realm of speculation, he not only imagines but also identifies with Velázquez's thoughts and feelings. The starting point for these digressions is nearly always drawn from the archival or scholarly material. In one of his readings of Antonio Palomino's eighteenth-century treatise on painting, Teodoro is captivated by a sentence in which the author claims that Velázquez's series of Pandora paintings destroyed in the Alcázar fire in 1734 conveyed "las aflicciones y desconsuelos y otras cosas que llegan con el matrimonio" (the afflictions, distress, and other things that come with marriage).[85] Very little is known about the painter's personal life, but Teodoro still wonders about Velázquez's "monótona vida matrimonial. . . . El matrimonio que agosta el deseo, que lo deseca" (monotonous married life. . . . Marriage that withers and desiccates desire), projecting the boredom he felt in his own first marriage.[86] But Teodoro's second wife's active social life and the embarrassment that he seems to cause her leads him to also adopt the perspective of Velázquez's wife, Juana Pacheco. Teodoro identifies with Juana languishing at home while her husband "se esponja, pinta, presume, luce galas, se avergüenza de ella, de esa coneja paridora que engorda en el hogar" (struts around, paints, brags, dresses up, and is ashamed of her, that fertile rabbit getting fat at home).[87] These ekphrastic descriptions do more than humanize figures from the past. Teodoro relies equally on story forms and history in these passages, and they demonstrate the lack of hierarchy between historical and literary intertexts that inform the novel. As Hutcheon reminds us, history and literature are "both part of the signifying systems of our culture. They both make and make sense of our world."[88] However, in Teodoro's profession, there is indeed a hierarchy, for, in his words, "la ficción . . . produce indignación en la Academia" (fiction . . . incites indignation in the academy).[89]

The limitations on the kind of writing that is accepted as research and that will lead to career advancement are one of the greatest dissatisfactions of Teodoro's academic life, but they are just one of many. The blending of the campus novel with historiographic metafiction highlights the importance of the narrator's enunciative situation, as well as the context in which the historiographic writing is produced. In the case of *Las manos de Velázquez*, this context is an indictment of the conditions of professorial life in an age defined by neoliberalism. The novel condemns the narrowing of the spirit, the curtailing of creativity, and the requiste mastery of the self—also defined as the discipline to accept a life without boundaries between work and leisure—that lead to isolation and frustration. Teodoro knows that writing a book in which the disciplines of fiction and history overlap too much is a transgressive act that will lead to sanction in the scholarly community. If one leaves the "pauta marcada" (indicated guidelines), as he would if he were to publish such a book, the consequence is "anonimato, silencio, olvido. Cuando no el castigo" (anonymity, silence, and obscurity. If not punishment).[90] To stray from the path would be to renounce the opportunity both to leave a mark on the field and to provide materially for himself and his family.

Ortiz's novel reveals the quotidian intensity of academic time and the labor involved in the day-to-day process of writing. Herself a professor of art history, Ortiz does not shy away from depicting what she has surely experienced firsthand: the agony of writer's block, the profound boredom and even disgust with one's chosen research topic, and the battle to carve out writing time in a profession (and a life) filled with other responsibilities. Teodoro's own vision of his work contrasts with notions held by other characters, who buy into that old professorial romance that bears little resemblance to reality. The way others see him confirms the mythified image of professorial work. Teodoro describes his image in the department—"Un profesor tan respetable y ligeramente excéntrico que se mantenía siempre distante, siempre ajeno al trajinar del mundo y de sus pompas, interesado en la verdad del Arte. Ja, ja, ja." (a respectable and slightly eccentric professor who always kept his distance, always removed from the workings of the world and its pretentiousness, interested only in the truth of art. Ha, ha, ha.).[91] His sarcastic laughter indicates what will be made apparent as the novel progresses: Teodoro is indeed status-seeking and competitive. He is neither altruistic nor disinterested, but a governable subject responding to a perceived responsibility to perform. When Mónica's friend Ignacio, a wealthy businessman and art collector, "se deshacía en elogios para la labor callada del investigador" (lavished praise on the quiet work of the researcher), he expresses another notion of academic labor's strangeness and articulates his envy for what he imagines to be Teodoro's control of his own time and his opportunity to engage in mentally gratifying work.[92] These visions of his labor—disinterested, lucky, autonomous, independent—do not resonate with Teodoro, who sees himself merely as a "funcionario," an employee who must "agachar la cabeza y cumplir el horario" (keep his head down and put in his hours).[93] In a "puñetero país de mierda" (shitty fucking country) like Spain, all he can expect from his university position is "burocracia, reuniones sin cuento, papeles que rellenar" (bureaucracy, irrelevant meetings, and forms to fill out).[94] The tower in which he resides is made not of ivory but rather "de inercias, componendas, clases y cursos repetidos" (of inertia, shady dealings, the same classes and courses over and over again).[95] His scholarship, even with all the emotional and intellectual difficulties it presents, is still the most worthwhile of the tasks in which Teodoro engages, but the bureaucracy, the meetings, the forms, and the courses fill his days at work, so the time and energy he needs to complete his book must be carved out from other parts of his life.

Discenna argues compellingly that the notion of "freedom" often associated with academic work should instead be seen as "an instrument of control used to extract ever increasing amounts of time and labor from the professoriate."[96] Control over their time is secured through professors' tacit agreement to "cede any differentiation between work and leisure" and to give up their time "'freely' in order to meet social or cultural goals."[97] Academics in the corporatizing university are expected to "take responsibility for working harder, faster, and better as part of [their] sense of personal worth."[98] Teodoro experiences this when, in a fit of self-loathing and fear that his book will never be finished, he questions his own worth as a scholar: "Es verdad que las circunstancias cuentan, pero el que puede, puede" (One's circumstances surely matter, but the person who can do it will do it regardless).[99] The toxic shame Teodoro feels for his inability to become a superstar professor, to transcend his existence as a "buen y comedido profesor de Historia del Arte, sin muchas publicaciones, sin grandes tratados" (good and respectable art history professor, without many publications, with no great treatises to his name), can only be remedied by working more and working harder.[100]

The responsibility he feels to constantly increase the quantity and quality of his work reaches such a point that physical infirmity appears to be the only way to find reprieve. When he falls ill one day, Teodoro pays lip service to the idea that he would rather be working than convalescing, and he lists the tasks going undone: the exams waiting to be graded, the meetings with advisees he has postponed, the conference paper not yet written. However, his illness offers him an excuse to rest. The narrator explains: "Agradece este respiro, esta mañana en que añora los mimos de Mónica, un caldito, una manzanilla, mucha atención, una caricia a tiempo." (He's thankful for this chance to breathe this morning when he's longing for Mónica's love, a little soup, some chamomile tea, a lot of attention, a caress at just the right time.)[101] When Teodoro is physically unable to work, the numbing effects of labor wear off, and he becomes aware of the desires he has pushed aside in order to remain efficient. It takes the excuse of his body's physical degradation to indulge feelings and desires that are unrelated to his own performativity. As he notes elsewhere in the novel, the separation he has built between his work and life is revealed when the work stops: "ahí está la vida, siempre nueva, cambiante, agitada, ahí están las pasiones, el dolor, los cambios" (there's your life, always new, changing, tumultuous, there are the passions, the pain, the shifts).[102] Ortiz shows that with the exception of these rare instances of clarity, all of Teodoro's waking moments have been colonized by the academic workplace.[103]

This notion of making academic labor visible, when it is often denied as labor at all, is allegorized in Teodoro's final conference presentation, partially transcribed in the final chapter. With a hypothesis he considers audacious for its lack of empirical grounding and its relationship to fiction, Teodoro compares Velázquez's hands to Rembrandt's in their respective self-portraits to claim they represent "dos maneras diferentes de enfrentarse a sí mismo, a su oficio" (two different ways to confront oneself and one's profession).[104] Teodoro cites no archival or academic source to verify that Rembrandt's blurred hands meant that he valued his gaze and his intellect over his hands, mere tools used to convey his message.[105] He has only an intuition that the status-seeking Velázquez insisted on and amplified his own hands in *Las meninas* (*The Ladies-in-Waiting*) in order to represent them as an instrument of manual labor worthy of respect.[106] According to Teodoro, Velázquez hoped to dignify his own hands "frente a todos los que niegan al trabajo manual del pintor el rango que se merece, el rango de artista caballero o noble" (before all those who deny the painter's manual labor the social status it deserves, that of a gentleman artist or nobleman).[107] Teodoro's identification with Velázquez throughout the text, his sense that they share that lowly title, *funcionario* (public servant), allows the reader to appreciate Teodoro's attempts to dignify his own labor, too.

This notion is mirrored in an ekphrastic passage that appears early in the novel, as Teodoro gazes at Velázquez's *Apolo en la fragua de Vulcano*

(*Vulcan's Forge*). This painting, completed in 1630, depicts an episode from Ovid's *Metamorphoses* in which Apollo, an orange-robed and brilliant figure, addresses himself to Vulcan to reveal his wife's adultery with none other than Mars, whose armor Vulcan is crafting. The primary function of this ekphrastic passage is to concretize Teodoro's abstract feelings of jealousy and bitterness that he is harboring for Mónica's friend and collaborator Beltrán, who works as a photographer. After seeing a series of nude photos that Beltrán took of Mónica, Teodoro becomes convinced that his wife is having an affair. He blames himself for neglecting her in favor of his book and for not supporting her work with Beltrán, whom he assumes must be mocking him behind his back. However, in Teodoro's personal identification with Velázquez's work, the ekphrastic passage on *Apolo en la fragua de Vulcano* also has the function of making his own scholarly labor visible. He imagines himself as Vulcan, the gruff and haggard worker, whom he describes as "paleto, desarmado, tal vez acomplejado por el brillo del otro, su parsimonia, un dios que baja de las alturas sin esfuerzo mientras él está allí, dale que dale, con el calor de la fragua y sobre su cabeza, en vez de cuernos, las armaduras del forjado" (coarse, defenseless, perhaps hung up on the brilliance of the other, his lack of urgency, a god who comes effortlessly down from on high while he is there day in and day out, with the heat of the forge and the forged armor over his head instead of horns).[108] The divine creature who appears from the heavens—Beltrán/Apollo—is "el guerrero, el vencedor" (the warrior, the victor), while he is just an old man, "puteado y renegrido, reconcomido por el trabajo agobiante, dando el callo" (screwed over and blackened with soot, tired of this oppressive work, working his fingers to the bone).[109] This passage, on the one hand, highlights Teodoro's anxiety about his age and his attractiveness to Mónica but, on the other, serves to reveal Teodoro's relationship to his work.

Teodoro's insistence on Vulcan's defining identity as laborer reflects how Teodoro sees his own work. Critics like Javier Portús have seen in Velázquez's painting an allegory of art, as Apollo illuminates the darkness of the forge with "the light of principal art forms . . . implying a discourse on the superiority of the world of ideas over that of mechanical labor."[110] In this case, as in his conference paper, Teodoro acknowledges and dignifies labor or, at the very least, hopes to incite sympathy for his plight. There is no way Teodoro's hands, with fingers worked to the bone like Vulcan's, can compare with "las manos que nunca han trabajado, manos de artista" (hands that have never worked, artist's hands) that belong to Beltrán.[111] Teodoro's work is separating him from his wife, whom he imagines prefers Beltrán's calmness and adaptability, which contrasts with his own rigidity and anxiety. His work has also divorced him from his own inner life, in large part because of the discourses of denial that operate to negate his labor as such, which means that the boundaries between his life and his work are porous to the point of nonexistence. His identification with Vulcan, and especially the image of his hands, makes Teodoro's labor visible while critiquing its effects on the quality of his life.

In her campus novel variant, Ortiz captures many of the dissatisfactions inherent in academic life with Teodoro's prolonged working days, diminished passions, and self-imposed isolation. As Arthur P. Bochner asserts, orthodox academic practices that permit the discipline, control, and perpetuation of the professoriate have the effect of "discouraging creativity, . . . making it difficult to take risks, and severing academic life from emotional and spiritual life."[112] These academic practices and discourses have the effect of "disciplining the erotic," controlling and tightly managing passion and pleasure in one's work, but also in the academic's private life.[113] When eros is lost in everyday life, it leads to what Franco Berardi has described as an "investment of desire in one's work, understood as the only place providing narcissistic reinforcement to individuals used to perceiving the other according to rules of competition, that is to say as danger, impoverishment and limitation, rather than experience, pleasure and enrichment."[114] The loss of passion in life and its re-investment in work has allegorical expression in *Las manos de Velázquez* as a romance plot that is unconventional for the campus novel. Teodoro does not find himself seduced by an ingenue or wooing a student; rather, his investment of eros in his work is signaled by the affair he has with another scholar while attending a conference.

As Dalton-Brown has noted, many campus novels use the academic's sexual behavior as a "parable of disempowerment." When the (male) academic finds his own will to power curtailed within the political and bureaucratic university, he turns to sexual predation.[115] Illicit sexual encounters represent a distraction from the idealized dedication to one's scholarly work, one pole in the dilemma between the life of the mind and the life of desires. The women, often students who are not fully enmeshed in the academic world, offer the temptations of the flesh and life outside the university. Teodoro's spouse, Mónica, once his graduate student, has been married to him for five years at the novel's opening; the story of seduction occupies a mere four pages in the first chapter. In some ways, though, she still represents the allure of the outside world and re-inforces the strangeness of his academic labor. Mónica, at more than twenty-five years his junior, throws into relief not just Teodoro's age but also the contrast between a nonacademic life and an academic one. At the time the novel begins, Mónica, once awed by Teodoro's mind, has lost interest in his work (still the same book after five years!) and even more so in "los pequeños incidentes en el departamento" (the little incidents in the department).[116] Mónica has stopped working on her own thesis in art history in order to pursue her goal of establishing a gallery. She tells her husband: "Yo no me meto en la enseñanza ni loca" (You couldn't pay me to become a professor).[117] All of these factors—Mónica's youthful exuberance and social grace, her lack of interest in Teodoro's work and abandonment of her own academic pursuits, as well as her frustration with her husband's "manias"—lead Teodoro to struggle with "temores y anhelos que [le] impiden centrar[se] en [su] trabajo" (fears and longings that keep him from focusing on his work).[118]

It appears that Teodoro's initial interest in Mónica was for her beauty and her age, but also because of her respect for and understanding of his profession. He sees himself as different from the "cretinos . . . que aprovechaban su situación para ligar con las alumnas" (creeps . . . who take advantage of their situation to hook up with students) and thought that he had found in Mónica not an escape from his rigidly constructed academic life but a partner who would understand and support his intellectual pursuits.[119] When the illusion of this support begins to crumble, Teodoro finds himself with two choices: to double down and re-entrench himself in the world of his research and writing or embrace, at least in part, what Monica embodies—the life outside academia, or, at the very least, an alternative way of conceptualizing the academic practices that define the discipline. But Teodoro has fully invested the eros of his life in his work, and it is *he* who is unfaithful to Mónica, even after years of worry that she will be unfaithful to him. Teodoro's affair with Caterina, an Italian early modern art historian, does not challenge the already blurred boundaries of work and leisure that define his life. His pleasure in the affair derives not only from sex but also from shared conversation about work and art. Rather than have an affair with someone who could help him escape from the academic world that confines him, Teodoro confirms that world's power over him through his affair with another scholar. This relationship, as well as his eventual completion and publication of his book (the reception of which is left unknown), confirms that his battle to stay in academia has been won, but at what cost?

Teodoro's tale seems to be a cautionary one, as his humiliation at the conference in the final chapter suggests. When, in the middle of his talk, Teodoro bursts into tears for the wife who has left him as he speaks of his beloved Velázquez before a packed room, he is shocked and surprised because he has spent the better part of his life using his academic practices and discourse to discipline his emotions. In this final instance, those emotions become too powerful to suppress. By spending his adult life repressing the commingling of the personal and the academic, Teodoro becomes alienated from himself and from those around him, giving into the "institutional depression that permeates academic discourse."[120] The book about Velázquez in which he had invested so much hope has lost all meaning by the end. As he sits with his tears dried, once again composed but unable to focus on the next speaker's talk, Teodoro softly closes his eyes and sighs, "Qué más da?" (What difference does any of it make?).[121]

As Dalton-Brown notes, often there is "remarkably little point to most of the work undertaken by academic protagonists" in the campus novel, though in this case Teodoro's disappointment seems rooted in the ways that his work has alienated him from his life.[122] The desire to know Velázquez and the obsession with finishing his book kept Teodoro from a full experience of his relationship with Mónica. In a way, his disappointment mirrors the kind Angeles Caso depicts in *El mundo visto desde el cielo* (discussed in chapter 1), when her artist protagonist Julio is left unsatisfied with the work to which he has passionately devoted years of his life. Teodoro has given himself to his project with a fervor equal to that of a charismatic artist like Julio, but he realizes that it is the university, not him, that is the ultimate beneficiary of his work and his time. Teodoro's completed book cannot return love as his wife did. The work is not and, he sees only now, has never been a satisfying substitute for a life richly lived. Rosalind Gill notes that sometimes the "pleasures of academic work (or at least a deep love for the 'myth' of what we thought being an intellectual would be like, but often seems at far remove from it) bind us more tightly into a neoliberal regime with ever-growing costs, not least to ourselves."[123] Ortiz emphasizes these costs in the postscript that announces the bibliography, which advocates for a balance in both academic life and historical writing: "La tarea del investigador es modesta y la vida rica, mentirosa, y trabucante. Nos desmiente y nos voltea. Eso es lo que la literatura añade, que no es poca cosa." (The researcher's work is modest and life is rich, mendacious, and messy. It shows us we're wrong and it turns us around. That is what literature gives us, which is no small thing.)[124] The "literary" aspects of Velázquez's life included in the novel—precisely the parts that Teodoro has sought to keep out of his academic book but that seduce him nonetheless—are those associated with emotion, sentiment, and intuition.

Ortiz ultimately celebrates these elements in historical fiction by combining historiographic and literary registers and also advocates for their necessary privileging in academic life.

---

The techniques of historiographic metafiction in these unique permutations of the campus novel ultimately stress the importance of the enunciative situation of the writer and at the same time highlight the circumstances in which the writer's labor is carried out. The effects of neoliberal capitalism on the fictional professors' work—and arguably on that of real professors, too—is undeniable: they are required to track their output and meet ever higher demands for publications, in addition to the other very real work required of them. In response to these new demands, many take refuge in the "myth of the academic good life," as Gill calls it, that both allows for survival as a justification for suffering at the same time that it increases complicity with the neoliberal structures within the university that depend on professors' self-exploitation to be successful.[125] Professors and artists are not so different after all, as both are prone to have very permeable boundaries between their lives and their work and both boast a deep investment that ties their work to their identities. As Sarah Brouillette has shown, more and more work that takes place outside of creative fields has become like artists' work.[126] Artistic work is imagined as "romantically honorable and free," and artists are seen as "flexible" and "self-managed" workers to be emulated by those who wish to work for themselves.[127] Teodoro's own identification with Velázquez explicitly underscores the connection between his profession and the artist's. However, that sense of self-management and the accompanying erosion of boundaries between work and leisure actually encourage a longer, even endless, working day, which responds indirectly to the desires and demands of the neoliberal university system. The adoption of some of the characteristics of artistic labor—especially the sense of freedom that comes from managing of one's own time and the privilege of engaging in mentally gratifying work—offers what Peter Bloom calls a "sheen of empowerment" that allows workers to entertain the fantasy that they dictate their own career choices, which leads them to exploit their own labor rather than offering it for direct exploitation by a boss.[128] For Bloom, this is a paradox in much contemporary work: "The contemporary subject of employability struggles not for the eradication of exploitation, but rather for their right to self-exploitation."[129] Working more like the charismatic artist allows scholars the illusion of taking control of their lives as they generate profit for their university at the same time. The uniqueness of artistic labor has been structured into the workings of the cultural field, a model that is now quite valuable to capitalism. Just like artists, professors are defined by what Brouillette calls "romantically aesthetic models of selfhood" that euphemize their capitulations to the university's market demands.[130] Ortiz's and Díaz-Mas's blending of the campus novel genre with historiographic metafictional techniques exposes the constructed textuality of historical discourse in order to reveal the reality of labor in neoliberal academia. However, neither Ortiz nor Díaz-Mas is very critical of the ways that the alternative model of artistic labor, informed by myths about the autonomous, creative labor of artists (that we have seen bears little resemblance to the work artists actually do), idealize and distort the labor of professors, presenting it as creative and liberating, which re-inforces the blurred boundaries between life and work and ultimately ensures that their labor becomes another instrument of control over their time and energy.

CHAPTER 4

# Affiliation Anxiety

## AVANT-GARDE IDENTITY AT DOCUMENTA(13) IN ENRIQUE VILA-MATAS'S *KASSEL NO INVITA LA LÓGICA*

In a metapoetic and self-referential poem titled "Confession," published in 1999, American poet Bob Perelman mused about having "lost his avant-garde card in the laundry" at some point since the beginning of his career in the 1970s. The poetic voice judges his own words in the rhetorical present, noting that "this writing seems pretty normal: // complete sentences; semi-colons; yada yada," suggesting, tongue firmly in cheek, that "avant-garde" identity can be ascertained by the presence of certain formal elements, vocabulary, or other immediately discernible outward characteristics.[1] In a 2010 article titled "My Avant-Garde Card" in which Perelman critically revisits his poem, he observes that the designation "avant-garde" has become for poets like him a "token of affiliation," a membership card of sorts for an exclusive literary club.[2] His fear that the card has been lost in the laundry, shredded to soppy bits amid socks and underwear in the most quotidian of activities, reveals to the author a decade later a particular lack of enthusiasm for "the whole enterprise [of the avant-garde]."[3] What is more, his words in the poem belie an anxiety about his identity as an avant-gardist—a fear of "not being sufficiently avant-garde"—or perhaps about the validity of the avant-garde as a meaningful category in the contemporary age. The reference is meant to be humorous, but, Perelman notes, "this dismissal of the avant-garde published by a poet," especially one closely associated with the "avant-garde," is not "simply a joke."[4]

Enrique Vila-Matas's narrator in his 2014 novel *Kassel no invita la lógica* is similarly concerned with the status of his "avant-garde card," and this trepidation betrays cultural anxieties that are also no laughing matter. This is evident in the novel's very first sentence, in which the narrator observes: "Cuanto más de vanguardia es un autor, menos puede permitirse caer bajo ese calificativo" (The more avant-garde an author is, the less he can allow himself to be labeled as such).[5] References to the "avant-garde" resurface continually throughout the novel, but what exactly does Vila-Matas mean when he uses this malleable term? As Perelman has shown, the term *avant-garde* has syntactically distinct uses, but in Vila-Matas's case, it can be understood as "an intensifying cognate for a host of words such as 'confrontational,' 'difficult,' 'advanced,' and 'new.'"[6] In the novel's first sentence, "vanguardia" references a normalized "practice" of the avant-garde that any self-respecting, "true" *vanguardista* needs to shun in order to continue as a card-carrying member. Though Vila-Matas has long been considered an avant-garde writer in Spain, this identity is put to the test when he is invited to participate as a sort of performance artist at Documenta(13), the large-scale quinquennial exhibition held in Kassel, Germany. In this chapter, I explore the diegetic repercussions of Documenta's challenge to the narrator–Vila-Matas's avant-garde identity as an autonomous artist, as well as the extradiegetic repercussions ascertainable in the very existence of the novel itself as a response to that challenge.

*Kassel no invita la lógica* is a fictionalized rendering of the author's real-life participation as an artist in Documenta(13) in 2012, the transformation of his experience with the visual arts into its own work of art.[7] Vila-Matas was invited to contribute to a generically ambiguous performance series titled *Chorality, on Retreat: A Writer's Residency*.[8] As the online exhibition catalogue puts it, the participating authors from around the world were invited to Kassel, "[to] simply do what they would normally do: write."[9] However, the word "retreat" of the title was intentionally deceiving, as the writing was not to take place in a secluded space or refuge. Rather, the curatorial team instructed the authors to work in a fully functional Chinese restaurant, located at the far end of Karlsaue Park in Kassel. There they would be on display for exhibition goers and restaurant patrons alike, and expected to interact with that public if approached by them, in compliance with one of the exhibition's themes of "interconnectedness." *Chorality*—and, ultimately, the narrator's rejection of it—serves as the pretext for the novel. It is fictionalized through the creation of the narrator–Vila-Matas, who is "[una] figuración del yo" ([an] imagined self), to use José María Pozuelo Yvancos's term for the shared nominal identity between character and author.[10] As such, this voice both belongs to the author—referring to actual people and events from his experience at Documenta—and exists independently by fictionalizing that experience through narrative emplotting. The discursive space generated frees the narrative voice from the "responsabilidad testimonial" to which it would be bound in an essay.[11] *Kassel no invita la lógica* is semi-fictional, and though the author's website categorizes it as a novel, Vila-Matas himself has described *Kassel* as a hybrid, using the terms "reportaje novelado" (novelized report) and "ensayo novelado" (novelized essay) to classify it.[12] The adjective "novelado" in both cases liberates Vila-Matas from the constraints of the referential plane and allows his actual experience in Kassel to serve as the springboard for this ambitious literary exploration of contemporary art and literature.[13] This freedom eventually allows Vila-Matas to use the novel to return the individual artist to his imagined privileged place of primacy that has been denied him in his relational experience at Documenta.

My analysis of Vila-Matas's novel in this chapter is twofold. First, I explore the narrator–Vila-Matas's ambivalent position with respect to avant-garde identity and the artist's role in society. The narrator boasts of adopting a "progressive" attitude for himself as both a practitioner and critic of the avant-garde. On the one hand, he claims to privilege *orthopraxis*, or a recovery of an originary avant-garde "experience" that can take myriad forms, over *orthodoxy*—the repetition of certain *practices* easily identifiable as "avant-garde."[14] On the other hand, the narrator's insistence on his difference from his contemporaries obsessed with orthodoxy does little more than betray his anxiety to prove his avant-garde affiliation. In an art world in which being an artist means being recognized and consecrated as such, he fears that not observing the avant-garde "doxa" strictly enough might impede his identification as a true avant-gardist. The progression of his experiences at Documenta highlights that the narrator actually feels comfortable with a more conservative conception of the avant-garde that exists "in circulation," which Richard Schechner describes as "the same items, ideas, techniques, and kinds of shows [that] go around and come around viewed by the same kinds of audiences."[15] I posit that the narrator's rejection of *Chorality* stems from the lack of control inherent in its setting and audience; the "connection" its relational format promotes is with a potentially general public whose interest in and respect for the material is not guaranteed, and the narrator worries that if he is off the avant-garde "circuit," he will not be seen at all. When his charismatic identity is challenged, he seeks refuge in orthodoxly "pure" artworks that encourage a type of connection that more closely aligns with his mythified conception of avant-garde. He concludes that connection between artist and audience is acceptable, as long as the artist's privileged position is not questioned.

Second, I consider the publication of the novel *Kassel no invita la lógica* as an attempt for Vila-Matas to recast his experience at Documenta. The novel offers an opportunity to recenter himself as a creator after being stripped of that privileged position through his participation in *Chorality*. The detailed ekphrastic descriptions of more than twenty contemporary artworks seen in Kassel—a sort of personal exhibition catalogue—combined with the intricate web of intertextual references common in Vila-Matas's work ensures an "elite" readership equivalent in many ways to the privileged audience one could expect to find on the biennial circuit, not the one who may haplessly stumble into a Chinese restaurant. In the form of the novel narrated by his fictionalized self, Vila-Matas scales the experience with relational art at Documenta through a concrete object under his control. Thus the novel we read is a tangible transformation of his experience into an art object and a means of reprivileging a charismatic identity that the actual experience at Documenta denied him through the relational experience of *Chorality*. More broadly, the entire trip to Documenta is, for Vila-Matas, a way to discover if the avant-garde world of art is in the same state as it is in literature: "Lo vanguardístico había perdido peso, por no decir que probablemente se había extinguido" (The avant-garde had lost ground, if not become almost entirely extinct).[16] Determining the health, perhaps even the existence, of the avant-garde is essential to someone as preoccupied with proving that his own "avant-garde card" is current.

Vila-Matas has said that, in the context of the novel, the depiction of the exhibition itself is but an excuse: "Kassel es un macguffin: el viaje y la performance como excusa para comentar la vida y el mundo" (Kassel is a Macguffin: travel and performance as an excuse to comment on life and the world).[17] In spite of a focus on the singulative experience—the detailed descriptions of the artworks seen at Documenta(13) and Vila-Matas's feelings as a result of interacting with them—the novel also more generally depicts the artist's changing role in a world in flux, perhaps even in crisis. Vila-Matas's conceptualization of the artist is deeply informed by the charismatic myth: it is clear that he still values the individual who disinterestedly produces unique works of art in the context of an "economic world reversed." In this formulation, the artist is one who pursues artistic novelty without evident strategic calculation and art has value that transcends its market price. Pamela M. Lee calls these characteristics typical of an "old model" of understanding the art world, exemplified by mid-century thinkers like Arthur Danto. She observes that the legacy of scholars like Danto, especially his 1964 article "The Artworld," is the still common notion that the art world is "a virtual space of both discursive and sociological separation, premised on a peculiar sense of distance" and "*spatialized* as a very particular kind of world: rarified, perhaps even sublime, held far above the crude workings of the earth."[18] Lee urges all those who work in and speak about the art world to engage with it, not from "some celestial perch" but rather from below, where it is possible to "question our own embeddedness in this world."[19] When the actors of the art world see themselves as both active agents and objects acted upon by global market forces, it becomes increasingly difficult to sustain the notion that art belongs in a separate, independent realm. Lee notes that the art world now "forgets . . . what made an art world such a distinct and singular 'world' in the first place," as the reality of globalization draws the art world from its place of exceptionality.[20]

Vila-Matas is made to reckon uncomfortably with this change as it is represented by *Chorality*, in which the realm of art is forced into direct and unavoidable contact with a heterogeneous audience and with the realm of commerce in a Chinese restaurant. *Chorality* asks him to offer up his supposedly avant-garde artistic craft in a commercial space, and thus serves as a catalyst for him to consider the collapsing distance between artistic labor and other kinds of work, a prospect made terrifying by his own belief in the centrality of art's autonomy. As Peter Bürger explains in his influential 1984 book *Theory of the Avant-Garde*, to consider art autonomous or independent from society means adopting the position that "art-for-art's-sake" is the true "nature" of art.[21] If disinterestedness is considered inherent to art's essence, then it is impossible to explain the historical and social constructedness of that "apartness."[22] Vila-Matas's narrator in *Kassel no invita la lógica* begins his trip to Documenta a firm believer in autonomy as central to the definition of "artist." As I demonstrate in the following pages, though he does revise his beliefs, he does so only insofar as his own authority as a creator is not challenged.

---

The biennial and other large-scale perennial exhibitions require brief definition and contextualization in order to understand Vila-Matas's experience depicted in *Kassel no invita la lógica*. Documenta occurs every five years and while it is not a biennial, strictly speaking, it belongs to the same family of art events. It is one of the longest-running perennial exhibitions, characterized as a category by their grandiose scale and by their predilection for discursive elements like "symposia, extensive publications, or even accompanying journals."[23] The global pretentions of biennials across continents are reflected in the way they share many of these characteristics, but Elena Filipovic, Marieke van Hal, and Solveig Øvstebø emphasize that the "founding stories" of most of these exhibitions are very embedded in the local fixtures of a city. To ignore their local specificity is to naïvely disregard the context that facilitates these events.[24] Founded in the German postwar reconstruction period, Documenta was considered instrumental in the literal and figural rebuilding and rebranding of Kassel as a cultural center, after the city had been nearly razed in the war.[25] The narrator of *Kassel no invita la lógica* arrives in the city failing to recognize Documenta's very site-specific context, but when he eventually does, it prompts him to reconsider his position that art and life must remain separate.

Some of the biennial's common characteristics discourage the recognition of that local context. Large-scale perennial exhibitions like Documenta occupy a liminal space in the field of artistic practice. They have an ambivalent relationship to both the market and the museum, and that liminal position can foster a bad-faith disavowal of biennial art's connections to commerce and tradition. Citing the curator Carlos Basualdo, Filipovic, van Hal, and Øvstebø refer to the biennial as a "fundamentally 'unstable institution,'" best defined by all the things it is not.[26] The biennial is freer and more open to change than the museum, as it celebrates and legitimates art of the moment rather than consecrating art of even the recent past.[27] In contrast to the museum's permanence, the biennial exists as a temporally bound *event* that allows its organizers to create what Ranjit Hoskote calls a "discursive environment: a theater that allows for the staging of arguments, speculations, and investigations concerning the nature of our shared, diversely veined, and demanding contemporary condition."[28] Despite these key differences, the biennial shares with the museum the same "white cube" exhibition styles that "extract the viewer from the world" through a presentation considered "neutral" and "pure."[29] Often, this approach has the effect of minimizing the importance of both the exhibition's local context and the curatorial hand involved in the organization of the exhibition.

At the same time, the biennial also stands in contrast to the market, as it is assumed to not operate by the same supply and demand logic, thus making it a more "pure" artistic space than the gallery or the art fair.[30] Vila-Matas initially refers to Documenta's "purity" in the novel when he expresses his admiration for one of the exhibition's unwritten rules: "su voluntad de mantener una débil relación con el mercado de arte" (to maintain a weak connection with the art market).[31] The narrator's opposition to *Chorality* rests on its connection to commerce that he would be more comfortable disavowing. Biennials' existence as non-selling events permits participants' strategic disavowal of their connection to the market, though exhibitions like this still deal in other forms of capital that allows participants to accrue economic capital in the long run. As Olav Velthuis notes, biennials "send out signals" that have a "relatively strong effect on the market because of their pure, fresh, independent and highly visible character."[32] The biennial as an institution generates the symbolic capital that offers legitimacy—and, for many, eventual market success—to the contemporary artists who exhibit there.

Finally, despite its claims to innovation, the biennial is also an institution suffering from what Lee calls a "fatal bout of sameness"—the same types of works, the same groups of artists, the same "jaded art world audiences."[33] Richard Schechner echoes this notion when he speaks of the "avant-garde in circulation," describing the "same items, ideas, techniques, and kinds of shows [that] go around and come around, viewed by the same kinds of audiences."[34] Given that, those audiences are familiar with the contemporary avant-garde "brand" and know what to expect. In sum, a large-scale exhibition like Documenta presents a unique space for a Spanish writer to explore questions of artistic autonomy. This is an event with global pretensions that is, nevertheless, embedded in the local. It is a non-selling event that presents itself as fresher and more adventurous than the museum and not directly associated with the market. However, despite variation in the works and artists exhibited, there is a predictability about these events as well that could be seen as comforting or boring according to one's disposition.

---

*Chorality* takes place within this biennial context, looking in many ways quite different from some of the other works at Documenta because of its attempts to disrupt established relationships. Vila-Matas's depiction of the *Chorality* project serves three complementary functions in the novel. First, the image of *Chorality* makes visible the commercialization of culture that Vila-Matas abhors. Second, the project serves as a springboard for a consideration of the meaning of *avant-garde* and the contemporary Spanish author's place in the international artistic community. Third, the relational nature of *Chorality* serves to denaturalize author-reader relationships, disrupting the hold of the charismatic artist over his public. By displacing the authors from their discrete realm and inserting them into the "vulgar" world represented by the commercial space of the Chinese restaurant, they are forced to reconceptualize their artistic identities.

The notion of "interconnectedness"—one of the theoretical bases of Documenta(13)—is fundamental to *Chorality*'s workings. In the context of *Chorality*, "interconnecting" meant communicating or interacting in some way with the public who entered the Chinese restaurant, interested in what Vila-Matas was writing, in his profession as a writer, or simply, as he says, in "qué diablos hacía yo perdido en aquel restaurante chino de las afueras de Kassel" (what on earth I was doing lost in that Chinese restaurant on the outskirts of Kassel).[35] This staging playfully interrogates the author's relationship to the (potential) reading public, here cast as *consumers* in the most literal sense as they enter the space as restaurant patrons. Even though *Chorality* still falls within the institutional and curatorial framework of Documenta, it invites a potentially heterogeneous audience not necessarily predisposed to be amenable—and perhaps even inclined to be hostile—to the installation in the Chinese restaurant. It was very possible that this general audience would not see *Chorality* through the lens the curators intended, described in the online exhibition catalogue as an investigation of the "possibilities of privacy in a public space," or "instances of mutual commitment" in the offering of a potential space in which "voices could meet and join together without the outright demand that they should" in order to resuscitate the "subvocalizations" dissolved by "our accelerated way of life."[36] Rather, those visitors to the Dschingis Khan, unaware that the writer sitting in one of the restaurant's red vinyl corner booths was a "great individual," might not acknowledge that greatness or, worse still, might ignore the writer's presence altogether. At the same time, *Chorality* probes the relationship of the author to the literary market, something made immediately apparent in the setup of the so-called retreat space in the Dschingis Khan, defined by "commercial obligations and customers."[37] *Chorality* forces authors to meet a potential reading public where they are rather than waiting for that public to come in search of their products and their personae in a separate realm. The format of *Chorality*, which swapped one writer out for another every few weeks for Documenta(13)'s duration, is even reminiscent of the buffet setup of the Chinese restaurant in which it took place, as customers could return time and again to sample different styles or stay away to avoid them.

Vila-Matas is drawn to Kassel and Documenta as a sort of "home" largely because his concept of "pure" avant-garde art entails a rejection of market-driven cultural production. Kassel is a last bastion of disinterestedness, he believes at first, so different from Spanish art fairs like ARCO, founded in 1982 during the height of the PSOE's investment in culture of all kinds. Vila-Matas has described ARCO as characterized by "superficialidad absoluta, mercadería, ventas" (total superficiality, merchandise, sales).[38] He believes Documenta immune to that hyperinflation of culture experienced in other sectors of the art world. The narrator observes that, in contrast to selling events like ARCO, Documenta preserves "cierto aroma romántico y duchampiano" (a certain romantic and Duchampian aura).[39] In comparison with other cultural events and endeavors, that romance is a relief to him because "en casi todo el resto del mundo lo intelectual había caído en picado y la cultura se había trivializado extraordinariamente" (all over the rest of the world the intellectual had taken a nosedive, and culture had become extraordinarily trivialized).[40] However, the art world of the twenty-first century in which Documenta takes place is neither the one of Marcel Duchamp's avant-garde nor that of the Romantic era, but rather is situated in a moment the art historian José Luis Brea calls "el tercer umbral: la era del *capitalismo cultural*" (the third threshold: the age of *cultural capitalism*).[41] The contemporary moment is defined by two forces acting upon each other simultaneously: culture is drawn toward the market as cultural industries become more powerful and the economy is pulled toward culture as it appropriates the power once held by culture to take part in processes of identity formation.[42] For the artist who defines him- or herself by the charismatic myth, this threshold is an uncomfortable space to inhabit because it casts him or her out of a space of exceptionality. Within that framework, artistic production is made available for public consumption, not just through a mercantile exchange of money for a cultural good, but also through economies of production and distribution that allow access to a cultural product with no change in the object's "ownership." *Chorality* dramatizes some of these characteristics and tendencies inherent in the "age of cultural capitalism."

*Chorality* does not resonate with Vila-Matas because the project consists of putting himself on display, in a "vulgar" place tainted by commerce, where he must wait for readers to seek him out and interact with him. He is scarcely able to overcome his dread as the time to write in the restaurant approaches and, upon his arrival, complains of feeling ridiculous as he contemplates his "verdadera situación" (true situation): "a la espera de que entrara algún cliente, bien despistado en mi ruinoso comercio. ¿Comercio? Sí, de un hombre de letras sentado en su propio cadalso" (waiting for some very absentminded customer to come into my disastrous business. Business? Yes, the business of a man of letters, seated at his own gallows).[43] When men of letters, especially those of the avant-garde variety like Vila-Matas, are forced to pander to the public, it is nothing short of a death sentence. He is especially opposed to promoting himself with the ragged sign that reads "Writer in residence" on the table before him. Sitting in the red booth, surrounded by bustling waiters and the smell of Chinese food, strikes the narrator as a contribution to Documenta unsuited for him. He considers *Chorality* discordant with the city he has understood as "un paraíso para los que amaban las conjeturas intelectuales, los discursos teóricos, la elegancia de algunas especulaciones" (a paradise for those who loved intellectual conjecture, theoretical discussions, and the elegance of certain speculations).[44]

However, the negative reaction that the narrator has to his experience as a "resident writer" in the Dschingis Khan cannot be explained solely by *Chorality*'s allusions to the market. *Chorality* ultimately skews the narrator's preconceptions of Documenta as a legendary place home to "obras de ruptura" (groundbreaking works).[45] Before his arrival, he says, "Kassel era . . . todo un mito de mis años de juventud, un mito no destruido" (Kassel was . . . legendary and has been since the days of my youth; it is an intact legend).[46] The invitation he receives to participate in Documenta is a means of confirming the narrator's longed-for place among the ranks of the contemporary, international avant-garde: "No podía olvidarme de que más de una vez había soñado que los vanguardistas me consideraban uno de los suyos y un día me invitaban a Kassel" (I couldn't forget that more than once I'd dreamed that the avant-garde considered me one of their own and would one day invite me to Kassel).[47] This invitation is a particular honor because he sees it as an international recognition of his avant-garde status. Though he has been called a *vanguardista* in Spain for decades, he considers the international avant-garde label a more prestigious one. The narrator believes himself different—more autonomous, more avant-garde—than many of his Spanish contemporaries, and he accepts the invitation to Kassel, the "home of the avant-garde," looking for the acceptance, fulfillment, and inspiration he claims is elusive in Barcelona or anywhere else in his home country.

However, his participation in *Chorality* only heightens the anxiety he feels about being a Spanish artist at a global exhibition. He wonders if *Chorality* is simply a repository for those second-rate avant-gardists and questions whether or not he can actually consider himself a good-faith member of the international avant-garde after all. He worries that Chus Martínez, the curator of Documenta who sought him out, will regret her decision to invite him, as he explains when he confesses: "Me doy cuenta de que en el fondo tenía miedo de que Chus me dijera que presentía que la habían engañado al decirle que yo era uno de los pocos vanguardistas que había en la amuermada España" (I think that underneath it all, I was afraid Chus would say she had a feeling they'd tricked her when they told her I was one of the few avant-garde people around in boring old Spain).[48] Luis Moreno-Caballud notes that these artists who are considered "avant-garde among their [own] people" want to "lead everyone to the long-awaited 'modernization,'" but at the same time, "their mission links them annoyingly to those 'backward' people—or at least, to an image of backwardness—from whom they want to differentiate themselves at all times."[49] The mention of Vila-Matas's "boring" home country and his de facto association with it speaks directly to this dilemma. Therefore, he justifies his presence in Kassel by differentiating himself from his backward Spanish contemporaries who scorn contemporary art and herald its death. Of course, the perspective that contemporary art has been exhausted is not limited to Spain. Jan Verwoert explains that the disdain with which many speak of contemporary art today is due to the avant-garde brand, the recognizable "codes" with which those works communicate.[50] When artworks can be identified categorically based on these shared codes, it diminishes the mark of the original author or assumes interested motives for adhering to established conventions, leading to their consideration as "derivative, calculating, and flat."[51] The people Vila-Matas knows think of contemporary art as "un verdadero desastre o una tomadura de pelo" (a real disaster or a swindle), but he assumes that he has been invited to participate in Documenta because his is not one of those detested voices: "voces agoreras, muy frecuentes en mi país, que hacían alarde de una supuesta lucidez y proclamaban con fatalismo cada dos por tres que en arte vivíamos un tiempo muerto" (ominous voices very common in my country that displayed their supposed lucidity and frequently proclaimed fatalistically that we were living in a dead time for art).[52] His difference from his contemporaries lies in the vow he has taken to never laugh at the avant-garde and its aspirations to create something original. And yet, in spite of that difference that he believes the invitation to Documenta and his worldview confer on him, he knows his nationality still links him to those people who scorn contemporary art, and he is plagued by doubt. Though he is tempted to give in and reject the invitation, he does leave Barcelona and heads for Kassel, "el centro mismo de la vanguardia contemporánea . . . a tratar de encontrar un hogar en mi camino" (the very center of the contemporary avant-garde . . . to try to find a home along the way).[53]

This idea of Kassel as "home" repeats at many points throughout the novel, and the narrator invests his search for a place of belonging there into a series of related intertextual images from various works of Franz Kafka. These passages dramatize the narrator's fear that he is a prophet without honor in his homeland—which explains his topophilic attraction to Kassel as an alternative "home"—but also a fraud whose "avant-garde card" has been misplaced or, worse, revoked. The first of these references appears after the narrator has accepted the proposal to participate in Documenta(13). As he walks home, the narrator recalls a letter Kafka wrote to his lover Felice Bauer during his stay in the spa city of Marienbad, a place with which he had become enamored during a vacation. In this letter, he declares, "I imagine if I were a Chinese and were about to go home (indeed I am a Chinese and I am going home), I would make sure of returning soon, and at any price."[54] Vila-Matas's narrator imagines himself living out this letter: "Anduve imaginado . . . que protagonizaba la frase kafkiana, es decir, que era chino y regresaba a mi hogar" (I walked along imagining . . . that I was enacting Kafka's phrase; in other words, that I was Chinese and I was going home).[55] Though the actual distance that Kafka would have had to travel from his home to Marienbad was not long, his reference in the letter to a long journey reflects what Mirjam Zadoff calls the "emotionally perceived distance" between a space of recreation—the spa town where he has been relaxing—and the world of his obligations and routine to which he must return.[56] Likewise, the journey that Vila-Matas's narrator will make in the novel from Barcelona to Kassel is, objectively speaking, not a long one, but the metaphorical and emotional distance between the "home of the avant-gardes" and Spain feels vast. The reference to himself as Chinese, which continues throughout the book and is intensified by his work in the Chinese restaurant in Kassel, betrays his fears that he is not an autochthonous member of the "avant-garde" society that makes Kassel its home every five years. As Zadoff observes, Kafka's use of "Chinese" in reference to himself is a "coded metaphor for foreignness" constructed in the letter as a "topos of longing."[57] Vila-Matas's narrator, too, longs for belonging in Kassel where he feels his foreignness, first, as a Spaniard in Germany, but more importantly as a writer among visual artists.

In a novel bursting at the seams with intertextual references, quotations, and glosses from other works of literature, film, and art, it might be easy to see the reference to Kafka as just another one of many. Yet Kafka in particular helps to illuminate the narrator's fears about not finding a space of acceptance as an avant-garde author. On the first night in his hotel room in Kassel, he wonders to himself if "Home-Coming," Kafka's 1923 short story, might not have been written just for him.

He reflects on the following passage from the story:

> I have returned, I have passed under the arch and am looking around. It's my father's old yard. . . . I have arrived. Who is going to receive me? Who is waiting behind the kitchen door? Smoke is rising from the chimney, coffee is being made for supper. Do you feel you belong, do

> you feel at home? I don't know, I feel most uncertain. . . . The longer one hesitates before the door, the more estranged one becomes. What would happen if someone were to open the door now and ask me a question? Would I not myself then behave like one who wants to keep his secret?[58]

Vila-Matas's narrator has arrived at what he has always presumed to be his home in Kassel, the place in which his own eccentricities and avant-garde label would be welcomed, but upon his arrival, the doubt he feels at being able to claim a filial relationship with the place is overwhelming. Is a Spanish avant-garde artist—especially one who rose to prominence in the context of the CT—really avant-garde? What will happen when he crosses the threshold of the Chinese restaurant and steps with both feet into the world of Documenta? Will the difference he feels from his countrymen be enough to allow him to stand out in this place? The project in which he has been asked to participate does not resemble the artistic endeavors that he had imagined when he thought of Documenta, and he, like Kafka's narrator, hesitates before the door, unsure whether or not to throw himself headlong into *Chorality.*

The greatest source of discomfort for the narrator with respect to *Chorality* is the disruption of the typical relationship between reader and author in the charismatic conception of artistic activity. *Chorality* can be defined as "relational art," a term coined by Nicolas Bourriaud in 1998 to describe works that "seek to establish intersubjective encounters (be these literal or potential) in which meaning is elaborated *collectively*, rather than in the privatized space of individual consumption."[59] Claire Bishop observes that relational artworks, often site-specific pieces or events, do not necessarily "transform a space" as much as they "insist upon *use* rather than contemplation."[60] A collective elaboration of meaning is precisely what *Chorality* encourages, but for a writer like Vila-Matas, leaving it up to others to recognize him as an artist is tantamount to a reconfiguration of his artistic identity. Giving the public an opportunity to "connect" with the narrator disrupts the relationship that he has with his readers. The description he offers of that relationship is telling of the power relations that underlie it: "No se escribe para entretener . . . ni se escribe para eso que se llama 'contar historias.' . . . Se escribe para *atar* al lector, para adueñarse de él, para seducirlo, para subyugarlo . . . para conquistarlo." (No one writes to entertain . . . no one writes to "tell stories." . . . One writes to *take the reader captive*, to possess, seduce, subjugate, . . . to win the reader's heart.)[61] This is a relationship based on control and domination, not collaboration. The site-specificity of relational art makes it somewhat unpredictable, "entirely beholden to the contingencies of its environment and audience," and therefore disruptive to the power dynamic based on control of the reader that the narrator is used to exerting.[62] Art critic Nick Thurston has observed that *Chorality* excelled at unsettling established relationships because the visitors to the Chinese restaurant were "potentially implicated in the live process of composition . . . before deciding whether or not [they] wished to be any kind of active reader."[63] The denaturalizing experience cut both ways, and there was a very real possibility for an exchange of ideas, contributing to the "choral" effect of what Thurston calls a "polyglossic ensemble." Even though *Chorality*'s purpose is to contribute to a shift in perspective by placing "los artistas fuera de sus doimicilios cerebrales habituales" (artists outside of their habitual mental comfort zones), for an artist whose identity is grounded in freedom from outside constraints and influences, a loss of power to determine the course of his narrative is unsettling.[64]

There is a parallel between the "uncontrolled" nature of the situation in the Chinese restaurant and the potential audience for Vila-Matas's novels. As Valerie Miles observes in the *New York Times* review of *The Illogic of Kassel* upon its translation to English in 2015, Vila-Matas's work has something of a cult following. Because it is "largely conceptual, and it can be an acquired taste," it requires a reader to "learn the handshake" that will get him or her into the club.[65] Vila-Matas's readers thus share important characteristics with Documenta visitors. The biennial's site-specific nature presupposes visitors who are very educated, literate, and interested in the "codes" of contemporary art and economically privileged enough to travel the world to see it. The audience is curated and cultured, like the ideal readership of a Vila-Matas novel. There is no control over the flow of tourists, restaurant patrons, and art aficionados alike into the Dschingis Khan, and therefore the security of recognition offered by being "in the club" disappears for Vila-Matas.

*Chorality* is depicted in the novel as trying to Vila-Matas's dignity and a test to his artistic mettle. After several hours with no visitors to the Chinese restaurant on his first day, he asks Pim, one of the organizers' assistants, if he can leave. Shocked by this question, Pim responds: "No todo consiste en que te vean" (It's not all about you being seen).[66] Vila-Matas interprets this response as a reproach for not holding up his end of the bargain, for not writing *disinterestedly* enough. If he is indeed the autonomous artist he believes himself to be, having an audience should be the least of his concerns. The relational art format of *Chorality* allows Vila-Matas to understand what he calls a "gran verdad" (great truth): "Necesitamos percibir que somos vistos por alguien, pues lo contrario es insufrible" (We need to feel like we are seen by someone, since the opposite is insufferable).[67] The uncomfortable reality is that when Vila-Matas feels "off the circuit," he is unsure he will be seen. The risk of going unrecognized as an artist is crushing to his ego and damaging to his understanding of himself, so his strategy to withstand the experience is to simply become someone else.

In order to better endure his trial by fire in the Dschingis Khan, the narrator invents two alter egos or personae he can embody while he serves his time. The first of these alter egos is aptly named "Autre," and the narrator describes him as his opposite: he is a "normal" writer who can relate to an "average" public, "un autor nada intelectual . . . lo que podía facilitar la comunicación con los que fueran a verle escribir en directo" (far from intellectual . . . this might make communication easier with people who came to see him write on the spot).[68] To be like Autre, a sort of anti-intellectual, "quedaba pésimo en Kassel" (was abominable in Kassel), but it is an advantage in the wider world, where "ser analfabeto o aparentarlo tenía un éxito enorme" (being illiterate, or appearing to be so, made one immensely successful).[69] The creation of Autre signals, first, the belief that places like Documenta stand apart from the rest of the world. But, it also speaks to the narrator's belief that *Chorality* is unrepresentative of his concept of Documenta as a place of artistic and intellectual "purity." Autre is an author who enjoys collaborating with his readers and feels no shame in putting himself on display for them, so the narrator's game of being Autre involves pretending, acting as if he were "un escritor en busca de la colaboración de sus admiradores" (a writer seeking the collaboration of his fans).[70] By stepping into this role, the narrator hopes to ward off the disgrace he anticipates his time in the Chinese restaurant will bring him.

Being someone else also allows Vila-Matas to free himself from expectations associated with his own consecrated status as a writer. When he continues his shape-shifting game by adopting yet another identity as "Piniowsky," named after a minor character in Joseph Roth's novella "The Bust of the Emperor" who is known and trusted for his simple worldview, he describes the liberating potential of divesting himself of the baggage of his own name: "Llamarme de aquella forma me liberaba de las presiones de mi propio nombre y me permitía, además, meditar con alguna alegría acerca de una posible última vertiente que le quedaría a la vanguardia" (For calling myself by that name liberated me from the pressures of my own, and that allowed me, moreover, to cheerfully ponder a possible final dimension remaining to the avant-garde).[71] As Vila-Matas, he feels compelled to live up to certain expectations his long "avant-garde" career has created, but as Piniowsky, he is freer to experience *Chorality*, to experiment with his own work, and to optimistically experience the work of others that he sees at the exhibition. The narrator creates both of these alter egos, Autre and Piniowsky, as a means of coping with being outside of his mental comfort zone in the Dschingis Khan.

---

Vila-Matas's negative experience of *Chorality* offers insight into his definition of autonomous "avant-garde" work, but it is just one side of the coin.

An examination of the works to which Vila-Matas is drawn when he is freed from the Chinese restaurant reveals how he conceptualizes the "true" avant-garde that has its mythified home at Documenta. He finds a respite in works by Tino Sehgal, Ryan Gander, and Pierre Huyghe that are marked by their anti-discursivity. For the narrator, the works' reluctance to speak indicates their independence from society, politics, or history. They are all site specific, noticeably intangible and nearly impossible to reproduce, which makes them more difficult to commodify as objects. To him, these works comprise the essence of art, but in a sort of mythified way that does not recognize the historically constituted nature of the "pure gaze" that sees "true" art as defined by its form rather than function. In addition to their supposed purity, the works he contrasts with *Chorality* all share another common thread: they encourage a lived sensorial experience for him as a consumer of art. *Chorality* encourages communication and connectedness that could force the narrator to explain his motivations or defend his authorial identity, but the works by Gander, Huyghe, and Sehgal are not nearly so direct. Yet another point of contact between the three works is their ability to reach out and make contact with him in a literal and physical way, prompting him to reconsider modes of connection between artists and their public.

All three of the narrator's favorite works exemplify the branded avant-garde that Schechner describes as having "gotten older, and certainly better in its uses of technology, media and the Internet and in quality of performing. But it is no longer, and has not been for many years, avant-garde in the common understanding of that term."[72] These works are already marketed, already known, already curated, but their familiarity and ability to be recognized as "avant-garde" makes them a source of comfort for the narrator. Even he is forced to admit that these works are not necessarily "new": "Y sólo cabía preguntarse . . . si había algo realmente nuevo entre todo lo visto. Y la respuesta era no." (And it only remained to be asked . . . whether there really was anything new in all that had been seen. The answer was no.)[73] *Chorality* is, in many ways, more innovative than the works by Sehgal, Gander, and Huyghe, but the narrator ultimately is not comfortable with the challenge that the relational work in which he participates presents him.

The narrator interacts most frequently with Tino Sehgal's piece titled *This Variation*, and it comes to hold high symbolic value for him. *This Variation* is not a material art object, but rather, like many of the artist's most recent works, a relational "constructed situation," in which "the viewer is no longer a passive spectator, but is drawn in and becomes a participant."[74] The piece, which has been staged elsewhere after its appearance at Documenta(13), consists of a room in which near total darkness hides from the spectators the "interpreters" who stand against the walls, waiting for the entrance of a visitor into the space.[75] These interpreters then interact variably with the spectators, singing, speaking, producing animalistic noises, engaging in a choreographed dance, and sometimes even touching those who have entered. All of these actions begin with a script of sorts that Sehgal provides them, a list of possibilities for the interaction, but the individual instances are improvised and singular.[76] A visitor could enter the space multiple times and have a different experience each time, as the narrator does in *Kassel no invita la lógica*. Each time, he encounters the work in a new variation, as its title suggests. *This Variation*, like many of Sehgal's works, is what Jessica van den Brand deems an "immaterial commodity," a piece of art for which he receives monetary compensation but which "negates its own status as a thing."[77]

The work's "radical dematerialization" is key to the narrator's sustained interest in it. For Sehgal, this dematerialization begins with the work itself as an ephemeral event, but it is perpetuated in the way his "situations" are collected and documented. As we have seen, the narrator objects to the commodification of his persona and his work as objects to be consumed, as they are when he participates in *Chorality*. Sehgal's work actively challenges this type of commodification, in that he expressly forbids the reproduction of the works in catalogues, and given that his work is sold only through oral transactions, he prohibits the existence of any sort of archival paper trail. The narrator admires Sehgal's desire to fly under the radar, as he notes that no evidence of Sehgal's work appears in the exhibition catalogue: "De aquella obra no quedaría constancia ni tan siquiera en el grueso catálogo de Documenta 13, pues Sehgal había pedido . . . que respetaran su deseo de ser invisible. Duchamp puro, pensé." (There wasn't even a record of that piece in the thick Documenta 13 catalogue, as Sehgal had asked . . . [that they] respect his desire to be invisible. Pure Duchamp, I thought.)[78] References to Duchamp in this text often serve as coded indications of those things the narrator considers "truly" avant-garde.[79] Unlike the narrator's "vulgar" exhibition and obligate promotion of self in the Dschingis Khan, Sehgal is able to remain invisible, even inhuman, which allows him to be elevated as a more "pure" avant-garde artist than the narrator can ever hope to be as he sits in the Chinese restaurant.

*Chorality* and *This Variation* are both relational art works that depend on collective experience, but the narrator's reactions to each are determined by the different subject-position he occupies with respect to each piece. To begin with, the works are housed in very different spaces. Sehgal's work inhabits an institutionally sanctioned space—one of the official exhibition locations in Kassel, while *Chorality* occupies the outskirts of the city and draws the world of art and the world of commerce uncomfortably close together. The nature of the interactions between the parties is also radically different in the two pieces. When Vila-Matas is asked to interconnect directly with the reading public, he must step down from his space of exceptionality into their world, where he can no longer control and dominate them, and invite them to be a part of the process as equals. Tim Edensor observes that Sehgal devises "scenarios where participants learn to share and take part in a temporary collective," even "gradually com[ing] to belong to a community."[80] In *Chorality*, the redistribution of relationships implies an equalizing between the author and the readers that stokes Vila-Matas's anxiety.

*This Variation*'s mode of communication is more suggestive than *Chorality*'s, less explicit and less demystifying. On the narrator's first visit to the space, which is located conveniently across the street from his hotel in the center of Kassel, one of the interpreters reaches out to him, touching his shoulder with intention. Yet, this seemingly insignificant action has a profound impact on him: "El roce, eso sí, no pude sacármelo de la cabeza en todo el día. . . . Salí de allí pensando que había sido todo más que curioso y que, según como se mirara, resultaba terrible comprobar la importancia de que a uno le roce el hombro una desconocida o desconocido." (For the rest of the day, I wouldn't be able to get the feel of that touch out of my head. . . . I walked out of there thinking it had all been more than odd and that, depending on how you looked at it, it was terrible to discover the significance of a stranger brushing against one's shoulder.)[81] This interaction serves as an impulse to think, question, and create, even though it transmitted no "message." His contact with the "true" avant-garde is made while literally fumbling about in the dark, arms outstretched, vulnerable to the experience that may result from an optimistic opening up of oneself to the possibilities. On his second visit to *This Variation*, the narrator tries unsuccessfully to orient himself in the dark room, first by attempting to articulate verbally his geographic location—he tells himself, "Estás en Alemania" (You are in Germany)—and then by trying to touch the room's walls.[82] He never makes contact, and as he flounders in the darkness, he embraces the sense of disorientation: "Me sentí perfecto fuera de este mundo" ([I felt] completely outside of this world).[83] Surrounded by the avant-garde, enveloped by it but unable to see or determine its actual shape or structure, the narrator feels at home. What is more, *This Variation* prompts the narrator to think about the limits of communication and indeed of language itself. His final visit dramatizes this inability to communicate fully when one of the interpreters whispers in his ear the mystifying words "Last bear." At first, the narrator is unsure if he has even heard or understood correctly these words in his nonnative language. He wonders if the interpreter meant something else ("last beer, la última cerveza?") or if the words are perhaps a reference to a film.[84] Though he frantically searches them for meaning, he ultimately determines that it is not worth his attempt to assign logic to the words. That unbinding of meaning from language and experience is, for him, a truly "avant-garde" experience.

Ryan Gander's work, *I Need Some Meaning I Can Memorise (The Invisible Pull)*, also has an impact on the narrator that heightens his optimism about the state of contemporary art. Gander was responsible for three "interventions" at Documenta(13), though the only one mentioned in the text is *The Invisible Pull*.[85] Like Sehgal's work, Gander's does not evade the institutional space of the museum and, in fact, was staged in the Fridericianum, the most iconic museum in Kassel. The exhibition hall in which the piece was located was left entirely empty, devoid of any visible artworks, but filled with a light breeze that the exhibition catalogue describes as "not immediately recognizable as artificial." However, once detected, this breeze is enough to "create a moment of wonder in the viewer while standing in what is considered the 'heart' of Documenta."[86] This is precisely the effect that this radically dematerialized work has on the narrator in the text, a suggestive experience of making physical contact with the avant-garde: "[La brisa] me permitió experimentar por momentos un atisbo de 'instante estético,' algo que recordé que era una de las cosas que había ido a buscar a Kassel: una especie de armonía que no sabía muy bien en qué consistía, pero que me interesaba catar." ([The breeze] allowed me to experience at moments a hint of an "aesthetic instant," something I recalled was one of the things I'd come to Kassel to find: a sort of instant of harmony. I didn't quite know what that might consist of, but I was keen to sample it.)[87] Though the experience with the breeze inspires the narrator with its subtlety, it also returns him to some of the preoccupations with his Spanish identity that have plagued him from the first moments of his trip. The narrator cannot help but compare his positive response to Gander's work with the reaction he expects his Spanish contemporaries would have to it. As Carlos Geli has noted, the novel as a whole appears to be "un velado ataque a los intelectuales españoles, que . . . sonríen condescendientes ante un arte que suelen no entender" (a veiled attack on Spanish intellectuals, who . . . smile condescendingly at art they don't usually understand), but here the critique is less than subtle.[88] When the narrator first realizes that the air current is intentional and part of the exhibition, he exclaims: "¡Alguien firmaba una corriente de aire! Maravilloso. Aunque, eso sí, no puede evitar tener un pensamiento para los detractores del arte contemporáneo: seguro que encontrarían en aquella placa inspiración para burlarse bien a fondo." (Somebody was putting their signature to a draft! Fantastic. Although, naturally, I couldn't avoid thinking of the detractors of contemporary art: no doubt they would find inspiration for all-out mockery in that plaque.)[89] The narrator feels the need to defend his own participation in Documenta as an avant-garde artist by vocally asserting his aesthetic enjoyment of the piece to contrast with the reaction he imagines his contemporaries would have. Gander's work represents the notion that in order to *be* avant-garde, rather than simply *look* avant-garde by adopting now-routinized attitudes and practices, one needs to become "una especie de ágil y muy móvil conjurado del bosque, ligero como la corriente más invisible del Fridericianum" (a sort of agile, very mobile forest conspiracy, as light as the most invisible breeze in the Fridericianum).[90]

The final artist whose work the narrator connects with is Pierre Huyghe, who perhaps best exemplifies the avant-garde identity to which he aspires, especially as that mutable and malleable nature is manifested in his work *Untilled*. Vila-Matas considers this piece "uno de los espacios principales de toda la Documenta" (one of the foremost spaces in the whole of Documenta).[91] As we have seen, the artworks to which the narrator feels the strongest attraction as he flees *Chorality* are those that are difficult to commodify, and *Untilled* is the maximum expression of this tendency. Located not just on the outskirts of Kassel in the Karlsaue Park (the same park in which the Dschingis Khan is located), but on the fringes of the park itself, *Untilled* is effectively a composting site that thrives on processes of construction and deconstruction, on the interactions between the animate—dogs, bees, plants, and other living creatures—and the inanimate—a concrete statue, an uprooted oak tree, and so on. The site-specific nature of this installation, as well as its dependence on living creatures, makes it even harder to replicate and more challenging to trade as a material good than other kinds of artworks.

The location of *Untilled* on the outskirts of the park strikes the narrator as highly symbolic, making the work an emblem of the avant-garde. Huyghe's work avoids the museum, and the narrator praises the artist's "discreta sagacidad" (discreet wisdom) indicated by his understanding that "un arte remoto en los márgenes del sistema y alejado de galerías y museos podía ser realmente innovador" (only art at the margins, distanced from galleries and museums, could be truly innovative).[92] Filipovic emphasizes that exhibitions like Documenta "offer a counterproposal to the regular programming of the museum as well as occasions for artists to trespass institutional walls and defy the neat perimeter to which the traditional institution often strictly adheres when it organizes exhibitions."[93] Alternative spaces and structures allow the curators and artists involved to disavow their connection to the "system" in a way that produces symbolic capital, the same symbolic capital that the narrator in *Kassel* buys into when he visits *Untilled* for the first time. The notion that Huyghe has created in *Untilled* "un homenaje a un hipotético arte de las afueras de las afueras" (a tribute to a hypothetical art of the outskirts of the outskirts) makes it a piece that is richly inspiring for him as a hopeful avant-gardist like the fictionalized Vila-Matas.[94]

*Untilled* contrasts sharply with *Chorality* in its utter indifference to spectator involvement. As Andy Weir notes, *Untilled* relies on "staged indifference to participation," in fact refusing to "prioritize a subject of experience."[95] Rather, its natural processes of decomposition and growth continue with or without the spectator's involvement. Weir describes the work as a place where "'stuff happens' . . . in which [the spectator] is implicated ecologically, while the work is not reduced to a stage for [his or her] experience, activation, or tension."[96] That "stuff" that is happening does not consider the spectator as a subject to be interpellated. Vila-Matas recognizes as much: "Había repetición, reacciones químicas, reproducción, formación y vitalidad, pero la existencia allí de un *sistema* era del todo incierta: los roles no estaban distribuidos, no había organización, ni representación, ni exhibición." (Chemical reactions, repetition, reproduction, formation, and vitality were all present in the work, but the existence of a system was quite uncertain. Nothing was allocated; there was no organization, no representation, no exhibition.)[97] The curators of Documenta(13) refer to works like *Untilled* as "circumstances that are readable by art."[98] This calls attention to the lack of any inherent artistic qualities that compose a work of art, instead privileging the socially constructed conditions of belief that allow one to perceive something like a composting site as avant-garde art. The narrator's encounter with *Untilled* re-inforces the impression he has had in all of his best experiences at Documenta: that the works of art do not need to be radically new or different or even "artistic" to have impact. He asks himself, as he contemplates this "untilled" landscape that Huyghe has created, "qué podía exactamente significar 'terrenos no hollados,' 'persona con ideas rupturistas'" (what exactly "unexplored territory" and "everybody with disruptive ideas" might mean).[99] These ideas, too, have become routinized clichés, he notes, but the experience produced can still be powerful; as long as contemporary art can provoke thought or inspire wonder, it is alive and well, even if the work itself is not radically innovative.[100]

Stirred by the notion that Documenta is an exhibition "que . . . *podía vivirse* [could also be *lived*]," the narrator wishes to place himself squarely inside *Untilled*.[101] He aspires to make contact with it, reach out and touch it even if (or perhaps because) it refuses to reach out for him. Again, this contrasts with his experience of *Chorality*. The intentional visitors (both potential and actual) who attend *Chorality* are presumably anxious to consume culture in the form of the author's laboring self. The best example of this is a rather absurd scene that takes place on one of the narrator's first days at the Dschingis Khan. In one of the episodes that prompts him to create "Autre" in order to withstand these interactions, a German woman enters the restaurant, with the express desire to see him and partake in the cultural spectacle he helps to constitute. To the narrator's horror, the woman enthusiastically makes her way toward him, reaching out to hug him and screaming in English at the top of her lungs: "*Writer, writer, writer!*"[102] In contrast, Huyghe's words about his piece in the Documenta catalogue suggest his attempts to frustrate such consumption: "In the compost of Karlsaue Park, artifacts, inanimate elements, and living organisms . . . plants, animals, humans, bacteria are left without culture."[103] Though it is more tangible than the dematerialized works like *This Variation* or *The Invisible Pull*, this "untilled" place, "aquel lugar sin cultivar [uncultivated place]," gets closer than any other work Vila-Matas sees at Documenta to fleeing the demands of art to be a specific thing.[104] The narration of his night in the park is winding, composed of a string of stream of consciousness associations that ultimately leave him feeling accomplished and one step closer to being accepted as an avant-garde artist: "De algún modo había logrado vivir y soñar en las afueras del arte, como un conspirador secreto en la noche de Kassel" (I had somehow managed to live and dream on the outskirts of the outskirts of art, like a secret conspirator in the Kassel night).[105] He finally feels he has earned a space in the international avant-garde and can proudly claim his affiliation, having transcended his Spanish identity to become a good-faith co-conspirator in its production of meaning.

---

*Kassel no invita la lógica* engages with Spain's role in the global art world by depicting Vila-Matas as a privileged traveler who represents his country on a global scale as he participates in Documenta(13). However, in his journey through the exhibition spaces when he is "off duty" from *Chorality*, he can be described as what Carol Becker refers to as a "cultural nomad," or a person who travels for pleasure in the era of artistic transnationalism.[106] Cultural nomads satisfy a hunger for culture on the biennial circuit while engaging very little with the local communities in which the traveling global exhibition with its itinerate white cube spaces is implanted. Vila-Matas's interactions with the works by Gander, Sehgal, and Huyghe are aesthetic and personal, and the works' anti-discursivity and resistance to conveying a "message" heighten the narrator's ability to see them as "el arte en sí" (art itself) because of their theoretical disconnect from real world concerns. The spaces of the large-scale exhibition bracket works like these and undermine "the impression that [they] might be related to, or the same as, the stuff of everyday life."[107] Cultural nomads have to "answer only to the art world," Becker notes, which is easier than "thinking of oneself as a citizen of one's own neighborhood, where the problems are messier and more immediate."[108] Vila-Matas's narrative emphasizes that there is a romance associated with this disconnection from history, from the social, and from the local, revealed by his consideration of Kassel as a mythified place that exists in his mind only to house the "universal" avant-garde.

The narrator has never considered the local realities of Kassel—the city that exists between the exhibitions and that existed for centuries before it—but his Documenta(13) guide, María Boston, makes sure that he puts Kassel in context. Shortly after his arrival in Kassel, María Boston takes the narrator to visit *The Brain*, a work composed of diverse art objects organized by Documenta curator Carolyn Christov-Bakargiev. The installation has a mission to "resumir las líneas de pensamiento desarrolladas en la Documenta 13" (represen[t] the puzzle posed by the whole huge exhibition).[109] As a sort of "summary" of the entire exhibition, *The Brain* contains a wide variety of objects from all over the world, from early twentieth-century paintings by Giorgio Morandi to objects damaged during the Libyan civil war. Yet, the most salient object for Vila-Matas is related to Germany's not-so-distant past: "el último frasco de perfume que perteneció a Eva Braun" (the last bottle of perfume that had belonged to Eva Braun).[110] He is confused by the combination of objects he sees in *The Brain* and disgusted by the presence of Braun's perfume bottle, so he rejects this tangible reminder of the past and seeks refuge in the intangible impulse, calling to mind Gander's inspiring breeze that he experienced for the first time moments before: "Miré físicamente hacia la brisa invisible, como si la brisa pudiera ser vista. . . . Quise mirar desesperadamente hacia delante." (I looked behind me toward the invisible breeze, as if it might be seen. . . . I suddenly wanted, desperately, to look forward.)[111] Seeing the perfume bottle causes disorientation as the political past encroaches on contemporary artistic expression. He attempts to "purify" his experience by returning his gaze and thoughts to Gander's air current, but it is a fruitless endeavor.

The breakdown of his understanding of Kassel as the atemporal "home of the avant-gardes" begins in this moment with a simple bottle of perfume and a question: "¿Crees que puede haber el más mínimo punto de relación entre vanguardia y perfume ario?" (Do you think there can be any point of connection between the avant-garde and Aryan perfume?)[112] María Boston responds angrily to the narrator's question and expresses her surprise that he agreed to participate in Documenta(13) without researching the exhibition's founding story that is so intertwined with German postwar reconstruction. It is clear that the narrator has considered the exhibition and the art it hosts each year as distinctly transnational. To think of Kassel is not to think of Germany, but rather to associate it with a sort of transnational or postnational art that has no home but the international art world.[113] *The Brain* is the jumping-off point for the narrator to see Documenta as a historically and geographically located place, but in what the narrator interprets as a punishment for his obliviousness, María Boston also leads him to visit two other installations that obligate him to see Kassel's locality. Scottish artist Susan Philipsz's *Study for Strings* and Canadian artists Janet Cardiff and George Bures Miller's *FOREST (For a Thousand Years)*, invisible sound installations in outdoor spaces, are both linked to Kassel's wartime past, and they are meant to make him appreciate that, as María Boston reminds him, "No estás en un país mediterráneo, sino profundamente trágico" (You're not in a Mediterranean country, but a profoundly tragic one).[114]

As he considers the German response to national tragedy and war crimes upon his experience of these installations, the narrator cannot help but compare Germany to his own country, and as he does, he recognizes that his aversion to the political in contemporary art is rooted in Spain's treatment of its own political issues. He muses about the ways the two nations have dealt with their collective guilt, and he observes: "En mi tierra . . . la culpa apenas existía, se dejaba esa cursilada para los ingenuos alemanes. Nadie perdía el tiempo con el remordimiento." (In my home country . . . guilt barely existed; that vulgarity was left to the ingenuous Germans. Nobody in Spain wasted time regretting.)[115] Without naming it directly, he refers to the oft-cited "pact of silence" seen in the early post-Franco years as a way for the country to turn over a new leaf and move forward, wiping the slate clean without holding anyone accountable. His experience in Kassel prompts the narrator to suggest that cultural producers should find a middle ground—creating with enough memory of the past to keep tragedy from happening again, but not so much that the nation remains "fieramente atrancad[o] en el horror del pasado" (firmly stuck in the horror of the past).[116] Vila-Matas never renounces his belief in the cultural producer's autonomy, but he recognizes the importance of seeing the context that offers a home to the international art world's itinerate citizens.

---

At the end of all this, an important question remains. Why has Vila-Matas chosen to novelize and fictionalize his experience at Documenta? Why chronicle the experience in a fictional form rather than in an essay, especially given the very essayistic nature of much of the novel? I posit that a possible answer to this question lies in the creative control that Vila-Matas was asked to relinquish through his participation in *Chorality* and that he can gain by recentering himself as an individual creator in *Kassel no invita la lógica*. First, some speculations about the "model reader" of Vila-Matas's novel lead to the conclusion that it is written in a way that creates an "elite" audience just as Documenta naturally does for the works exhibited there, and which *Chorality* attempted to decenter and even democratize. In this case, Vila-Matas's model reader is someone interested enough in contemporary art to read over two hundred pages filled with catalogue-like descriptions of nearly thirty different works of art. But it is also someone predisposed to appreciate Vila-Matas's now-recognizable style. It is a reader who is intentional, educated, and intelligent, but over whom Vila-Matas, through his masterful grasp of citations and references, is still able to exert his "power" as an individual creator. It is the audience he sets out to seduce and subjugate, not to entertain. Whereas the patrons at Documenta (at least those outside of the context of *Chorality*) are part of that "audience in circulation," the potential readers of Vila-Matas's book are much more diverse. His representation of the experience at Documenta can be read as a means of controlling an audience that may not self-select as easily as the one who shows up for an international art exhibition.

On the other hand, the novel is a way to turn an experience like *Chorality*—one that has not been sufficiently "artistic" for the narrator's liking—into a work of art. That is, Vila-Matas is given an opportunity to scale a large and unsettling experience through a more concrete and controllable "object" that is the novel itself. The narrator exclaims in the text that he desires to remember the experience "con la misma perfección con la que podía recordar . . . una obra de arte" (with the same exactness I remembered a work of art).[117] Through his ekphrastic descriptions in the novel of the things he has seen and experienced at Documenta, he is able to make good on his desire to "convertir el tiempo en espacio" (turn time into space), preserving and even petrifying experiences intended (in many cases) by their creators precisely to resist this kind of chronicling.[118] Both in the construction of the novel and in the presence of his autofictional narrator who reluctantly interacts with his audience and finds hope in the works he deems most "pure," *Kassel no invita la lógica* becomes a performance of avant-garde identity, an attempt to allay his fears with respect to affiliation through an embodiment of those elements that constitute the avant-garde "doxa" in his mind.

Ultimately, we can read *Kassel no invita la lógica* as indicative of Vila-Matas's rather ambivalent position with respect to the avant-garde and charismatic identity in the contemporary era. By rejecting one element of the "doxa"—namely, novelty for novelty's sake—which has been so central to the conception of the avant-garde, he tries to position himself as a progressive believer in "orthopraxis," that is, in the desire to recover an "originary experience" of the avant-garde. In an interview, Vila-Matas suggested that he is drawn to the world of contemporary art because it helps him, in his words, to "salvarme de mis mundos literarios" (save me from my literary worlds).[119] However, despite this affirmation, the contact with the art at Documenta seems to plunge him into a self-reflexive exploration of precisely those literary worlds he ostensibly wants to escape. The novel itself betrays his obsession with his (literary) avant-garde affiliation, which requires not just an embodied experience he can feel but rather an outward sign, discernible by others, that he is avant-garde, either in his cultural products or in his identity as a creator. The novel is a definitive attempt to demonstrate that his "avant-garde card" is still current, even if *Chorality* put his membership in doubt.

# Conclusion

Decades have now passed since Spanish governments, both regional and national, began their strategic investment in culture. Scores of new museums have been built and art fairs like ARCO are now consecrated, but what has been the long-term effect of this investment? Has "culture," heralded as a panacea, delivered in the way it promised for Spanish democracy? The investment in museums and art fairs in particular was meant to appeal to international nomadic cultural tourists, much like the narrator of *Kassel no invita la lógica*, in the post-Transition era. The Guggenheim Museum in Bilbao stands as a particularly salient example of a pilgrimage site for other nomads and a reference point for the success, or lack thereof, of Spanish cultural policy. The museum's collection of American art does not encourage the average foreign tourist to engage with local Basque culture, as Carol Becker relates: "The art traveler's word on Bilbao is: 'See the museum, eat. You can do it in a day, two at the most.'"[1] Comments like these suggest that the museum has not (yet) had the power to transform Bilbao into a cosmopolitan European destination in the way of Barcelona. As María Alvarez Saínz points out, one "trophy building" cannot make up for the dearth of a "critical mass of attractions to take it from a provincial post-industrial town to a global cosmopolitan city."[2] Beatriz Plaza and Silke N. Haarich suggest that the Guggenheim's success when considered in the context of the local economy is partial at best. The fact that nearly one million people—only about 38 percent of them from Spain—visit the museum each year confirms that it "has succeeded as a tourist magnet and an image-making device," but its larger impact on the city is more ambivalent, as "it has failed to restructure the region's uneven development and inequality."[3] Despite projections that the museum would grow the cultural industry in the area, the jobs that have been created since the museum's arrival to Bilbao have been most heavily concentrated in business and real estate.[4] The Guggenheim was also criticized for its exclusion of Spanish and Basque artists. Though the museum did respond to those criticisms with several early twenty-first-century landmark exhibitions of local artists' work, as well as a support program for young local artists founded in 2012, they reflect a more general lack of backing for artists.[5] As Jorge Luis Marzo and Tere Badia assert, especially after 1996 when the Partido Popular came to power, the development of a "política cultural de exteriores" (foreign cultural policy) hurt the development of "una política interna, afectando especialmente a las perspectivas educativas" (a domestic policy, especially affecting educational opportunities).[6] Promoting Spain as a cultural mecca in the wider world and investing in drawing those "nomads" to the country took precedence over helping Spanish artists establish themselves.

After several decades of full incorporation into global markets and participation in the transnational art circuit, it seems safe to say that the initial shine has worn off for Spanish writers and artists alike. It is significant to note that the majority of the novels about the art world studied in this book were published in the post-Transition (that is, after 1992) but before 2008, in a time of relative political stability and economic prosperity, but also when culture was being marketed heavily in new ways and for varied ideological ends. Therefore, these novels can be understood in two complementary ways. They offer their authors the opportunity to navigate the shifting contemporary relationship between art and commerce through their artist characters. As they explore how authors respond to the opportunity to make money, the ways their desires clash with mythologized understandings of their profession, and the inherent contradictions that characterize cultural production today, the authors vacillate between expressions of concern and celebration of the new conditions for making art, sometimes within a single text. The novels also stand as concretized pieces of symbolic capital, which may be one of an author's many cultural "investments" that make known his or her position with respect to the market and the profession. By allowing the readers to access the erstwhile hermetic artists through their books and turning them into relatable characters struggling to find the living and working conditions that will foment their best and therefore most authentic selves, these authors can capitalize on trends and benefit materially from that culture bubble growing larger and larger around them. These novels are ambivalent because the authors work to critique a process in which they are deeply embedded and that is itself contradictory. If autonomy is the normative principle of this labor process, it means that authors' and artists' work is never fully reducible to capitalist demands, even if it undoubtedly responds to and is organized by them.

As the twenty-first century advances and Spain continues to recover from the disastrous 2008 financial crisis, the narratives about culture and its power in the age of the Transition and post-Transition are being revisited and reshaped. In a short time, all of Spain's efforts to integrate culturally and economically into Europe were shattered when, according to Olga Bezhanova, the country moved from being a "model member of the EU" to "the ranks of states that are seen as dispensable to the European project."[7] It remains to be seen whether or not the boom of artist novels will continue into the post-crisis era, but what does appear true is that the crisis has paved the way for authors to engage more openly and even antagonistically with the capitalist systems that exacerbated inequalities and lost public trust after 2008—something the artist novels, as products of the Culture of the Transition, do in more covert ways, if at all. Like Bezhanova, Pablo Valdivia refers to the emergence of "novelas de la crisis" (novels of the crisis) in which characters take on "un proceso de visibilización como sujetos históricos" (a process of being made visible as historical subjects) that allows them to own their "radical historicidad, negada por la construcción pública interesada de los discursos hegemónicos de poder institucional" (radical historicity, which the public interest in hegemonic discourses of institutional power has denied them).[8] Valdivia observes that this has manifested itself in a rise in detective fiction and dystopian fiction that take this period as their backdrop, as well as in novels that deal quite blatantly with the repercussions of the crisis, returning Spanish literature very much to the *local*. There are novels that openly critique the economic crisis, like Rafael Chirbes's *En la orilla* (2013), and those that deal with the precariousness of life in a capitalist society, like Elvira Navarro's *La trabajadora* (2014).

As these novels proliferate as a category, it remains to be seen how the artist novel will fare in this literary environment. It is worth recalling that during the Franco era, namely, the era of social realism, there was a sharp decline in the number of artist novels published in Spain. Even though Valdivia is quick to point out that the "novels of the crisis" are not a rewriting of the social realist novels that arose in the early postwar period in Spain, certain parallels may certainly be drawn. As Spanish literature today moves toward a renewed political engagement that it shunned in the post-Transition, will the artist novel still hold the same appeal in a climate of increased social urgency? Will authors continue to depict the same kind of tension between a potentially beneficial creative economy and the charismatic myth of the artist in an era in which neoliberalism has lost its luster for many? Will culture be used once again as an avenue of resistance rather than complicity? Bezhanova notes that many novelists of the crisis, especially younger ones, insist that the only way to stop the suffering caused by the crisis and the neoliberal burden of personal responsibility is by forming "networks of solidarity."[9] In this context, will the individual artist protagonist, with his or her individualistic and aesthetic preoccupations, continue to be of interest? Perhaps the artist novel will undergo yet another transformation in the post–financial crisis era.

None of this is certain, but it can be said that the artist novel boom explored in this book is a product of a very particular moment in Spain, that window of post-Transition (after 1992) and pre-crisis (before 2008) when the creative economy began to blossom in earnest. The study of the eight novels in this book shows that there is no definitive way that authors respond to the shifts happening around them, and trying to articulate a decisive position that authors have taken with respect to this creative economy would be limiting. What is clear is that each of the positions expressed in the novels—a nostalgic embrace of a utopic, anticapitalist autonomous ideal only possible at the expense of social bonds; a celebration of the opportunities the market offers creatives (especially to women) and subsequent revelation of the ways that those opportunities are unevenly distributed; a certain lamenting of the way academic labor modeled on the artist's flexible, intrinsically motivated style of work leads to fatigue and burnout; or even the use of the novel to scale and control uncomfortable interactions with the market—is in some context marketable and appealing to readers. Whether for its exemplarity as a critique of the market or its complicity with it, each of these positions can prove profitable for the authors. The recognition of the "marketable antimarket gesture," as Sarah Brouillette calls it, raises concerns for the authors and other cultural producers around them about the notion of artistic autonomy, even if belief in a totally autonomous or disinterested pole no longer exists.[10] The artist novel and its long history of dramatizing the tensions inherent in the creation of cultural work thus serves as an ideal vehicle for authors to examine critically both the instrumentalization of their creativity and their own fluctuating responses to it.

# Acknowledgments

I have many people to thank for the existence of this book. Because this project began at the Pennsylvania State University, I must first express my gratitude to everyone there who believed in me and helped shape me, a first-generation college student, into a scholar. Special thanks are due to Matthew J. Marr, whose guidance as an adviser in graduate school and beyond has been truly invaluable. I must also thank Bob Blue for warm and compassionate mentorship and for validating my persistent interest in art and literature. For her contributions to the early stages of this project, I am grateful to Guadalupe Martí-Peña, who helped introduce me to so many wonderful works of literature about art. The insightful questions that Charlotte Houghton asked me about my research lingered long in my mind and helped me transform this book into what it has become.

While this book was born in Pennsylvania, it became what it is today in Milwaukee, Wisconsin. It would not exist were it not for the thoughtful and intelligent advice of the women in my Milwaukee writing group—Kay Wells, Sarah Schaefer, Sarah Carter, Tara Daly, and Jodi Eastberg—who have read every word of this manuscript and reminded me continually of its intellectual merit. They helped me consider a wider audience for this book with the breadth of their interdisciplinary perspectives, making it better in every way. I am most thankful, though, for their scholarly camaraderie and friendship that helped me see this project through.

I am thankful to the anonymous external reviewers whose comments helped me transform the manuscript. An earlier version of some of the research in chapter 1 appears in "Before the Bubble Burst: The Artist and the *Cultura de la Transición* in Julio Llamazares's *El cielo de Madrid*," *Hispanic Studies Review* 2, no. 2 (2017): 302–313. The feedback received on this article helped me reshape the first chapter of the book. I am also immensely grateful to Beth Marino for her astute and penetrating comments on many of these chapters.

I am privileged to have so many friends and colleagues to thank for their support through the years it took this project to mature. Carolyn Lee, Kay Wells, and Sarah Carter have been my most dependable support system in Milwaukee. I am lucky to know such strong and accomplished women. I am always indebted to Charlie Nagle, who, since those days in Madrid many years ago, believed in me long before I believed in myself. He has been helping me see myself as a scholar for more than a decade. I am grateful to Gurkirat Singh Sekhon for his intellectual companionship and shared vulnerability over many a cup of Colectivo coffee. Special thanks are due to John Gilligan for championing my work and for consistently showing up as my Martín Gaite style interlocutor. Our conversations over lunch at Café Lulu always leave me seeing my work and myself more clearly. Matt Reynell also deserves my appreciation for always reminding me of the freedom that lies in letting go of perfectionism. Kallan Picha, Liz Heywood, and David Anderson have always buoyed my spirits through this process from afar. Finally, I would be remiss if I did not thank my community at Urban Om for letting me show up exactly as I am and honoring all of me.

None of this would be possible without the sacrifice of my family, especially my parents, Mike and Pat, and my grandparents, Gus and Audrey. From my youngest days, they instilled in me the value of hard and honorable work and have believed unwaveringly in my success. Their support of a journey they have not always understood has meant the world to me. I am also grateful to my brother, Danny, for his encouragement (especially when it came in the form of *Simpsons* GIFs) and for helping me stay grounded.

The journey to this book has been long and sometimes painful, but ultimately it has been a rewarding one. To Adam, whose capacity for love and support continually amazes me: I could not have finished this book without you.

# Notes

## INTRODUCTION

1. Reig, "Desde dentro de la burbuja."
2. Reig.
3. Reig.
4. Reig.
5. High-profile Spanish authors like Emilia Pardo Bazán (*La quimera*, 1905), Vicente Blasco Ibáñez (*La maja desnuda*, 1906), and Gabriel Miró (*La novela de mi amigo*, 1908) published artist novels at the turn of the twentieth century. Artists also feature prominently in works like Miguel de Unamuno's *Abel Sánchez* (1917) and Pío Baroja's *Camino de perfección* (1902).
6. Some of these studies that enumerate artist novels published in contemporary Spain include a chapter in Francisco Calvo Serraller's book *La senda extraviada del arte* (1992) titled "La pintura narrada: La novela actual en busca del arte perdido" and Mercedes Rodríguez Pequeño's 2009 essay "Referentes artísticos y literarios en la novela española actual." Rodríguez Pequeño in particular focuses in her work on a subset of historical artist novels that has risen parallel to the fictional and contemporary ones discussed here. See Rodríguez Pequeño, "La novela histórica culturalista."
7. Banks, "Autonomy Guaranteed?," 251.
8. Banks, 253.
9. Banks, 252.
10. Banks, 252.
11. Banks, 251.
12. Banks, 254.

13. For more on the different critical responses to cultural industries, see O'Connor, "Cultural and Creative Industries," 27–29; and Banks, "Autonomy Guaranteed?," 255–259.

14. Banks, "Autonomy Guaranteed?," 257.

15. Susen, "Bourdieu and Adorno," 173.

16. O'Connor, "Cultural and Creative Industries," 28. Raymond Williams could also be included in this group of thinkers interested in the "material 'industrial' conditions of cultural production and their historical trajectories" (28).

17. Johnson, "Editor's Introduction," 9.

18. Røyseng, Mangset, and Borgen, "Charismatic Myth," 1.

19. Bourdieu, *Field of Cultural Production*, 29.

20. Bourdieu, 40.

21. Bourdieu, 75.

22. For Bourdieu, the cultural field is always the locus of struggle between two "autonomous" and "heteronomous" poles of hierarchization. The "autonomous pole," represented at its most extreme by the avant-garde, contrasts with the "heteronomous one" that is dominated by large-scale cultural producers whose products are aimed at a bourgeois audience. Some critiques of Bourdieu argue that this vision of the field is too rigidly structured. See Susen, "Bourdieu and Adorno," 40–41.

23. Banks, "Autonomy Guaranteed?," 259.

24. Brouillette, *Literature and the Creative Economy*, 14.

25. Brouillette, 38.

26. Brouillette, 52.

27. Huehls and Smith, "Four Phases of Neoliberalism," 9.

28. Brown, *Undoing the Demos*, 9.

29. Graham and Sánchez, "Politics of 1992," 411. The authors find it important to unpack the meaning of "Europe" and Spain's desire to join symbolically what they already belong to geographically. The market-based explanation of Europe helps to resolve the question they pose: "Which Europe? For there are and have always been many different Europes, often mutually incompatible" (411).

30. Harvey, *Brief History of Neoliberalism*, 2.

31. Huehls and Smith, "Four Phases of Neoliberalism," 11–12.

32. McVeigh, "Embedding Neoliberalism," 92–93.

33. McVeigh, 91.

34. Carlos Prieto del Campo describes the change in the party this way: "The PSOE rapidly developed into an institutionally embedded and well-rewarded career structure for those espousing faintly progressive, liberal-capitalist views," leaving behind its origins as a "historic activist formation with a firm grass-roots commitment to social democracy." See "Spanish Spring?," 55.

35. McVeigh, "Embedding Neoliberalism," 98.

36. Marzo and Badia, "Las políticas culturales," 2.

37. Brouillette, *Literature and the Creative Economy*, 3.

38. For more on MACBA's impact in the community as a tool for urban renewal, see P. Smith, *Contemporary Spanish Culture*, 69.

39. Marzo and Badia, "Las políticas culturales," 4.

40. Vila-Matas, *Kassel*, 64–65. I have used the following translation by Anne McLean and Anna Milsom for this and all following quotations in English: Vila-Matas, *Illogic*, 42–43.

41. Manchado, "Cultural Memory," 92.

42. O'Connor, "Cultural and Creative Industries," 33.

43. Carmona, "La pasión capturada," 147.

44. Stapell, *Remaking Madrid*, 110–121. Madrid's local government, headed at the time by mayor Enrique Tierno Galván, "was attracted to the movida because it represented a plural, democratic movement that embraced a wide spectrum of styles and groups" (106). As it promoted and sponsored the cultural activity associated with the movida, the government could herald the city's "culturally vigorous present," rather than looking to the past (121).

45. Stapell, 109.

46. Stapell, 171–172.

47. Luis Moreno-Caballud has studied this change in groups and cultural collective movements that have emerged in the post–financial crisis context. These groups "tienden a sustraerse a las dinámicas elitistas y mercantilizadoras propias de lo que podríamos llamar 'la CT editorial'" (tend to avoid the elitist and commercializing dynamics characteristic of what we could call "the editorial CT"). See "Cuando cualquiera escribe," 14.

48. Echevarría, "La CT," 33.

49. Martínez, "El concepto CT," 16.

50. H. Rosi Song situates Martínez's work within a recent group of texts that seek to "narrate the behavior, values, and belief systems of the Spanish people during the years of the *Transición*." For Song, Martinez's essay collection "articulates a generational position" by recognizing both the negative effects of the perceived failures of intellectuals and artists of the time to transform Spanish society and the existence of "a specific cohort affected by these shortcomings." See Song, *Lost in Transition*, 6.

51. Moreno-Caballud, "Cuando cualquiera escribe," 13.

52. Martínez, "El concepto CT," 16.

53. Gopegui, "CT," 208.

54. Varsamopoulou, *Poetics of the* Künstlerinroman, xi.

55. Beebe, *Ivory Towers and Sacred Founts*, 8. Beebe bases this concept of the divided self on Carl Jung's theory of creativity. He cites Jung, saying that "the artist is not a person endowed with free will who seeks his own ends, but one who allows art to realize its purposes through him" (10).

56. Calvo Serraller, *La senda extraviada del arte*, 52.

57. Martín Nogales, "Literatura y mercado," 182.

58. Freixas, *Literatura y mujeres*, 49–50.

59. Gómez López-Quiñones, "La península ingrávida," 56.

60. Lozano Mijares, *La novela española posmoderna*, 231.

61. Brouillette, *Literature and the Creative Economy*, 13.

62. Brouillette, 13.

63. Røyseng, Mangset, and Borgen, "Charismatic Myth," 3.

64. In *Rise of the Creative Class* (first published in 2002), Richard Florida explains that he understands the term *creative professional* to be expansive enough to include those who work in "business and finance, law, [and] health care" (8). For Florida, any worker who needs "independent judgment" and "high levels of education or human capital" can be considered a creative worker (8).

65. Brouillette, *Literature and the Creative Economy*, 14.

66. Brooks, *Bobos in Paradise*, 136.

67. Brooks, 138.

68. Showalter, *Faculty Towers*, 4.

## CHAPTER 1 — THE WEIGHT OF FAME

1. Lozano Mijares, *La novela española posmoderna*, 220.

2. Lozano Mijares, 222.

3. Lozano Mijares, 223.

4. Herzberger refers specifically to postwar Spanish novels by the likes of Carmen Martín Gaite and Juan Goytisolo. Herzberger, 66.

5. Herzberger, *Narrating the Past*, 67.

6. Herzberger, 85.

7. Lozano Mijares, *La novela española posmoderna*, 317.

8. París-Huesca, "El espacio de la memoria," 130. Gopegui's work is much more overtly political than either of the novels by Caso and Llamazares discussed here, and she is more critical of the failures of the radical Left in the Transition era. More than twenty years after Franco's death, Gopegui's work urged progressives to recognize that "el capitalismo ha vencido gracias a nosotros, y negarlo sólo implica mentir" (capitalism has triumphed thanks to us, and denying it is just a lie). See Lozano Mijares, *La novela española posmoderna*, 320.

9. Lozano Mijares, *La novela española posmoderna*, 231.

10. Huyssen. *Twilight Memories*, 7–14.

11. Huyssen, 14.

12. R. Smith, *Affect and American Literature*, 1–2.

13. Cited in Huehls and Smith, "Four Phases of Neoliberalism," 9. By "novel of identity," Michaels refers to texts concerned with their protagonists' "place in the culture," rather than in the economy. He observes that "questions about who we are rather than about how much (or little) we own . . . [have] come to play an absolutely central role" in American literature and criticism today. He goes on to argue that "the focus on identity functions not just to distract people from the increase in inequality but to legitimate it" and that these novels often share the concerns of both liberal and conservative institutions. See Michaels, "Neoliberal Novel," 1017, 1027.

14. Worden, "Memoir," 171. Worden points out that despite this ethical public perception of the memoir, many memoirists actually "seize on the memoir to dramatize the inability to even formulate an ethical bond with others" (172).

15. R. Smith, *Affect and American Literature*, 32.

16. R. Smith, 38–39.

17. Calvo Serraller, *La senda extraviada del arte*, 51–52.

18. R. Smith, *Affect and American Literature*, 39–40.

19. R. Smith, 38.

20. Brouillette, *Literature and the Creative Economy*, 50.

21. Brouillette's assertions resemble Pierre Bourdieu's theory of the cultural field as an "economic world reversed." Within the most autonomous sectors of the cultural field, in which producers produce for other producers, the refusal of capital or economic profit is "misrecognized and thereby recognized, hence legitimate, a 'credit' which, under certain conditions, and always in the long run, guarantees 'economic' profits." See Bourdieu, *Field of Cultural Production*, 75. Indeed, Brouillette notes in her introduction that her work's focus is "the afterlife and telling persistence of the art-commerce dialectic that forms the generative heart of Bourdieu's whole scholarly endeavor." Brouillette, *Literature and the Creative Economy*, 17.

22. Brouillette, *Literature and the Creative Economy*, 52.

23. Harrison C. White and Cynthia A. White explain that the growth of the middle class "created a larger internal market for paintings," while the number of "great collector-connoisseurs" declined. White and White, *Canvases and Careers*, 76–90, 78. For more on the crisis of legitimation, see Bätschmann, *Artist in the Modern World*, 58–67.

24. B. Smith, *Death of the Artist as Hero*, 21.

25. Brouillette, *Literature and the Creative Economy*, 53.

26. Brouillette, 14.

27. Brouillette, 49.

28. Rachel Greenwald Smith observes that neoliberal individualism is expansive enough to include relationships, especially familial ones. She notes that investing energy in family and children is "consistent with economic goals" and that "time spent developing emotional attachments within the family is . . . figured as an activity that can be undertaken with an entrepreneurial spirit." See *Affect and American Literature*, 40.

29. Brouillette, *Literature and the Creative Economy*, 53.

30. The "ontological" is the final of four stages in neoliberal development identified by Huehls and Smith. In this phase, neoliberalism is no longer simply a "set of ideological beliefs or deployable rationalities," but rather it "becomes what we are, a mode of existence defined by individual self-responsibility, entrepreneurial action, and the maximization of human capital." See "Four Phases of Neoliberalism," 9.

31. Brouillette, referring to César Graña's 1964 book on bohemia, notes that the desire to be antibourgeois was often expressed through an adherence to communist or socialist politics. *Literature and the Creative Economy*, 52.

32. Goñi, "Angeles Caso."

33. Goñi.

34. Caso, *El mundo*, 151.

35. Caso, 19.

36. Caso, 15–16.

37. Caso, 81.

38. Herzberger, *Narrating the Past*, 79.

39. Caso, *El mundo*, 73.

40. Caso, 95.

41. Caso, 95.

42. Jean-Luc promotes Julio in his gallery as "un hombre del sur, una verdadera fuerza de la naturaleza" (a man from the south, a true force of nature) (Caso, 22), despite the fact that Julio is from Asturias, "la tierra de caseríos encaramados en las montañas . . . que nada tenía que ver con ese Mediterráneo ardiente que le llenaba la boca" (the land of hamlets perched upon the mountains . . . that was nothing like the fiery Mediterranean he couldn't stop talking about) (22). This description reflects what Paul Julian Smith calls fetishization of the Spanish artist outside of Spain in the post-Franco era. It feeds on "stereotypes of a 'typically Spanish nature': the image of instinct, fierceness, and a heated expressivity with classical touches." See P. Smith, *Contemporary Spanish Culture*, 73.

43. Caso, *El mundo*, 161. Bourdieu explains that dealers always serve as a "protective screen between the artist and the market," but at the same time, their pres-

ence links artists to the market and so "provoke[s], by their very existence, cruel unmaskings of the truth of artistic practice." Bourdieu, *Field of Cultural Production*, 79.

44. Caso, *El mundo*, 161.
45. Caso, 213.
46. Beebe, *Ivory Towers and Sacred Founts*, 97.
47. Caso, *El mundo*, 94.
48. Caso, 105.
49. Caso, 94.
50. Brouillette, *Literature and the Creative Economy*, 52.
51. Caso, *El mundo*, 20.
52. Brouillette, *Literature and the Creative Economy*, 52–53.
53. Caso, *El mundo*, 42.
54. Caso, 109.
55. Caso, 180. Colors serve as a loose structuring device in the novel as they help to mark different phases in Julio's life and career. Yellow is the color of his childhood, red the color of his passionate affair with Aurea, and green the color that heralds the beginning of the end—when he knows his relationship with Aurea is troubled and that he will eventually leave her, hence the reference to a disconcerting "greenish" hue that surrounds him.
56. Caso, 181.
57. Caso, 168.
58. In an interview with Alejandro Luque in *El País* a year after the publication of *El mundo visto desde el cielo*, Caso was asked how it felt to have been named a finalist for the Premio Planeta. Her response is an example of the same sort of tactical downplaying that Julio displays throughout the novel: "Nunca me había planteado ganar este premio" (I never set out to win this prize). Caso gains symbolic capital in the short term by "throwing away a gift" that could lead to long-term consecration in more elite sectors of the field. See Caso, "Angeles Caso escritora."
59. Caso, *El mundo*, 47.
60. Caso, 47.
61. Caso, 183.
62. Caso, 134.
63. Caso, 158.
64. Caso, 100.
65. Herzberger, *Narrating the Past*, 69.
66. Herzberger, 67.
67. Caso, *El mundo*, 220.

68. Hagman, *Artist's Mind*, 14.

69. Caso, *El mundo*, 207.

70. R. Smith, *Affect and American Literature*, 40–41.

71. The realization that Julio needs others corresponds to a trend Lee T. Lemon has observed in artist novels published in other parts of Europe after World War II, in which the artist is "primarily an ordinary human being" and that he must learn "slowly and painfully, that the artist cannot be more than human without being at least human." See *Portraits of the Artist*, xiii, xiv.

72. Llamazares has said that the addition of the references to Dante, in the titles and epigraphs of each section, was made late in his process of writing the novel, after he had chosen to name the bar Carlos frequents with his friends "El Limbo." Llamazares explains: "[Ese nombre] me hizo recordar *La Divina Comedia*. . . . Yo añadí esa primera parte que en *La Divina Comedia* de Dante es el primer círculo del infierno. . . . He hecho un homenaje explícito." ([That name] made me think of *The Divine Comedy*. . . . I added that first part that in Dante's *Divine Comedy* is the first circle of hell. . . . The homage was explicit.) Llamazares, "Entrevista," 255.

73. Llamazares, *El cielo*, 227.

74. Llamazares, 254.

75. Llamazares, 162.

76. Llamazares, 42.

77. Llamazares, 46.

78. Llamazares, 80, 251, 20.

79. Llamazares, 20.

80. Llamazares, 77.

81. Llamazares, 78.

82. Stapell, *Remaking Madrid*, 110.

83. Stapell, 79. Teresa M. Vilarós describes the generational clash with respect to politics in *El mono del desencanto*, 39–40.

84. Stapell, *Remaking Madrid*, 105–106.

85. Stapell, 103–104.

86. Llamazares, *El cielo*, 127–129.

87. In the earliest days of the Transition, Tierno Galván had separated himself from the national PSOE party, as he was opposed to its rejection of Marxism and its embrace of neoliberalism. Stapell, *Remaking Madrid*, 31–41. Stapell summarizes the mayor's program as "a combination of often contradictory lines of leftist political and philosophical thought: utopianism, libertarianism, Marxism, elitism, and populism" (41).

88. Stapell, 168.

89. Stapell, 171.

90. Llamazares, *El cielo*, 122.

91. Llamazares, "Entrevista," 255. The title of the novel holds a double meaning, of course. It refers to the "paradise" that Carlos finds in the last section of the novel, his "cielo." But it also refers to Madrid's literal sky overhead. In 1991, Llamazares wrote an article titled, "El cielo de Madrid," for the magazine *Lápiz* in which he praised the sky's beauty and explained that everyone who arrives in Madrid from elsewhere, just as he did, "llegamos a esta ciudad para conquistar el cielo. No el que nos cubre, . . . sino el que debajo de él, a todos nos esperaba o al menos las circunstancias nos llevaron a creerlo" (arrived in this city to conquer the sky. Not the one above us, . . . but rather the paradise below it, the one we all believed was waiting for us, or at least that our circumstances led us to believe in) (25). This pursuit of "paradise" looks different for everyone. It could be "la simple supervivencia o la consecución del bienestar económico" (simple survival or attaining economic well-being), or it could be "el triunfo professional" (professional success), but Madrid, covered by its sky that Llamazares sees as so unique, exists, as he says, to "acoge[r] todos nuestros esfuerzos y todos nuestros deseos" (accommodate all of our efforts and all of our desires) (25). The story of Carlos and his friends in the novel mirrors Llamazares's earlier musings about Madrid's sky. They have different paths and desires, but Madrid is the place where anything is possible.

92. Llamazares, *El cielo*, 79.

93. Llamazares, 79.

94. Llamazares, 155.

95. Moreno-Caballud, *Cultures of Anyone*, 82.

96. Moreno-Caballud, 82.

97. Llamazares, *El cielo*, 119.

98. Llamazares, 129.

99. Carlos's retreat to Miraflores offers a showcase for Llamazares's characteristic treatment of rural scenes. The vast majority of Llamazares's earlier novels linger over detailed representations of rural spaces. The natural world depicted in the "Purgatorio" section is both beautiful and ultimately inhospitable, similar to the landscapes found in Llamazares's *Luna de lobos* or *La lluvia amarilla*. Carlos's years in Miraflores are strikingly similar to the one of Andrés, the protagonist of *La lluvia amarilla*, but Carlos is able to let go and return to Madrid, while Andrés "paga con la muerte en soledad el apego al pasado y a la tierra" (pays with a solitary death his attachment to the past and to the land). See Cárcamo, "Del aforismo a la ficción."

100. Moreno-Caballud, "Cuando cualquiera escribe," 19–20.

101. Llamazares, *El cielo*, 208.

102. Llamazares, 224.
103. Llamazares, 211.
104. Llamazares, "Entrevista," 257.
105. París-Huesca, "El espacio de la memoria," 140.
106. Brooks, *Bobos in Paradise*, 10–11.
107. Brouillette, *Literature and the Creative Economy*, 38.
108. Llamazares, *El cielo*, 243.
109. Llamazares, "Entrevista," 254.
110. R. Smith, *Affect and American Literature*, 42.
111. Banks, "Autonomy Guaranteed?," 259.
112. Banks asserts that the attempt to "balance the impacts and necessity of economic motives while attempting to devise and apply some means of retaining autonomous artistic ambitions" is a much more realistic depiction of how "being an autonomous artist is actually lived." See Banks, 263.

## CHAPTER 2 — THE POSTFEMINIST TURN IN THE ARTIST NOVEL BY WOMEN

1. Huf, *Portrait of the Artist*, 4. Huf's book on the female artist novel is one of the most influential studies on the topic, but her approach has been critiqued as essentializing in the same way that Maurice Beebe's is. Evy Varsamopoulou notes that "rejecting male stereotypes," as Huf does, "is laudable enough," but she observes that Huf presents "merely the reverse of a dominant stereotype." Varsamopoulou, *Poetics of the* Künstlerinroman, xx.
2. There is not a long history of studying women's artist novels—or women's literature in general—in Spain. Laura Freixas admits as much in her 2000 book *Literatura y mujeres*: "Mientras que en otros países (anglosajones especialmente) la investigación académica sobre la literatura escrita por mujeres tiene una importante presencia en la opinión pública, en España raramente traspasa las fronteras de la Universidad" (While in other countries [English-speaking ones in particular] scholarly research about women's literature is important in public opinion, in Spain it rarely leaves the university setting) (39).
3. Nochlin, "Women Artists," 265.
4. Nochlin, 265.
5. Beebe articulates the difference between these two sorts of artistic experience as represented in fiction of the twentieth and twenty-first centuries. For Beebe, the artist of the "Ivory Tower" "exalts art above life and insists that the artist can make use of life only if he stands aloof," whereas the artist of the "Sacred Fount" "equates art with experience and assumes that the true artist is one who lives not

less, but more fully and intensely than others." See *Ivory Towers and Sacred Founts*, 13–17.

6. DuPlessis, *Writing beyond the Ending*, 84.

7. See R. White, *Studio of One's Own*, 31.

8. R. White, 14.

9. See Budgeon, "Contradictions of Successful Femininity," 280–281.

10. Tasker and Negra, "Introduction: Feminist Politics," 1.

11. Tasker and Negra, 4.

12. McRobbie, "Postfeminism and Popular Culture," 32.

13. Agawu-Kakraba, *Postmodernity*, 19.

14. Lidia Falcón, the founder of Spain's Feminist Party, lamented that after nearly ten years of democracy, no real social reform for women had been achieved: "Al fin y al cabo todo es lo mismo. Se trata de despreciar a las mujeres, negándoles el derecho a su propio cuerpo, a la enseñanza liberadora y progresista y a su propia dignidad." (When it comes right down to it, everything is the same. It's still about disparaging women, denying them the rights to their bodies, to a progressive and liberating education, and to their own dignity.) See *El alboroto español*, 90.

15. Bonet, "Radiografía del posfeminismo."

16. Swanson, "Poll." Interestingly, just three years later, another poll conducted by the *Washington Post* and the Kaiser Family Foundation found that 17 percent of women surveyed identified as "strong feminists" and another 43 percent considered themselves "feminists." See Cai and Clement, "Feminism Today."

17. Scharff, *Repudiating Feminism*, 52.

18. Pérez and Pérez, "Postfeminism in Hispanic Literature," 14. Stephanie Harzewski, in her study on "chick lit" and postfeminism, cites the HBO show *Sex and the City* and Helen Fielding's novel *Bridget Jones's Diary* as cultural projects that popularized this kind of character, "a typically single, urban media professional." She observes that often postfeminism operates in these texts "through the 'stylistic alibi' of irony, its hip style masking conservative ideologies." See Harzewski, *Chick Lit and Postfeminism*, 4–9.

19. Tasker and Negra, "Introduction: Feminist Politics," 6–7.

20. Bette J. Kauffman asserts that women artists (in life and literature) are "caught between two cultural constructs: the mythic 'artist as male hero' on the one hand and the stereotypical dabbling lady painter on the other." See Kauffman, "'Woman Artist,'" 95.

21. Tasker and Negra, "Introduction: Feminist Politics," 12. Scharff cites one woman's rejection of feminism, related to her in an interview, as being rooted in her "optimism": "[Her] investment in being an optimist and in attending to the

bright sides of life are pitched against feminism[,] which allegedly highlights lack and the hardships suffered by individuals." See Scharff, *Repudiating Feminism*, 57.

22. See Freixas, "Mujeres artistas," 74.

23. Henseler, *Contemporary Spanish Women's Narrative*, 14.

24. Henseler, 2.

25. In a 2016 interview with Bárbara Ayuso, Spanish author Sara Mesa explained clearly the reason why literary prizes are essential to budding authors, especially women: "Yo empecé así porque no me quedaba otra: empezar con premios. Mandando a premios. Yo no quería ganar premios, quería publicar libros, pero la única manera de conseguirlo era a través de premios." (I started that way because I had no other option: start with prizes. Submitting to prizes. I didn't want to win prizes, I wanted to publish books, but there was no other way to do that except by way of prizes.) Mesa, "Sara Mesa."

26. Henseler, *Contemporary Spanish Women's Narrative*, 10.

27. Henseler, 10.

28. See Freixas, *Literatura y mujeres*, 23.

29. Bermúdez, "Let's Talk about Sex," 231.

30. As Deborah Barker argues in her book on "portraits of the woman artist" in nineteenth- and early twentieth-century American literature, women employed the figure of the artist protagonist to "circumvent their problematic relationship to high culture," to "signal the aesthetic seriousness of their own writing and explore issues of creativity and sexuality that often conflicted squarely with the limitations of feminine decorum." See *Aesthetics and Gender*, 11.

31. McRobbie, "Postfeminism and Popular Culture," 38.

32. McRobbie, 38.

33. Stèphanie Genz uses the term "conflicted actors," which she in turn borrows from Patricia Mann, to describe women's occupation of "multiple agency positions." She insists that these subject positions are sometimes assumed consciously, sometimes deemed "natural," and at other times instilled from a range of sources and linked to individual familial or social backgrounds. *Postfemininities in Popular Culture*, 3.

34. Planeta de Libros España, "Todo fue nada."

35. Tsuchiya, "Gender," 240–241.

36. Scharff, *Repudiating Feminism*, 10.

37. Tsuchiya, "Gender," 241.

38. DuPlessis, *Writing beyond the Ending*, 90–91.

39. Budgeon, "Contradictions of Successful Femininity," 281.

40. Herrero, *Todo fue nada*, 145.

41. Herrero, 200.

42. Herrero, 208.
43. Herrero, 210.
44. Herrero, 210.
45. Herrero, 208.
46. Freixas, "Mujeres artistas," 79.
47. Herrero, *Todo fue nada*, 146.
48. Budgeon, "Contradictions of Successful Femininity," 284.
49. Budgeon, 285.
50. Herrero, *Todo fue nada*, 130.
51. Herrero, 77–78.
52. Herrero, 145.
53. DuPlessis, *Writing beyond the Ending*, 94.
54. Herrero, *Todo fue nada*, 231.
55. Gill, "From Sexual Objectification," 103.
56. Herrero, *Todo fue nada*, 326.
57. Rosenfelt, "Contemporary Women's Fiction," 270.
58. Tsuchiya, "Gender," 242.
59. Bermúdez, "Let's Talk about Sex," 229.
60. Bermúdez, 229.
61. Grandes, "'Un ejercicio de nostalgia.'"
62. Grandes, *Castillos*, 74.
63. Grandes, "'Un ejercicio de nostalgia.'"
64. Grandes, *Castillos*, 26.
65. Grandes, 27.
66. Grandes, 28.
67. Grandes, 32.
68. Grandes, 32.
69. Gill, "From Sexual Objectification," 100.
70. Gill, 103.
71. Grandes, *Castillos*, 40.
72. Agawu-Kakraba, *Postmodernity*, 72.
73. Grandes, "'Un ejercicio de nostalgia.'"
74. Grandes, *Castillos*, 164.
75. Grandes, 43–46.
76. Grandes, 164.
77. Budgeon, "Contradictions of Successful Femininity," 285.
78. Gill, "From Sexual Objectification," 104.
79. Grandes, "'Un ejercicio de nostalgia.'"
80. Grandes.

81. Boden, *Creative Mind*, 271.

82. FIL Guadalajara, "Clara Usón es ganadora."

83. Usón, "Entrevista."

84. Usón stresses that she feels a greater sympathy for Fede /Juan than she does for Marta: "Fede es mejor persona que Marta, sin embargo ella por prudencia no hace nada malo" (Fede is a better person than Marta, though she is too prudent to do anything bad). Usón, "Entrevista."

85. Usón, *Corazón*, 53.

86. Usón, 61.

87. Usón, 61. Barker, in her book about women artist protagonists in early twentieth-century American literature, explains that male authors often represented women painters as copyists in their artist novels to "indicate what was considered inartistic," implying that women's artistic capacities were limited to replication. Many women authors at the time wrote specifically to combat this vision of female creativity by representing "original, professional [women] artists" in their own texts. See Barker, *Aesthetics and Gender*, 28.

88. Moreno-Caballud. *Cultures of Anyone*, 80.

89. Usón, *Corazón*, 101.

90. Usón, 101.

91. Usón, 102 (parentheses in original).

92. Usón, 102.

93. Usón, 102.

94. Usón, 120. Marta invokes Hirst's famous 1991 piece *The Physical Impossibility of Death in the Mind of Someone Living*, calling to mind the shark floating in formaldehyde next to the sign displaying its "pomposo título" (pompous title). When she thinks of it, especially in light of her own failures to establish herself, she exclaims: "Me tiro de los pelos. ¿Por qué no se me ocurrió a mí eso?" (I want to pull out all my hair. Why didn't I think of that?) (101).

95. Freixas, "Mujeres artistas," 77.

96. Usón, *Corazón*, 19–20.

97. Usón, 19.

98. Usón, 365.

99. Usón, 354.

100. Freixas, "Mujeres artistas," 79.

101. Usón, *Corazón*, 357–358.

102. Freixas, "Mujeres artistas," 79.

103. Henseler, *Contemporary Spanish Women's Narrative*, 3–4.

104. Usón, *Corazón*, 359.

105. Usón, "Entrevista."

106. Usón, *Corazón*, 367.

107. Tasker and Negra, "Introduction: Feminist Politics," 10.

108. Usón, *Corazón*, 312.

109. Usón, 320, 312.

110. Scharff speaks of the frequency with which the young women interviewed about their relationship with feminism "expressed their desire for a 'traditional' home." In her description of a young participant named Asena, she explains: "Asena demonstrates gender awareness by using the disclaimer 'I am still very traditional' which does the postfeminist trick of taking feminist ideas into account while distancing herself from them at the same time." *Repudiating Feminism*, 33.

111. McRobbie, "Postfeminism and Popular Culture," 33.

112. Usón, *Corazón*, 312.

113. McRobbie, "Postfeminism and Popular Culture," 37.

114. Usón, *Corazón*, 320.

115. Usón, 324.

116. Freixas, "Mujeres artistas," 79.

117. FIL Guadalajara, "Clara Usón es ganadora."

118. Freixas, *Literatura y mujeres*, 41.

## CHAPTER 3 — THE ART HISTORIAN AS NEOLIBERAL SUBJECT

1. Scott, "It's a Small World," 83.

2. Mark Winegardner draws a parallel between academic fiction and war stories, noting that the outsiders drawn to both genres are morbidly obsessed with what happens inside—the trauma of battle, the life inside that closed world of the university. The insiders read the same fiction to find out if the "author's inventions can compare with their own stories." Cited in Scott, "It's a Small World," 85.

3. Discenna, *Discourses of Denial*, 6.

4. Discenna, 56.

5. Hutcheon, "Historiographic Metafiction," 3.

6. Showalter, *Faculty Towers*, 8.

7. Showalter, 121. Showalter notes that she has not found a campus novel in English that accomplishes this mix of the different realities of professorial time.

8. Ortiz has held a permanent position as a professor of art history and theory at the Real Escuela Superior de Arte Dramático since 1976. See Morgado, "Estudio preliminar," 14–16.

9. Hutcheon, *Poetics of Postmodernism*, 123 (emphasis in original).

10. Ball, "Performativity," 17–19.

11. Scott, "It's a Small World," 83.

12. Showalter, *Faculty Towers*, 4.

13. Ball, "Performativity," 17.

14. Dalton-Brown, "Is There Life Outside," 592.

15. Dalton-Brown, 592.

16. Showalter, *Faculty Towers*, 118.

17. Showalter offers earlier examples such as George Eliot's *Middlemarch* (1872) and Willa Cather's *The Professor's House* (1925) to demonstrate that a lack of meaning and a depletion of energy have been common complaints of the fictional professoriate for some time. See Showalter, *Faculty Towers*, 5–6.

18. La Berge, "Humanist Fix," 295.

19. Dalton-Brown, "Is There Life Outside," 591.

20. Showalter, *Faculty Towers*, 4.

21. La Berge identifies representation of the updated and institutionalized "sexual politics of campus" as an amended thematic concern of the campus novel published in the twenty-first century. She provides several examples, among them Jonathan Franzen's *The Corrections* and Francine Prose's *Blue Angel*, in which male professors are fired or otherwise punished for violating the codes of "political correctness" in the form of sexual harassment or hate speech, leaving them to "plot an unsuccessful return to the real world." The political correctness that constitutes the discursive limits of these texts does not make its way into the Spanish campus novel in the same way it does in the American examples La Berge discusses. See La Berge, "Humanist Fix," 296–297.

22. Dalton-Brown, "Is There Life Outside," 591.

23. Gil-Albarellos, "La novela de campus," 197.

24. Marr, "Stepping Westward," 110.

25. Marr, 110–111.

26. Dalton-Brown, "Is There Life Outside," 592.

27. Hutcheon, *Narcissistic Narrative*, 22.

28. Hutcheon, 29.

29. See Hutcheon, "Historiographic Metafiction," 8.

30. Hutcheon, 11.

31. Hutcheon, *Narcissistic Narrative*, 29.

32. Hutcheon, 20.

33. Hutcheon, 25.

34. Hutcheon, 29.

35. Hutcheon, "Historiographic Metafiction," 11.

36. Hutcheon, 12.

37. Amago, *True Lies*, 18.

38. Amago, 14.

39. Amago, 16.

40. Rosalind Gill takes on what she calls a "culture of silence" in academia surrounding the effects of "audit culture," or the need to render everything "knowable and calculable in terms of quantifiable outputs." The subject of audit culture is one capable of self-management, "in a manner that is a far more effective exercise of power than any imposed above by employers." "Breaking the Silence," 42.

41. Elkins, *Why Are Our Pictures Puzzles?*, 13.

42. Dalton-Brown, "Is There Life Outside," 596.

43. Ball, "Performativity," 19.

44. Heffernan, *Cultivating Picturacy*, 44.

45. Discenna, *Discourses of Denial*, 15. At the end of the introduction to *Discourses of Denial*, Discenna reflects on how the book is "profoundly *interested*" as a work that "will leave some imprint or trace upon the world" but also that it will contribute to his own family's material well-being (15). The same is true for Teodoro in *Las manos de Velázquez*, and it is arguably also true for the vast majority of those of us who write scholarly work.

46. Becerra Mayor, *La Guerra Civil*, 65.

47. Becerra Mayor, 66–67.

48. Hutcheon, *Theory of Parody*, 34.

49. Díaz-Mas, *El sueño*, 50. This quotation is taken directly from the source text, *Lazarillo de Tormes*.

50. In an interview with Ofelia Ferrán, Díaz-Mas admitted she initially did not consider the painting a link between the chapters: "Sí, eso que parece el tema fundamental de la novela [el cuadro] es una idea que me surgió cuando ya la tenía avanzadísima, casi terminándola." (Yes, the thing that seems to be the fundamental theme of the novel [the painting] is an idea that came to me when it was very far along, when I had almost finished it). Díaz-Mas, "La escritura y la historia," 332.

51. Coll-Tellechea, "España a examen," 63.

52. Folkart, "El arte apropiado," 98.

53. Díaz-Mas, *El sueño*, 221.

54. Spires, "*El sueño de Venecia*," 395.

55. Berger, "Fictions of the Pose," 88–89.

56. Hutcheon, "Historiographic Metafiction," 8.

57. Díaz-Mas cleverly reminds the reader of this detail when the art historian expresses confusion over the evidence that tropical insects had attacked the wood to which the canvas had been attached. *El sueño*, 207.

58. Díaz-Mas, 220.

59. H. White, *Tropics of Discourse*, 86.

60. H. White, 86.

61. Díaz-Mas, *El sueño*, 220.

62. Díaz-Mas, 220. Angeles Saura's short 2001 novel *La duda* also positions a Spanish scholar against a foreign one, with dramatic results. The novel tells the story of the art historian César Rinconeda, whose research saves a (fictional) Spanish baroque still life painter, Francisco Meltán, from oblivion. He is challenged by a Nordic Hispanist named Brunhild, who maintains that one of the paintings César has identified as Meltán's is actually that of an Italian woman painter. Incensed by this allegation, César invites Brunhild to his house in order to kill her and thus protect his own research and his scholarly reputation.

63. Bourdieu, *Field of Cultural Production*, 118.

64. Spires, "*El sueño de Venecia*," 395.

65. Discenna clarifies three different terms sometimes used interchangeably in the literature of economic and institutional critique of the "crisis" in American higher education—marketization, academic capitalism, and corporatization. He notes that while *marketization* is often used to refer to the "institution's outreach and self-presentation to students (consumers)" and *corporatization* to refer to "structural changes in university administrative practices," *academic capitalism* is generally used to analyze "differing modes of capital accumulation in the contemporary university." See *Discourses of Denial*, 3–4.

66. The novel's title represents precisely this potency of words to create worlds. It refers to the stories Pablillos's first master, the Italian painter, tells him about life in Venice, which seems to him too fantastic to be real. Pablillos believes that the ultimate sign of his master's love for him is the invention of this fantastical world. Despite the fact that Venice is indeed a real place, Pablillos's limited experience of the world does not allow him to understand it as such. In a similar way, the very real experience of Ana de Alfarache, who lived her life as Gracia de Mendoza, seems too fantastic for the art historian to see as plausible. Through the language used in the essay, another alternative version of this world is created.

67. Dalton-Brown, "Is There Life Outside," 591–592.

68. Hutcheon, *Poetics of Postmodernism*, 105.

69. Ortiz, *Las manos*, 8.

70. Ortiz, 8 (ellipsis in original).

71. Robinson, *Narrating the Past*, 31.

72. Hutcheon, "Historiographic Metafiction," 4.

73. Ortiz, *Las manos*, 152.

74. Ortiz, 152.

75. Ortiz, 152.

76. Ortiz, 7, H. White, 82.

77. H. White, *Tropics of Discourse*, 82 (emphasis in original).

78. Ortiz, *Las manos*, 347.

79. James A. W. Heffernan offers a definition of *ekphrasis* he calls "simple in form but complex in its implications: ekphrasis is the verbal representation of graphic representation." See "Ekphrasis and Representation," 299.

80. Robillard, "In Pursuit of Ekphrasis," 59.

81. Ortiz, *Las manos*, 114.

82. Ortiz, 114–115.

83. Ortiz, 115.

84. Touton, "El Siglo de Oro," 208. According to Touton, Velázquez is one of the most commonly represented early modern figures in Spanish historical novels published after 1996 (198).

85. Ortiz, *Las manos*, 262.

86. Ortiz, 263.

87. Ortiz, 267.

88. Hutcheon, "Historiographic Metafiction," 28.

89. Ortiz, *Las manos*, 152.

90. Ortiz, 13.

91. Ortiz, 17.

92. Ortiz, 132.

93. Ortiz, 9.

94. Ortiz, 9.

95. Ortiz, 55.

96. Discenna, *Discourses of Denial*, 63.

97. Discenna, 65–66.

98. Ball, "Performativity," 19–20.

99. Ortiz, *Las manos*, 270.

100. Ortiz, 9.

101. Ortiz, 295.

102. Ortiz, 56.

103. Discenna uses the phrase "colonization of time" in the context of the academic workplace to describe how the "publish or perish" imperative, driven by "the neoliberal assault on higher education and facilitated by the denial of labor on the part of academics," impinges on professors' daily lives. *Discourses of Denial*, 68.

104. Ortiz, *Las manos*, 339.

105. Given the extensive bibliography included at the end of *Las manos de Velázquez*, the absence of Svetlana Alpers's influential book on Rembrandt is surprising considering that she does speak of Rembrandt's depiction of hands. See Alpers, *Rembrandt's Enterprise*.

106. Spanish painters in the seventeenth century, unlike their Italian counterparts, were constantly forced to defend the intellectual value of their work. This tension was manifested in their attempts to refuse the *alcabala*, the taxes the government expected them to pay on their works. As Javier Portús explains, their rejection of these taxes was rooted in their belief that "lo que daba valor a sus obras no era el material con el que estaban realizadas o el esfuerzo físico que requería su ejecución, sino su trabajo intelectual" (what gave their work value was not the material it was made with or the physical labor that its execution required, but rather their intellectual labor). See *Pintura y pensamiento*, 88.

107. Ortiz, *Las manos*, 340.

108. Ortiz, 72.

109. Ortiz, 74.

110. Portús, *Velázquez*, 301.

111. Ortiz, *Las manos*, 75.

112. Cited in Discenna, *Discourses of Denial*, 69.

113. Discenna, 69–70.

114. Cited in Discenna, 74.

115. Dalton-Brown, "Is There Life Outside," 593.

116. Ortiz, *Las manos*, 35.

117. Ortiz, 182.

118. Ortiz, 22–23.

119. Ortiz, 17.

120. Discenna, *Discourses of Denial*, 70.

121. Ortiz, *Las manos*, 346.

122. Dalton-Brown, "Is There Life Outside," 595.

123. Gill, "Breaking the Silence," 52.

124. Ortiz, *Las manos*, 350.

125. Gill, "Breaking the Silence," 51.

126. Brouillette, *Literature and the Creative Economy*, 34.

127. Brouillette, 2.

128. Bloom, "Fight for Your Alienation," 786.

129. Bloom, 787.

130. Brouillette, *Literature and the Creative Economy*, 45.

## CHAPTER 4 — AFFILIATION ANXIETY

1. Perelman, "My Avant-Garde Card," 889.

2. Perelman, 881.

3. Perelman, 877.

4. Perelman, 877.

5. Vila-Matas, *Kassel*, 9. This English translation and all of the following ones come from McLean and Milsom's 2015 translation of Vila-Matas's novel. Vila-Matas, *Illogic*, 1.

6. Perelman, "My Avant-Garde Card," 880. *The* avant-garde often refers to the historical, early twentieth-century movement; using the indefinite article indicates that one considers avant-gardes to be recurring phenomena (878–880).

7. This connection to reality outside the fiction is typical of Vila-Matas's broader oeuvre. He deftly fuses fiction with his own lived experiences in novels like *París no se acaba nunca* (2003), which depicts his time in Paris as a young man, and *Marienbad eléctrico* (2016), a literary rendering of his verbal-visual collaboration with the French artist Dominique González-Foerster. In all of these texts, it becomes nearly impossible, and arguably unnecessary, to distinguish objective facts from fictionalizations.

8. In addition to the days he spent participating in *Chorality*, Vila-Matas gave a talk at Documenta(13) titled "Archivo de huellas" (Archive of Footprints). The narrator of the novel, Vila-Matas, gives a totally improvised and mystifying talk titled "La conferencia sin nadie" (Lecture to nobody).

9. Documenta(13), "Chorality, on Retreat."

10. Pozuelo Yvancos, *Figuraciones del yo*, 30. Many of Vila-Matas's novels have been considered examples of "autofiction," although this is a term that the author himself has rejected. In his book on "autoficción," Pozuelo Yvancos cites Jacques Lecarme to define the term: "La autoficción es en primer lugar un dispositivo muy simple: se trata de un relato cuyo autor, narrador, y protagonista comparten la misma identidad nominal y cuyo intitulado genérico indica que se trata de una novela" (Autofiction is, in the first place, a very simple device: it is a story whose author, narrator, and protagonist share the same nominal identity and whose title indicates that it is a novel) (17).

11. Pozuelo Yvancos, 30.

12. Geli, "Vila-Matas, en un chino."

13. Vila-Matas has cited as precedents to his novel other fictionalized "exhibition catalogues" in the Spanish tradition, such as Eugenio d'Ors's *Tres horas en el Museo del Prado* and Ramón Gómez de la Serna's "anécdota" in *La sagrada cripta del Pombo* titled "Yo he estado en el Museo de noche" (I was in the museum at night) (1924). See Vidal-Folch, "El autor y su personaje."

14. Perelman elaborates on this distinction this way: "In such a binary landscape, orthodoxy would be a primary enemy [of the avant-garde]; the avant-garde attacks inherited forms and established aesthetic protocols—decorum in general. . . . Thus the avant-garde has to be orthopractic." Yet, is an artist able to determine what that "originary avant-garde experience" actually is, much less know

if he or she is experiencing it? He asks, "How can this be ascertained without recourse to a history, a tradition, historical examples to be mastered?" "My Avant-Garde Card," 891, 892.

15. Schechner, "Conservative Avant-Garde," 901.

16. Vila-Matas *Kassel*, 17; Vila-Matas, *Illogic*, 7.

17. Cited in Geli, "Vila-Matas, en un chino."

18. Lee, *Forgetting the Art World*, 17–19 (emphasis in original).

19. Lee, 17–19.

20. Lee, 4–5.

21. Bürger, *Theory of the Avant-Garde*, 35.

22. Bürger, 35. According to Bürger, the historical avant-garde of the early twentieth century rejected this apartness, instead proposing a "sublation of art," an attempt to "organize a new life praxis from a basis in art" that can be seen as an attack on the institution of art. The historical avant-gardists believed that art and life should not entirely collapse into each other, as the loss of distance would also cause the loss of a capacity to criticize; rather, art would be "transferred to the praxis of life where it would be preserved . . . in a changed form," something that Bürger maintains the early twentieth-century avant-garde failed to do (49–50).

23. Filipovic, van Hal, and Øvstebø, "Biennialogy," 14.

24. Filipovic, van Hal, and Øvstebø, 18.

25. Lee describes the relationship of biennials to their historical context in terms of a "nexus of cultural self-determination and belated nation-building" and the biennial itself as a "cultural paroxysm of the modern nation-state." See *Forgetting the Art World*, 12.

26. Filipovic, van Hal, and Øvstebø, "Biennialogy," 19.

27. Filipovic, van Hal, and Øvstebø, 20.

28. Cited in Filipovic, "Global White Cube," 328.

29. Filipovic, "Global White Cube," 323.

30. Filipovic, van Hal, and Øvstebø, "Biennialogy," 20.

31. Vila-Matas, *Kassel*, 28; Vila-Matas, *Illogic*, 16. Vila-Matas expresses relief in the novel when he suggests that Documenta(13) is much more "pure" in this regard than Documenta(12) (held five years earlier), having "superado con creces la edición anterior" (far surpassed the previous occasion). Vila-Matas, *Kassel*, 28; Vila-Matas, *Illogic*, 16. Documenta(12) had gone off course according to other critics, too. Oliver Marchart observes that the 2007 exhibition "wanted to help the educated petty bourgeoisie regain its right to enjoy art" by de-emphasizing the political and making the focus of the pieces represented more Eurocentric. See Marchart, "Hegemonic Shifts," 471.

32. Velthuis, "Venice Effect," 122.

33. Lee, *Forgetting the Art World*, 10.

34. Schechner, "Conservative Avant-Garde," 901.

35. Vila-Matas, *Kassel*, 21; Vila-Matas, *Illogic*, 10.

36. Documenta(13), "Chorality, on Retreat."

37. Thurston, "dOCUMENTA (13)."

38. Cited in Geli, "Vila-Matas, en un chino."

39. Vila-Matas, *Kassel*, 99; Vila-Matas, *Illogic*, 68.

40. Vila-Matas, *Kassel*, 99; Vila-Matas, *Illogic*, 68.

41. Brea, *El tercer umbral*, 20.

42. Brea, 21.

43. Vila-Matas, *Kassel*, 123–124; Vila-Matas, *Illogic*, 86.

44. Vila-Matas, *Kassel*, 99; Vila-Matas, *Illogic*, 68.

45. Vila-Matas, *Kassel*, 13; Vila-Matas, *Illogic*, 4.

46. Vila-Matas, *Kassel*, 13; Vila-Matas, *Illogic*, 4.

47. Vila-Matas, *Kassel*, 15; Vila-Matas, *Illogic*, 6.

48. Vila-Matas, *Kassel*, 143; Vila-Matas, *Illogic*, 102.

49. Moreno-Caballud, *Cultures of Anyone*, 90. Moreno-Caballud cites Javier Marías as a prime example of this mind-set, someone who "couldn't help but be happy despite himself when someone occasionally told him he 'didn't seem Spanish'" (90). This is because "the image of the country, 'which, when all is said and done, is what counts in times like these, much more than the country itself for all intents and purposes,' often keeps reproducing, out of sheer inertia, the backwardness and folkloric vulgarity that has been expected of it 'for the last couple of centuries,' despite the fact that in the last few years there has been 'an awareness that such an image was not easily compatible with modern—or postmodern—aspirations.'" (90). Vila-Matas echoes these sentiments in the novel when he speaks of "países incultos y deprimidos como el mío" (uncultured, depressed countries like mine). *Kassel*, 273; *Illogic*, 200.

50. Verwoert, "Curious Case of Biennial Art," 185. Verwoert designates three categories or modes in which biennial art attempts to communicate by selling cultural difference. The first is as "thrill," performed by the artist who adopts the role of "joker," making an audience feel "charmed, but not so demanding that they feel excluded" (190). The second is performed by the artist acting as "thief," who opts for "clandestine ways of rarification" by "dealing in secrets," namely, by pointing a spotlight at a hidden "cultural identity centered around an undecipherable trauma" (190). Finally, in the third, the "Boy/Girl Scout" artist sells cultural difference as a "piece of information," there to help the audience learn about the world in which they live (190). These *types* and their reproducibility are linked to the tendency to mock biennial art as a genre.

51. Verwoert, 187.

52. Vila-Matas, *Kassel*, 46; Vila-Matas, *Illogic*, 29.

53. Vila-Matas, *Kassel*, 45; Vila-Matas, *Illogic*, 28.

54. Kafka, *Letters to Felice*, 468.

55. Vila-Matas, *Kassel*, 25; Vila-Matas, *Illogic*, 13.

56. Zadoff, *Next Year in Marienbad*, 77.

57. Zadoff, 78.

58. Kafka, "Home-Coming," 445–46.

59. Bishop, "Antagonism and Relational Aesthetics," 54.

60. Bishop, 54.

61. Vila-Matas, *Kassel*, 44; Vila-Matas, *Illogic*, 27.

62. Bishop, "Antagonism and Relational Aesthetics," 54–55.

63. Thurston, "dOCUMENTA (13)."

64. Vila-Matas, *Kassel*, 17; Vila-Matas, *Illogic*, 7.

65. Miles, "Review."

66. Vila-Matas, *Kassel*, 129; Vila-Matas, *Illogic*, 91.

67. Vila-Matas, *Kassel*, 240; Vila-Matas, *Illogic*, 175.

68. Vila-Matas, *Kassel*, 111; Vila-Matas, *Illogic*, 78.

69. Vila-Matas, *Kassel*, 111; Vila-Matas, *Illogic*, 78.

70. Vila-Matas, *Kassel*, 121; Vila-Matas, *Illogic*, 85.

71. Roth, "Bust of the Emperor," 233. Vila-Matas, *Kassel*, 222; Vila-Matas, *Illogic*, 161.

72. Schechner, "Conservative Avant-Garde," 898.

73. Vila-Matas, *Kassel*, 168; Vila-Matas, *Illogic*, 121.

74. Van den Brand, *Tino Sehgal*, 3.

75. Sehgal prefers the word *interpreter* to *performer* because, rather than following a choreographed script to the letter, the interpreters "develop a particular approach to the event following the loose instructions of the artist." See Edensor, "Light Art," 152.

76. Edensor, 152.

77. Van den Brand, *Tino Sehgal*, 11. Sehgal's work is a situation made "readable" by art. Only within the institutional framework of the museum (or, in this case, the art exhibition) are such works legitimized. As van den Brand notes, Sehgal "does not aim to evade the market or museum," but rather attempts to redefine his relationship with it (9).

78. Vila-Matas, *Kassel*, 55; Vila-Matas, *Illogic*, 35.

79. Bürger opines that Duchamp's ready-mades "negate the category of individual production," which sends the message that "all claims to individual creativity are to be mocked." *Theory of the Avant-Garde*, 51. For Bürger, the ultimate provoca-

tion in Duchamp's work is its decentering of the creator, the "very principle of art in bourgeois society," in an attempt to create a new life praxis that is based in art. However, once that piece is "accepted as an object that deserves a place in a museum, the provocation no longer provokes" (52). His refusal to appear in the exhibition catalogue does not necessarily decenter Sehgal as the creator of the work, but rather solidifies the "brand" he is creating for himself within the institution.

80. Edensor, "Light Art," 152.

81. Vila-Matas, *Kassel*, 56; Vila-Matas, *Illogic*, 36.

82. Vila-Matas, *Kassel*, 108; Vila-Matas, *Illogic*, 75.

83. Vila-Matas, *Kassel*, 108; Vila-Matas, *Illogic*, 75.

84. Vila-Matas, *Kassel*, 279; Vila-Matas, *Illogic*, 204.

85. One of Gander's other projects at Documenta, titled *I Had a Message from the Curator*, relates very closely to *Chorality* in a variety of ways. It was also staged in a public space, this time a café, where an actor sat reading a book about improvisation. If approached by a visitor, the actor was instructed to identify himself as a playwright writing a script about an actor who has died and been resurrected and will play himself, looking back on his life with the privilege of hindsight. See Christov-Bakargiev, "Ryan Gander," 66.

86. Christov-Bakargiev, "Ryan Gander," 66.

87. Vila-Matas, *Kassel*, 65; Vila-Matas, *Illogic*, 43.

88. Geli, "Vila-Matas, en un chino."

89. Vila-Matas, *Kassel*, 65; Vila-Matas, *Illogic*, 43.

90. Vila-Matas, *Kassel*, 223; Vila-Matas, *Illogic*, 161.

91. Vila-Matas, *Kassel*, 138; Vila-Matas, *Illogic*, 98.

92. Vila-Matas, *Kassel*, 146; Vila-Matas, *Illogic*, 104.

93. Filipovic, "Global White Cube," 327.

94. Vila-Matas, *Kassel*, 146; Vila-Matas, *Illogic*, 104.

95. Weir, "Myrmecochory Occurs," 29.

96. Weir, 33. Weir claims that *Untilled* actively challenges the "regime" of participatory art in order to "question [its] political claims and philosophical limitations," which it does by "deprioritizing the sensible as the primary category of engagement without this deprioritization itself being recuperated as the central focal point" (38).

97. Vila-Matas, *Kassel*, 140; Vila-Matas, *Illogic*, 100.

98. Weir, "Myrmecochory Occurs," 39.

99. Vila-Matas, *Kassel*, 158; Vila-Matas, *Illogic*, 113.

100. Distancing the artist and author from the cult of novelty, or novelty for the sake of novelty, is a recurring theme throughout the novel. For example, in an essay the narrator reads by Documenta curator Chus Martínez, she exclaims: "El

arte no es creativo ni innovador. Eso dejémoslo para el mundo del zapato, los coches, de la aeronáutica, es el vocabulario industrial." (Art is neither creative nor innovative. That we leave to the world of shoes, cars, aeronautics. It's an industrial vocabulary.) Vila-Matas, *Kassel*, 56; Vila-Matas, *Illogic*, 36.

101. Vila-Matas, *Kassel*, 237; Vila-Matas, *Illogic*, 173.

102. Vila-Matas, *Kassel*, 117 (emphasis in original).

103. Christov-Bakargiev, "Pierre Huyghe," 262.

104. Vila-Matas, *Kassel*, 246; Vila-Matas, *Illogic*, 179.

105. Vila-Matas, *Kassel*, 252; Vila-Matas, *Illogic*, 183.

106. Becker, "Romance of Nomadism," 27.

107. Filipovic, "Global White Cube," 323.

108. Becker, "Romance of Nomadism," 28.

109. Vila-Matas, *Kassel*, 69; Vila-Matas, *Illogic*, 47.

110. Vila-Matas, *Kassel*, 69; Vila-Matas, *Illogic*, 46.

111. Vila-Matas, *Kassel*, 71; Vila-Matas, *Illogic*, 47–48.

112. Vila-Matas, *Kassel*, 77; Vila-Matas, *Illogic*, 52.

113. Becker, "Romance of Nomadism," 22. Becker asks, "What happens when artists from all over the world . . . position themselves as transnational or postnational but then are selected by curators to represent their point of origin in such contexts as international biennials, to the exclusion of those who have never left?" (22).

114. Vila-Matas, *Kassel*, 85; Vila-Matas, *Illogic*, 58. *Study for Strings* was staged on a platform of Kassel's train station, from which thousands of German Jews were sent out of the city during World War II, and featured isolated cello and viola parts from Czech musician Pavel Hass's orchestral piece composed while he was in the concentration camp of Theresienstadt. *FOREST (For a Thousand Years)* was staged in a wooded area of Kassel, where speakers mounted in trees played the sounds of World War II air raids followed by defining silence.

115. Vila-Matas, *Kassel*, 73; Vila-Matas, *Illogic*, 49.

116. Vila-Matas, *Kassel*, 74; Vila-Matas, *Illogic*, 49.

117. Vila-Matas, *Kassel*, 260; Vila-Matas, *Illogic*, 189.

118. Vila-Matas, *Kassel*, 256; Vila-Matas, *Illogic*, 186.

119. Cited in Geli, "Vila-Matas, en un chino."

## CONCLUSION

1. Becker, "Romance of Nomadism," 25.
2. Alvarez Saínz, "(Re)building an Image," 116.
3. Plaza and Haarich. "Guggenheim Museum Bilbao," 1457.
4. Plaza and Haarich, 1459.

5. Plaza and Haarich, 1466.

6. Marzo and Badia, "Las políticas culturales," 14.

7. Bezhanova, *Literature of Crisis*, xiii. When Spain was cast as one of the derisively named PIGS countries—Portugal, Italy, Greece, and Spain—after the crisis, for being unable to bail out its failing banks, it signaled what Arturo Guillén calls "creeping contradictions from the beginning of the European integration process." See Guillén, "Europe," 59.

8. Valdivia, "Narrando la crisis financiera," 24.

9. Bezhanova, *Literature of Crisis*, xviii.

10. Brouillette, *Literature and the Creative Economy*, 208.

# Bibliography

Agawu-Kakraba, Yaw. *Postmodernity in Spanish Fiction and Culture*. Cardiff: University of Wales Press, 2010.

Alpers, Svetlana. *Rembrandt's Enterprise: The Studio and the Market*. Chicago: University of Chicago Press, 1988.

Alvarez Saínz, María. "(Re)building an Image for a City: Is a Landmark Enough? Bilbao and the Guggenheim Museum, 10 Years Together." *Journal of Applied Social Psychology* 42, no. 1 (2012): 100–132.

Amago, Samuel. *True Lies: Narrative Self-Consciousness in the Contemporary Spanish Novel*. Lewisburg, Pa.: Bucknell University Press, 2006.

Ball, Stephen J. "Performativity, Commodification and Commitment: An I-Spy Guide to the Neoliberal University." *British Journal of Education Studies* 60, no. 1 (2012): 17–28.

Banks, Mark. "Autonomy Guaranteed? Cultural Work and the 'Art-Commerce Relation.'" *Journal for Cultural Research* 14, no. 3 (2010): 251–269.

Barker, Deborah. *Aesthetics and Gender in American Literature: Portraits of the Woman Artist*. Lewisburg, Pa.: Bucknell University Press, 2000.

Bätschmann, Oskar. *The Artist in the Modern World: The Conflict between Market and Self-Expression*. Translated by Eileen Martin. Cologne: DuMont, 1997.

Becerra Mayor, David. *La Guerra Civil como moda literaria*. Madrid: Clave Intelectual, 2015.

Becker, Carol. "The Romance of Nomadism: A Series of Reflections." *Art Journal* 58, no. 2 (1999): 22–29.

Beebe, Maurice. *Ivory Towers and Sacred Founts: The Artist as Hero in Fiction from Goethe to Joyce*. New York: New York University Press, 1964.

Berger, Harry, Jr. "Fictions of the Pose: Facing the Gaze of Early Modern Portraiture." *Representations*, no. 46 (1994): 87–120.

Bermúdez, Silvia. "Let's Talk about Sex? From Almudena Grandes to Lucía Etxebarria, the Volatile Values of the Spanish Literary Market." In *Women's Narrative and Film in Twentieth-Century Spain: A World of Difference(s)*, edited by Ofelia Ferrán and Kathleen M. Glenn, 223–237. New York: Routledge, 2002.

Bezhanova, Olga. *Literature of Crisis: Spain's Engagement with Liquid Capital*. Lewisburg, Pa.: Bucknell University Press, 2017.

Bishop, Claire. "Antagonism and Relational Aesthetics." *October*, no. 110 (2004): 51–79.

Bloom, Peter. "Fight for Your Alienation: The Fantasy of Employability and the Ironic Struggle for Self-Exploitation." *Ephemera: Theory and Politics in Organization* 13, no. 4 (2013): 785–807.

Boden, Margaret. *The Creative Mind: Myths and Mechanisms*. 2nd ed. London: Routledge, 2004.

Bonet, Joana. "Radiografía del posfeminismo." *El País Semanal*, June 1, 2013. https://elpais.com/elpais/2013/05/30/eps/1369925141_966414.html.

Bourdieu, Pierre. *The Field of Cultural Production: Essays on Art and Literature*. Edited by Randal Johnson. New York: Columbia University Press, 1993.

Brea, José Luis. *El tercer umbral: Estatuto de las prácticas artísticas en la era del capitalismo cultural*. Murcia: Cendeac, 2004.

Brooks, David. *Bobos in Paradise: The New Upper Class and How They Got There*. New York: Simon and Schuster, 2000.

Brouillette, Sarah. *Literature and the Creative Economy*. Stanford, Calif.: Stanford University Press, 2014.

Brown, Wendy. *Undoing the Demos: Neoliberalism's Stealth Revolution*. New York: Zone Books, 2015.

Budgeon, Shelley. "The Contradictions of Successful Femininity: Third-Wave Feminism, Postfeminism and 'New' Femininities." In *New Femininities: Postfeminism, Neoliberalism and Subjectivity*, edited by Rosalind Gill and Christina Scharff, 279–292. Basingstoke: Palgrave Macmillan, 2011.

Bürger, Peter. *Theory of the Avant-Garde*. Edited by Jochen Schulte-Sasse. Translated by Michael Shaw. Minneapolis: University of Minnesota Press, 1984.

Cai, Weiyi, and Scott Clement. "What Americans Think about Feminism Today." *Washington Post*, January 27, 2016. https://www.washingtonpost.com/graphics/national/feminism-project/poll/.

Calvo Serraller, Francisco. *La senda extraviada del arte: Ensayos sobre lo excéntrico en las vanguardias*. Madrid: Mondadori, 1992.

Cárcamo, Silvia. "Del aforismo a la ficción: La memoria en Julio Llamazares." *Espéculo*, no. 33 (2006). http://www.ucm.es/info/especulo/numero33/afollama.html.

Carmona, Pablo. "La pasión capturada: Del carnaval underground a 'La Movida madrileña' marca registrada." *Desacuerdos* 5 (2009): 147–158.

Caso, Angeles. "Angeles Caso escritora: 'No admito más presión que mi propia exigencia.'" Entrevista por Alejandro Luque. *El País*, August 8, 1998.

———. *El mundo visto desde el cielo*. Barcelona: Planeta, 1997.

Christov-Bakargiev, Carolyn, curator. *Documenta(13)*. Vol. 1. Exhibition catalogue. Ostfildern: Hatje Cantz, 2012.

———. "Pierre Huyghe." In *Documenta(13)*, 1:262–263. Exhibition catalogue. Ostfildern: Hatje Cantz, 2012.

———. "Ryan Gander." In *Documenta(13)*, 1:65–66. Exhibition catalogue. Ostfildern: Hatje Cantz, 2012.

Coll-Tellechea, Reyes. "España a examen: *El sueño de Venecia* y la memoria histórica en un caleidoscopio picaresco." *Confluencia* 13, no. 2 (1998): 61–68.

Dalton-Brown, Sally. "Is There Life Outside of (the Genre of) the Campus Novel? The Academic Struggles to Find a Place in Today's World." *Journal of Popular Culture* 41, no. 4 (2008): 591–600.

Díaz-Mas, Paloma. *El sueño de Venecia*. Barcelona: Anagrama, 1992.

———. "La escritura y la historia: Entrevista con Paloma Díaz-Mas." Por Ofelia Ferrán. *Anales de la literatura española contemporánea* 22, no. 1–2 (1997): 327–345.

Discenna, Thomas. *Discourses of Denial: The Rhetoric of American Academic Labor*. New York: Routledge, 2018.

Documenta(13). "Chorality, on Retreat: A Writer's Residency." Updated September 15, 2012. Accessed July 25, 2016. http://d13.documenta.de/#/programs/the-kassel-programs/chorality-on-retreat-a-writers-residency/.

DuPlessis, Rachel Blau. *Writing beyond the Ending: Narrative Strategies of Twentieth-Century Women Writers*. Bloomington: Indiana University Press, 1985.

Echevarría, Ignacio. "La CT: Un cambio de paradigma." In *CT o la Cultura de la Transición*, edited by Guillem Martínez, 25–36. Barcelona: Debolsillo, 2012.

Edensor, Tim. "Light Art, Perception, and Sensation." *Senses and Society* 10, no. 2 (2015): 138–157.

Elkins, James. *Why Are Our Pictures Puzzles? On the Modern Origins of Pictorial Complexity*. New York: Routledge, 1999.

Falcón, Lidia. *El alboroto español*. Barcelona: Fontanella, 1984.

FIL Guadalajara (Feria Internacional del Libro de Guadalajara). "Clara Usón es ganadora del Premio Sor Juana 2018." Updated October 29, 2018. Accessed December 5, 2018. https://www.fil.com.mx/prensa/boletin.asp?ids=1&id=2360.

Filipovic, Elena. "The Global White Cube." In *The Biennial Reader: An Anthology on Large-Scale Perennial Exhibitions of Contemporary Art*, edited by Elena

Filipovic, Marieke van Hal, and Solveig Øvstebø, 323–345. Bergen: Bergen Kunsthall, 2010.

Filipovic, Elena, Marieke van Hal, and Solveig Øvstebø. "Biennialogy." In *The Biennial Reader: An Anthology on Large-Scale Perennial Exhibitions of Contemporary Art*, edited by Elena Filipovic, Marieke van Hal, and Solveig Øvstebø, 12–27. Bergen: Bergen Kunsthall, 2010.

Florida, Richard. *The Rise of the Creative Class*. Rev. ed. New York: Basic Books, 2012.

Folkart, Jessica. "El arte apropiado: La reproducción de la identidad en *El sueño de Venecia* de Paloma Díaz-Mas." *Symposium* 58, no. 2 (2004): 93–107.

Freixas, Laura. *Literatura y mujeres*. Barcelona: Destino, 2000.

———. "Mujeres artistas: Los dados trucados." *Claves de razón práctica* 203 (2010): 74–79.

Geli, Carlos. "Vila-Matas, en un chino." *El País*, February 22, 2014. https://elpais.com/ccaa/2014/02/21/catalunya/1393011155_068892.html.

Genz, Stèphanie. *Postfemininities in Popular Culture*. Basingstoke: Palgrave Macmillan, 2009.

Gil-Albarellos, Susana. "La novela de campus en España 2000–2015." *Cuadernos de investigación filológica* 43 (2017): 191–207.

Gill, Rosalind. "Breaking the Silence: The Hidden Injuries of Neoliberal Academia." *Feministische Studien* 34, no. 1 (2016): 39–55.

———. "From Sexual Objectification to Sexual Subjectification: The Resexualization of Women's Bodies in the Media." *Feminist Media Studies* 3, no. 1 (2003): 100–106.

Gómez López-Quiñones, Antonio. "La península ingrávida: Sobre la novela española contemporánea." *Anales de la literatura española contemporánea* 32, no. 1 (2007): 37–93.

Goñi, Javier. "Angeles Caso se pone en la piel de hombre en su tercera novela." *El País*, April 4, 1997. https://elpais.com/diario/1997/04/04/cultura/860104808_850215.html.

Gopegui, Belén. "CT: ¿Para olvidar qué olvido?" In *CT o la Cultura de la Transición*, edited by Guillem Martínez, 207–216. Barcelona: Debolsillo, 2012.

Graham, Helen, and Antonio Sánchez. "The Politics of 1992." In *Spanish Cultural Studies: An Introduction*, edited by Helen Graham and Jo Labanyi, 406–418. Oxford: Oxford University Press, 1995.

Grandes, Almudena. *Castillos de cartón*. Barcelona: Tusquets, 2004.

———. "'Esta novela es un ejercicio de nostalgia': Entrevista a Almudena Grandes." Por Rosa Mora. *El País*, February 4, 2004. https://elpais.com/diario/2004/02/04/cultura/1075849201_850215.html.

Guillén, Arturo. "Europe: The Crisis within a Crisis." *International Journal of Political Economy* 41, no. 3 (2012): 41–68.

Hagman, George. *The Artist's Mind: A Psychoanalytic Perspective on Creativity, Modern Art, and Modern Artists*. London: Routledge, 2010.

Harvey, David. *A Brief History of Neoliberalism*. Oxford: Oxford University Press, 2005.

Harzewski, Stephanie. *Chick Lit and Postfeminism*. Charlottesville: University of Virginia Press, 2011.

Heffernan, James A. W. *Cultivating Picturacy: Visual Art and Verbal Interventions*. Waco, Tex.: Baylor University Press, 2006.

———. "Ekphrasis and Representation." *New Literary History* 22, no. 2 (1991): 297–316.

Henseler, Christine. *Contemporary Spanish Women's Narrative and the Publishing Industry*. Urbana: University of Illinois Press, 2003.

Herrero, Nieves. *Todo fue nada*. Madrid: Martínez Roca, 2005.

Herzberger, David K. *Narrating the Past: Fiction and Historiography in Postwar Spain*. Durham, N.C.: Duke University Press, 1995.

Huehls, Mitchum, and Rachel Greenwald Smith. "Four Phases of Neoliberalism and Literature: An Introduction." In *Neoliberalism and Contemporary Literary Culture*, edited by Mitchum Huehls and Rachel Greenwald Smith, 1–18. Baltimore: Johns Hopkins University Press, 2017.

Huf, Linda. *A Portrait of the Artist as a Young Woman: The Writer as Heroine in American Literature*. New York: Frederick Unger, 1983.

Hutcheon, Linda. "Historiographic Metafiction: Parody and the Intertextuality of History." In *Intertextuality in Contemporary American Fiction*, edited by Patrick O'Donnell and Robert Con Davis, 3–32. Baltimore: Johns Hopkins University Press, 1989.

———. *Narcissistic Narrative: The Metafictional Paradox*. Waterloo, Ontario: Wilfred Laurier University Press, 1980.

———. *A Poetics of Postmodernism: History, Theory, Fiction*. New York: Routledge, 1988.

———. *A Theory of Parody: The Teachings of Twentieth-Century Art Forms*. Urbana: University of Illinois Press, 1985.

Huyssen, Andreas. *Twilight Memories: Marking Time in a Culture of Amnesia*. New York: Routledge, 1995.

Johnson, Randal. "Editor's Introduction: Pierre Bourdieu on Art, Literature and Culture." In *The Field of Cultural Production*, by Pierre Bourdieu, 1–25. New York: Columbia University Press, 1993.

Kafka, Franz. "Home-Coming." Translated by Tania Stern and James Stern. In *The Complete Stories of Franz Kafka*, edited by Nahum N. Glatzer, 445–446. New York: Schocken Books, 1988.

———. *Letters to Felice*. Edited by Erich Heller and Jürgen Born. Translated by James Stern and Elisabeth Duckworth. London: Secker and Warburg, 1973.

Kauffman, Bette J. "'Woman Artist': Between Myth and Stereotype." In *On the Margins of Art Worlds*, edited by Larry Gross, 95–120. Boulder, Colo.: Westview, 1995.

La Berge, Leigh Claire. "The Humanist Fix: How the Campus Novel Sustains the Neoliberal University." In *Neoliberalism and Contemporary Literary Culture*, edited by Mitchum Huehls and Rachel Greenwald Smith, 291–315. Baltimore: Johns Hopkins University Press, 2017.

Lee, Pamela M. *Forgetting the Art World*. Cambridge, Mass.: MIT Press, 2012.

Lemon, Lee T. *Portraits of the Artist in Contemporary Fiction*. Lincoln: University of Nebraska Press, 1985.

Llamazares, Julio. "El cielo de Madrid." *Lápiz*, no. 79 (1991): 24–25.

———. *El cielo de Madrid*. Madrid: Punto de Lectura, 2006.

———. "Entrevista a Julio Llamazares a propósito de *El cielo de Madrid*." Por Salwa M. Mahmoud. *Siglo XXI: Literatura y cultura españolas*, no. 3 (2005): 251–267.

Lozano Mijares, María del Pilar. *La novela española posmoderna*. Madrid: Arco, 2007.

Manchado, Trinidad. "Cultural Memory, Commerce and the Arts: The Valencian Institute of Modern Art (IVAM)." In *Contemporary Spanish Cultural Studies*, edited by Barry Jordan and Rikki Morgan-Tamosunas. London: Arnold, 2000.

Marchart, Oliver. "Hegemonic Shifts and the Politics of Biennialization: The Case of Documenta." In *The Biennial Reader: An Anthology on Large-Scale Perennial Exhibitions of Contemporary Art*, edited by Elena Filipovic, Marieke van Hal, and Solveig Øvstebø, 467–483. Bergen: Bergen Kunsthall, 2010.

Marr, Matthew J. "Stepping Westward from Spain: Literary and Cultural Reversal in Recent Transatlantic Academic Novels by Josefina Aldecoa, Javier Cercas, and Antonio Muñoz Molina." *Anales de la literatura española contemporánea* 33, no. 1 (2008): 105–126.

Martín Nogales, José Luis. "Literatura y mercado en la España de los 90." In *Entre el ocio y el negocio: Industria editorial y literatura en la España de los 90*, edited by José Manuel López de Abaida, Hans-Jörg Neuschäfer, and Augusta López Bernasocchi, 179–194. Madrid: Verbum, 2001.

Martínez, Guillem. "El concepto CT." In *CT o la Cultura de la Transición*, edited by Guillem Martínez, 13–23. Barcelona: Debolsillo, 2012.

Marzo, Jorge Luis, and Tere Badia. "Las políticas culturales en el estado español." *Revista Espais*, 2006, 1–26.

McRobbie, Angela. "Postfeminism and Popular Culture: Bridget Jones and the New Regime." In *Interrogating Postfeminism: Gender and the Politics of Popular Culture*, edited by Yvonne Tasker and Diane Negra, 27–39. Durham, N.C.: Duke University Press, 2007.

McVeigh, Paul. "Embedding Neoliberalism in Spain: From Franquismo to Neoliberalism." In *Internalizing Globalization: The Rise of Neoliberalism and the Decline of National Varieties of Capitalism*, edited by Susanne Soederberg, Georg Menz, and Philip G. Cerny, 90–105. Basingstoke: Palgrave Macmillan, 2005.

Mesa, Sara. "Sara Mesa: 'Por escribir libros mi opinión no está más cualificada ni mejor que la de alguien que no escribe.'" Entrevista por Bárbara Ayuso. *Jot Down*. Updated October 17, 2017. Accessed November 27, 2018. https://www.jotdown.es/2017/10/sara-mesa-por-escribir-libros-mi-opinion-no-esta-mas-cualificada-ni-es-mejor-que-la-de-alguien-que-no-escribe/.

Michaels, Walter Benn. "Model Minorities and the Minority Model—the Neoliberal Novel." In *The Cambridge History of the American Novel*, edited by Leonard Cassuto, Clare Virginia Eby, and Benjamin Reiss, 1016–1030. Cambridge: Cambridge University Press, 2011.

Miles, Valerie. "Review: Enrique Vila-Matas Plots His Own Awakening in 'The Illogic of Kassel.'" *New York Times*, August 12, 2015. https://www.nytimes.com/2015/08/13/books/review-enrique-vila-matas-plots-his-own-awakening-in-the-illogic-of-kassel.html.

Moreno-Caballud, Luis. "Cuando cualquiera escribe: Procesos democratizadores de la cultura escrita en la crisis de la Cultura de la Transición española." *Journal of Spanish Cultural Studies* 15, no. 1–2 (2014): 13–36.

———. *Cultures of Anyone: Studies on Cultural Democratization in the Spanish Neoliberal Crisis*. Translated by Linda Grabner. Liverpool: Liverpool University Press, 2015.

Morgado, Nuria. "Estudio preliminar." In *Voces de mujer*, by Lourdes Ortiz, 11–80 Madrid: Iberoamericana, 2007.

Nochlin, Linda. "Why Have There Been No Great Women Artists?" In *The Feminism and Visual Culture Reader*, edited by Amelia Jones, 263–267. New York: Routledge, 2010.

O'Connor, Justin. "The Cultural and Creative Industries: A Critical History." *Ekonomiaz: Revista vasca de economía* 78, no. 3 (2011): 25–45.

Ortiz, Lourdes. *Las manos de Velázquez*. Barcelona: Planeta, 2006.

París-Huesca, Eva. "El espacio de la memoria en *El cielo de Madrid*." *Lucero* 21, no. 1 (2010): 130–142.

Perelman, Bob. "My Avant-Garde Card." *New Literary History* 41, no. 4 (2010): 875–894.

Pérez, Janet, and Genaro J. Pérez. "Postfeminism in Hispanic Literature: An Introduction." *Monographic Review / Revista Monográfica* 23 (2007): 7–46.

Planeta de Libros España. "Todo fue nada." Last modified October 18, 2005. Accessed May 23, 2019. https://www.planetadelibros.com/libro-todo-fue-nada/326.

Plaza, Beatriz, and Silke N. Haarich. "The Guggenheim Museum Bilbao: Between Regional Embeddedness and Global Networking." *European Planning Studies* 23, no. 8 (2015): 1456–1475.

Portús, Javier. *Pintura y pensamiento en la España de Lope de Vega*. San Sebastián: Nerea, 1999.

———. *Velázquez*. Exhibition catalogue, Kunsthistorisches Museum Wien. Edited by Sabine Haag. Munich: Hirmer, 2014.

Pozuelo Yvancos, José María. *Figuraciones del yo en la narrativa: Javier Marías y E. Vila-Matas*. Valladolid: Cátedra Miguel Delibes, 2010.

Prieto del Campo, Carlos. "A Spanish Spring?" *New Left Review* 31 (2005): 42–68.

Reig, Rafael. "Desde dentro de la burbuja." *El Diario*, November 12, 2012. https://www.eldiario.es/Kafka/dentro-burbuja_0_78392198.html.

Robillard, Valerie. "In Pursuit of Ekphrasis (An Intertextual Approach)." In *Pictures into Words: Theoretical and Descriptive Approaches to Ekphrasis*, edited by Valerie Robillard and Els Jongeneel, 53–69. Amsterdam: Vu University Press, 1998.

Robinson, Alan. *Narrating the Past: Historiography, Memory and the Contemporary Novel*. Basingstoke: Palgrave Macmillan, 2011.

Rodríguez Pequeño, Mercedes. "La novela histórica culturalista." *Siglo XXI: Literatura y cultural españolas* 2 (2004): 219–238.

———. "Referentes artísticos y literarios en la novela española actual." In *Musas hermanas: Arte y literatura en el espejo del relato*, edited by Susana Gil-Albarellos and Mercedes Rodríguez Pequeño, 7–25. Valladolid: Cátedra Miguel Delibes, 2009.

Rosenfelt, Deborah S. "Feminism, 'Postfeminism,' and Contemporary Women's Fiction." In *Tradition and the Talents of Women*, edited by Florence Howe, 268–291. Urbana: University of Illinois Press, 1992.

Roth, Joseph. "The Bust of the Emperor." 1935. In *The Collected Stories of Joseph Roth*, 227–247. Translated by Michael Hofmann. New York: Norton, 2002.

Røyseng, Sigrid, Per Mangset, and Jorunn Spord Borgen. "Young Artists and the Charismatic Myth." *International Journal of Cultural Policy* 13, no. 1 (2007): 1–18.

Scharff, Christina. *Repudiating Feminism: Young Women in a Neoliberal World.* Farnham, U.K.: Ashgate, 2012.

Schechner, Richard. "The Conservative Avant-Garde." *New Literary History* 41, no. 4 (2010): 895–913.

Scott, Robert F. "It's a Small World, after All: Assessing the Contemporary Campus Novel." *Journal of the Midwest Modern Language Association* 37, no. 1 (2004): 81–87.

Showalter, Elaine. *Faculty Towers: The Academic Novel and Its Discontents.* Philadelphia: Pennsylvania University Press, 2005.

Smith, Bernard. *The Death of the Artist as Hero: Essays in History and Culture.* Melbourne: Oxford University Press, 1988.

Smith, Paul Julian. *Contemporary Spanish Culture: TV, Fashion, Art, and Film.* Cambridge, U.K.: Polity, 2003.

Smith, Rachel Greenwald. *Affect and American Literature in the Age of Neoliberalism.* Cambridge: Cambridge University Press, 2015.

Song, H. Rosi. *Lost in Transition: Constructing Memory in Contemporary Spain.* Liverpool: Liverpool University Press, 2016.

Spires, Robert. "*El sueño de Venecia* and the Information Age: Deceiving Facts and Validating Fictions." *Revista Hispánica Moderna* 56, no. 2 (2003): 387–397.

Stapell, Hamilton. *Remaking Madrid: Culture, Politics, and Identity after Franco.* New York: Palgrave Macmillan, 2010.

Susen, Simon. "Bourdieu and Adorno on the Transformation of Culture in Modern Society: Towards a Critical Theory of Cultural Production." In *The Legacy of Pierre Bourdieu: Critical Essays*, edited by Simon Susen and Bryan S. Turner, 171–202. London: Anthem, 2011.

Swanson, Emily. "Poll: Few Identify as Feminists, but Most Believe in Equality of the Sexes." *Huffington Post*, April 16, 2013. https://www.huffpost.com/entry/feminism-poll_n_3094917.

Tasker, Yvonne, and Diane Negra. "Introduction: Feminist Politics and Postfeminist Culture." In *Interrogating Postfeminism: Gender and the Politics of Popular Culture*, edited by Yvonne Tasker and Diane Negra, 1–25. Durham, N.C.: Duke University Press, 2007.

Thurston, Nick. "dOCUMENTA (13): Writing's Retreat into the Context of Contemporary Art." *Afterall.* Last updated October 25, 2012. Accessed April 10, 2016. https://www.afterall.org/online/documenta-13-writing-s-retreat-into-the-context-of-contemporary-art#.WC9wL2RViko.

Touton, Isabelle. "El Siglo de Oro bajo el prisma de la novela histórica contemporánea: Aprensión e interpretación de una imagen." In *El Siglo de Oro en la España contemporánea*, edited by Hanno Ehrlicher and Stefan Schreckenberg, 195–211. Madrid: Iberoamericana; Frankfurt am Main: Vervuert, 2011.

Tsuchiya, Akiko. "Gender, Sexuality, and the Literary Market in Spain at the End of the Millennium." In *Women's Narrative and Film in Twentieth-Century Spain: A World of Difference(s)*, edited by Ofelia Ferrán and Kathleen M. Glenn, 238–255. New York: Routledge, 2002.

Usón, Clara. *Corazón de napalm*. Barcelona: Seix Barral, 2009.

———. "Entrevista a Clara Usón en Literaturas.com." Por Jordi Corominas. *Jordi Corominas i Julián* (blog), September 18, 2009. http://corominasijulian.blogspot.com/2009/09/entrevista-clara-uson-en-literaturascom.html.

Valdivia, Pablo. "Narrando la crisis financiera de 2008 y sus repercusiones." *452°F*, no. 15 (2016): 18–36.

van den Brand, Jessica. *Tino Sehgal: Art as Immaterial Commodity*. Saarbrücken: Lambert, 2015.

Varsamopoulou, Evy. *The Poetics of the* Künstlerinroman *and the Aesthetics of the Sublime*. Burlington, Vt.: Ashgate, 2002.

Velthuis, Olav. "The Venice Effect." In *The Market*, edited by Natasha Degen, 121–127. London: Whitechapel Gallery, 2013.

Verwoert, Jan. "The Curious Case of Biennial Art." In *The Biennial Reader: An Anthology on Large-Scale Perennial Exhibitions of Contemporary Art*, edited by Elena Filipovic, Marieke van Hal, and Solveig Øvstebø, 184–197. Bergen: Bergen Kunsthall, 2010.

Vidal-Folch, Ignacio. "El autor y su personaje: Enrique Vila-Matas y Chus Martínez conversaron en Fabra i Coats." *El País*, April 4, 2014.

Vila-Matas, Enrique. *The Illogic of Kassel*. Translated by Anne McLean and Anna Milsom. New York: New Directions, 2015.

———. *Kassel no invita la lógica*. Barcelona: Seix Barral, 2014.

Vilarós, Teresa M. *El mono del desencanto: Una crítica cultural de la transición española (1973–1993)*. Madrid: Siglo Veintiuno, 1998.

Weir, Andy. "Myrmecochory Occurs: Exhibiting Indifference to the Participating Subject in Pierre Huyghe's *Untilled* (2012) at Documenta 13." *Postgraduate Journal of Aesthetics* 10, no. 1 (2013): 29–40.

White, Harrison C., and Cynthia A. White. *Canvases and Careers: Institutional Change in the French Painting World*. Chicago: University of Chicago Press, 1993.

White, Hayden. *Tropics of Discourse: Essays in Cultural Criticism*. Baltimore: Johns Hopkins University Press, 1985.

White, Roberta. *A Studio of One's Own: Fictional Women Painters and the Art of Fiction*. Madison, N.J.: Fairleigh Dickinson University Press, 2005.

Worden, Daniel. "The Memoir in the Age of Neoliberal Individualism." In *Neoliberalism and Contemporary Literary Culture*, edited by Mitchum Huehls and Rachel Greenwald Smith, 160–177. Baltimore: Johns Hopkins University Press, 2017.

Zadoff, Mirjam. *Next Year in Marienbad: The Lost Worlds of Jewish Spa Culture*. Translated by William Templer. Philadelphia: University of Pennsylvania Press, 2012.

# Index

# About the Author

Katie J. Vater is an assistant professor of Spanish at the University of Wisconsin–Milwaukee. Her research interests include the contemporary Peninsular novel, with special emphasis on representations of cultural labor and the effects of neoliberalism on cultural production. *Between Market and Myth* is her first book.

